Getting
Noticed

Getting Noticed

*A Musician's Guide
to Publicity and
Self-Promotion*

James Gibson

Writer's
Digest
Books

Cincinnati, Ohio

Library of Congress Cataloging-in-Publication Data

Gibson, James, 1944-
　Getting noticed: a musician's guide to publicity and self-promotion

　Bibliography: p.
　Includes index.
　1. Music trade—Vocational guidance. 2. Arts publicity. I. Title.
ML3790.G54 1987　　659.1'978　　87-23130
ISBN 0-89879-285-1

Design by Christine Aulicino

The following page is an extension of this copyright page.

Public sentiment is everything.
With public sentiment nothing can fail,
without it nothing can succeed.

—Abraham Lincoln

To my family—especially Chris and Laura—and friends, who love making music.

ACKNOWLEDGMENTS

Lots of people helped with this book, and I thank them all. Special thanks to those musicians who allowed the use of their publicity material as examples. More special thanks to Patricia Elaine Pierce for her usual great graphic help, and to Eddie Reddick for turning rough ideas into great illustrations.

Thanks, finally, to Carol Cartaino for giving this book the chance to get noticed, to Julie Wesling Whaley for nurturing the idea into a manuscript, and to Beth Franks, who gave coherence to the manuscript with good humor and uncanny understanding.

CONTENTS

ABOUT THE AUTHOR

James Gibson has worked as a full-time freelance pianist/keyboardist for more than twelve years, performing both with bands and in solo acts. He has successfully used the techniques in this book to promote himself and to book performing jobs at banquets, dances, shows, award presentations, grand opening ceremonies, ground-breakings, weddings, promotion and retirement parties, and many other kinds of special events. He is also the author of *How You Can Make $30,000 a Year as a Musician Without a Record Contract*.

INTRODUCTION

DO THEY KNOW who you are?

The right people, that is. Your clients, audiences, peers—people who can hire you, buy your records or songs, and help you make a living in music. Do they know who you are? And, do they know what you can do? Have they heard you lately? In fact, have they *thought about you* lately?

Do you want to make a living—or a better living—in music? Welcome, then, to Real-Life Music 101, where the struggle to survive meets the hopes and dreams of every performer. This is the world where whom you know, and who knows you, is important.

Sometimes, unfair as it seems, *whom* you know is more important than *what* you know. Being a good performer isn't enough. You have to practice music, of course, but you also have to practice good public relations. You have to know how to make people notice you.

"But," you say, "how can I do that? I'm a performer, not an advertising person. I don't have the time or money to prepare a publicity campaign for myself. I don't even know what's involved. What is publicity anyway, and what does it have to do with being a musician?"

Good questions. This book offers some answers.

All performers—not just musicians, but actors, jugglers, speakers, dancers, mimes (and politicians)—have the same concerns. We all need to get noticed. It doesn't matter whether you're a classical violinist, a country fiddler, a fusion keyboardist, the lead singer in a top-forty group, or a college band director. You've got to find your audiences and clients and tell them what you do.

Every Hollywood star has a press agent and every recording company has an office full of publicity people. Every successful actor or actress has public relations consultants on the payroll. What about you?

If you can't afford the services of publicity professionals, what should you do? Save your money? Forget about public relations? Actually, there's good news about getting noticed. You, yourself, can make it happen.

You'll create for yourself, your band, or your organization, a publicity program that ranges from business cards to feature articles. And you'll plan special events to call attention to your music. You'll write, photograph, and record to produce exactly the materials your campaign needs, and you'll even learn how to think like a publicist—and turn ordinary events into good publicity for yourself and your group.

Big companies—and small ones—know that publicity is crucial to their success. Doctors, attorneys, and other professionals spend a lot of time building their publicity programs. You can, too.

PART
======

ONE

How to Create Publicity Tools

CHAPTER 1

If You Don't Tell Them, Who Will?

YOU'RE A PERFORMER—a musician, a singer, an actor, a dancer. You make your living—or plan to—with your talent. You know the profession isn't easy, but it makes you happy and it's what you want to do.

The first thing you need is an audience. You could play music in your own home, of course, or for your friends, but if you're a professional you must play for others. And, if you're professional, your audience also pays you. Whether they're called clients, patrons, fans, or bosses, they're necessary for your success.

Your audience can be formally dressed, seated in a concert hall, awaiting your virtuoso performance with the symphony. Or your audience can be a crowded dance floor of couples enjoying your rock band on Saturday night. Your audience may be a huge convention hall full of people from around the world. It may be the local Lions club, a fraternity, a country club, or even a group of record-company executives.

Your audience may be a corporate officer who's booking the entertainment for a training seminar. Before you can perform your music you may have to perform as a salesperson, convincing him that he should hire your group. So the first step to a profitable musical performance may be your sales performance, and it can be as important to your career as your stage presence.

DON'T BE AFRAID TO TOOT YOUR OWN HORN

For most performers, working on publicity is not a luxury. It's not optional, something you do in your spare time. Getting noticed is a survival skill; if your publicity works, you'll flourish; if it doesn't, your career may not survive.

Your mother probably said, "Don't brag about yourself, don't toot your own horn." But the reality of the music marketplace is different. You have to toot your own horn, pull your own strings, sing your own praises, because *if you don't, who will?*

The world is full of hungry musicians who can play with unbelievable skill. Your community probably has its share. In fact, there may be people nearby who play, sing, or perform better than you. Fortunately, the real struggle for survival in the performing world isn't a talent competition alone. Much more is involved than just music. There are audiences, agents, accountants, advertisers, authors, and artists to work with—and that's just the "a's."

The Bible warns us not to put our light under a bushel where it can't be seen. An old cliché says, "The squeaky wheel gets the grease." What does that mean? It means that first, before anything else can happen, you've got to *get noticed.*

Let's say you're the best reed player around. You can sight-read fly specks from fifty paces. You have fifteen thousand dollars invested in flutes, saxophones, clarinets of every description. Your intonation is impeccable, your tone pure. You sit at home on Saturday night and wonder why no one calls.

Or maybe your rock band is really superior, with a perfect blend of standards and strong original material. You have computer-driven lights, drum machines, and synthesizers. Nobody hires you, and you may have to get a day job to make the payments to the music store.

Or perhaps you just got your master's degree in piano and have opened a teaching studio in your hometown. You know the literature, the methods. You'll be a great teacher. But you don't have any students—or income.

Musical professionals need to be noticed by the right people—bandleaders, club owners, parents of beginning piano students. But how? Should they advertise?

Probably not. In these cases, and maybe in your own, a carefully planned publicity program can solve lots of problems and may be more effective than advertising. Publicity, properly done, creates an image that propels your career upward. It keeps your name before the right audiences. It tells the world, "This is the best musician for you to hire."

Why get noticed? At the most basic level, if they don't know you, they can't hire you. That's simple—but it's the foundation of your career.

WHAT IS PUBLICITY?

There are basically two ways of letting people know about you and your music: you can advertise or you can publicize yourself. Advertising and publicity are two entirely different things, and each has its place. Most musicians, especially at the local level, will do very little advertising. Most musicians, on the other hand, should constantly work at creating good publicity.

Advertising is expensive. One small ad in the newspaper might cost your band hundreds of dollars. One well-done thirty-second commercial on a local TV station costs thousands to produce and run. And, for reasons we'll talk about later, such ads probably wouldn't do you much good.

Fortunately, you probably don't need such advertising. What you *do* need is lots of publicity. *Publicity* includes all the ways you can get noticed without buying expensive ad space or time. Publicity makes people talk, think, read, and hear about you—and it costs little or nothing.

Almost everything you do as a professional performer can be turned to good publicity, from the design of your letterhead and business cards to the production of demo tapes, from writing brochures and bio sheets to writing feature stories for newspapers and magazines. Even your hobbies and nonmusical activities can play a part.

Publicity includes good client relations—the idea that the customer is always right. It involves word-of-mouth recommendations. It's usually free, but it's effective; publicity ultimately gets you jobs.

The best news is that, for most performers, publicity is *better than advertising*. Everybody suspects advertising because they know it's paid for, but they'll assume that the publicity they see and hear is true.

Does publicity work? Ask Tiny Tim and Madonna—and Jimmy Carter.

As a musician, you are like every business with a product to sell. You have to find customers (in your case, an audience), and convince them they should buy the product (in your case, music). That's all there is to it—but that's a lot. This book will help, because you'll learn how to define your audience, to decide *exactly* who needs to know about you; you'll also learn how to use publicity tools and techniques to reach that precise group. Just having the tools and knowing how to use the media, however, isn't all there is to a good publicity program. There's lots more.

We'll talk about making video and audio demo tapes. We'll discuss publicizing your concerts and appearances with T-shirts, bumper stickers, posters, and banners. We'll cover sales calls—the dreaded necessity. You'll learn how to make effective presentations and phone calls and how to write all kinds of letters—introduction, solicitation, confirmation, and thanks. We'll even discuss advertising—the inexpensive sort that may work for you.

Getting Noticed is divided into two parts. The first is about the publicity tools you'll need, creating them yourself or finding professional help. Essentially, your publicity tool kit will include several kinds of printed materials, a few recorded items, photos, and perhaps some simple advertising ideas. You'll develop a logo to identify your group and project an *image* that will help all your publicity efforts work effectively.

Part Two concentrates on using those tools to let people know what you do. These chapters discuss working with the media, writing press releases, getting feature stories about your music in the paper, calling on clients, and devising other ways to get noticed.

Throughout this book there are activities to increase your working knowledge of publicity, and add to your stockpile of helpful material. If you spend the time to do these projects, this book will help your career. While these procedures aren't perfect or magical, they do supply information and experience. Don't just say, "Oh yeah, that sounds pretty interesting." Take a pencil and paper and *do the activity.* There's a lot of difference between simply thinking about something and actually getting involved.

One tool we'll frequently use is *brainstorming.* This is a simple technique, requiring nothing more than paper, a pencil, and an active imagination. The idea is to create a "storm" in your brain that will penetrate the habits that usually limit your thoughts. Brainstorming can lead to new ideas, fresh concepts, even breakthroughs.

And, throughout, we'll concentrate on how you can do it yourself—from laying out your own brochures to writing your own press releases. Why limit your creativity to music? The publicity field isn't mysterious or particularly difficult to master. Once you understand what works, you can make it work for you.

Is Your Image Right?

Your publicity tools will reflect your personality and musical ability, even when you yourself aren't around. Carefully produced letterheads, business cards, invoices, brochures, resumes, bio sheets, tune lists, demo tapes, and letters demonstrate that you're a professional who knows, and cares, about your image.

What kind of image do you have? Good? Poor? Indifferent?

"Image?" you ask. "Won't reality take care of that? Why should I worry about my 'image'?"

Everybody has an image that's known by friends and, in your case, audiences. The way you dress, talk, conduct yourself, the car you drive, your demeanor, all help determine how people see you. So will your professional activities.

What do you want people to think about you? That you're the best, most professional musician in town? That you're a hard worker, an innovator, an achiever? That you're laid back, relaxed? That you're an artist who isn't concerned with business?

Why not think about how you'd like to be perceived and work toward that goal? You can use the methods and materials discussed in this book to consolidate an image that will advance your career.

Is that dishonest? Won't you be manipulating people? Of course not. An image without underlying reality won't last. You'll never convince bandleaders that they should hire you if you can't play or don't show up on time. You'll never achieve the image of the "best party band in town" if your music isn't appropriate.

Publicity can do a lot, and your carefully cultivated image will help, but your product—music—must be of excellent quality and what your audience wants. Otherwise, all the publicity and advertising in the world won't help. Remember the Edsel and New Coke.

As you read this book and do the suggested activities, remember the image you'd like to convey. At the same time, of course, keep working on your music or performance. Image without substance is as pointless as performance without an audience. Each is necessary for success.

Publicity Practice

In this activity we'll work on your image, and we'll use brainstorming as the technique to create new ideas. Take a pencil and paper and find a quiet place where you won't be disturbed.

At the top of your paper, write something like this: "I'd like to be seen as. . . ."

Now, list the qualities and attributes you'd like to have. It doesn't matter whether you have them, or are likely to acquire them. In brainstorming you don't try to be realistic. And don't worry about being silly—nobody's going to see the list but you.

Maybe you've always wanted to play rock and roll on a stage swirling with smoke-machine fog and elaborate special effects—you want to be a rock star. Or maybe you'd really like to be friends with the wealthy party people in your town, and play sophisticated show tunes at all their soirees. These ideas, wishes, hopes, and dreams should be on your list.

Does your music lend itself to sophistication, or uncontrolled frenzy? Would your audience expect you to be disciplined or unrestrained? Should you be refined or macho? Do you want to be seen as living in the future—or living in the past? Do you see yourself as New Wave, or as a figure from the forties? Is your hair pink or neatly styled? Do you jump, twist, and shout when you play, or is your music quiet and understated?

Obviously, this list will be unique to *you*. The beginning piano teacher will develop an entirely different image from the cutting-edge punk musician, and the dixieland banjo player will have a different image from the Broadway singer. The idea is not to create a false image, but to work with the one you already have, to refine it and become aware of it as you pursue new publicity efforts.

Think about your audiences—the ones you have and the ones you'd like to have. Consider your clients. Think about your music, your talent, your general approach to life, your business goals. Write down all the ideas that pertain to the way you'd like to be seen. This will be your *image list*. Keep it. You'll use it from time to time.

GETTING NOTICED—THE PLAN

Now that you're thinking about your image, here's how we'll advance it. Your publicity tools will help you to get mentioned, talked about, written about, and generally noticed in lots of media—newspapers, radio, TV, and others. "But," you say, "how can *I* get this kind of publicity? I don't know any writers or broadcasters. Why would they ever notice me and my music?"

Here's a revolutionary idea: *the media need you*. Every day, radio and TV stations have hours and hours to fill. Every day, week, and month, newspapers and magazines need interesting news and features. You just have to learn how to play by their rules—to give them what they expect.

Can you do this? Of course. It's done every day. The results of other people's publicity efforts are literally all around you.

Publicity Practice

Start by enrolling in the free *media university*. Get a file folder or large envelope and a pair of scissors. Every day, go through the newspaper and clip (and save) all the articles, reviews, notices, news stories, and calendar listings of arts activities in your area. Don't limit yourself to music; include plays, school activities, church projects, artists, and craftspeople's activities, and so on. Anytime you see an article about a person or group in these categories, put it in your clip file.

Some of these clips will be nothing more than the "Morningside Band to hold bake sale this Saturday," type of listing. Go ahead and save such pieces, because you'll want similar listings before long.

Others will be full feature articles and personality profiles on individuals and groups. Some may be reviews of performances. Keep them all in your file. Eventually, you may even need several specialized files because you'll accumulate so much material. You may have one folder for sample calendar listings, another for feature articles, and a third for performance reviews.

You'll be surprised at how many articles your local paper runs about arts and community-oriented groups. Soon, you'll be among them.

As you become more expert at planning your own publicity, you'll only clip outstanding articles and really great new ideas—but for now save everything that relates to your field—because your beginning publicity program will need all the input you can find.

Such a growing file will demonstrate clearly that the publicity vehicles are there. Other people are getting noticed every day, and your file shows what works in your area. Your job is to do the same for yourself or your group.

Your clip file will be a source of ideas and inspiration. When you worry about your publicity, look at what others have done, and ask, "If they have done it, why can't I?"

You can.

Painter and singer join forces for art

By Barbara McKenzie
Special to The Journal-Constitution

When music is in the air at art openings, it's usually soothing, cerebral and in the background. Not so at the opening of Beth Bolgla's paintings at the Municipal Gallery.

Music was provided by New York singer-actress Angel Dean, who belted out songs written by the likes of Loretta Lynn, Hank Williams or members of her own band, Last Roundup.

Art Review

The two women have been friends since 1973 when they were both involved in theater in Augusta. For the past two years, Ms. Dean has been the subject of a series of paintings by Ms. Bolgla. In significant ways, the singer-actress serves as an alter ego for the artist.

"When Angel sings, she personifies the individual up against the forces which challenge our very existence," Ms. Bolgla says. "That's why I've chosen to paint her time and time again. Her performance here was a way to share with the public that which has inspired me." Seventeen oil paintings, four featuring Ms. Dean, and one charcoal drawing are on display at Municipal.

Ms. Bolgla is a ceramicist-turned-painter. At first, she painted pots and flowers arranged as still lifes. Gradually, the flowers became imaginary and took on human qualities. Next came the paintings of Angel and, along with them, a series of self-portraits that make up the majority of the works on exhibition.

The self-portraits are a visual diary. They are head-and-shoulder paintings made from photographs — usually photo booth pictures where the "instant" process strips away details. But other photographs have served as the basis for portraits — including one taken for a subway pass in London.

"That photograph really scared me. I looked so pale and depressed. I thought I was feeling OK about myself. Obviously I wasn't," she says. In the portrait, she paints herself sitting in front of a blue draped curtain. She is positioned too low in the frame as if the seat had been adjusted for someone taller. The painting translates vividly the emotional and physical state of aloneness.

The portraits of Ms. Dean are done full figure. Ms. Bolgla views Angel as both vulnerable and strong. "She doesn't put up too many walls — that interests me," she says.

The contrasting themes of vulnerability and strength are depicted most vividly in "Heartland X," a painting that measures 7 feet by 10 feet. In it, Ms. Dean is standing in an imaginary landscape surrounded by a decoratively painted arch. Close by is a large vase with flowers in three stages of their life cycle. Occupying the foreground is a large cow turned so that it faces Ms. Dean, who is wearing a brightly colored peasant-type skirt. Behind them are treeless fields traversed by winding roads. Sharp green cones, rather than soft grass, lie at their feet.

The symbolism in the painting is personal but clear. The fragile, beautiful flowers are loving, emotional forces. Their vase connotes female sexuality, as does the cow. The cones represent the sharp and threatening forces that surround us. The arch offers protection, but it also entraps. A road, leading to an undisclosed destination, snakes through a barren landscape. Ms. Dean is hemmed in by both the cow and the arch. "She can't move," Ms. Bolgla observes, "and the cow can't lie down."

"I can paint flowers," Ms. Bolgla says, "but they don't interest me right now. I want to express the things I am feeling." Self-honesty and directness are important to her. And, most importantly, she has found a way to express them in her art.

This isn't a music review—it's an art review. But the creative mixture of music and art results in an interesting article and is good publicity for both the artist and the musician. "Special to the Journal/Constitution*" indicates that the review is a freelance submission, and wasn't produced by a staff writer.*

What You Need to Get Started

You're going to meet lots of people and generate lots of information as you create your publicity program. Notes, letters, articles, contracts, business cards, and brochures will accumulate on your desk, in your pockets, and in your instrument case. If you keep up with this information flow you won't get frustrated. On the other hand, if you are haphazard you'll probably neglect your publicity efforts and your career will suffer.

A special, well-organized workspace will help you be efficient as you pursue publicity and career goals. Use a desk, if one's available, or clear a shelf in a bookcase, or designate the side of a countertop or dresser as your work area. It will help if there's a telephone handy, and you'll work smarter if you have all your office needs at your fingertips. Sharing your work area with roommates, or a spouse, or even children will cause you to waste time looking for files, phone numbers, clippings, or other essentials. A clean, well-lighted workplace is one advantage most office workers have over people who work from home, so you should strive to create an "office" of your own—even if it's just a drawer in the kitchen cabinet.

To stay organized from the start you need several things from the office supply store. They include:

1. *A good datebook.* Of course you have one now, to keep up with dates you've booked, but as your publicity projects get under way, you'll have lots of advance planning to do—letters, press releases, reminders to send. So get a large datebook to keep track of it all—maybe a desk size. Popular brands include the Day-at-a-Glance series and the Daytimers line (see the Appendix).

2. *A wall calendar.* You need a quick overview of what's happening, and when. The details go in your datebook or file, of course, but a large calendar quickly shows upcoming deadlines and events.

3. *A Rolodex,* or some other kind of card file. As you meet more and more people, you'll need a quick reference system for locating names, phone numbers, and addresses. Most businesspeople use some form of the Rolodex system because it can be instantly updated and changed, but if you like three by five-inch index cards, that's fine too. Keep them in a small file box, and you'll have an inexpensive system.

4. *A business-card file.* You might prefer to incorporate business cards into your Rolodex system, or you can use a book-style business-card holder from the office-supply store. These holders have little plastic sleeves to hold business cards and are a simple way to keep up with all the cards that are now stuffed in your wallet and tossed in the top desk drawer. You'll find that business cards are ubiquitous—everybody uses them, and they'll advance your network-building activities. They won't be helpful at all, though, if you can't find them when you need them.

5. *A file system* of some sort. You can use a cardboard box, a plastic

modular unit like the Decofile, or a standard filing cabinet, but you must have a system for keeping up with contracts, correspondence, and notes. There are several different systems for setting up a file. You can simply file everything alphabetically, or you can set up separate subcategories, perhaps in different file drawers or boxes, to give different subjects their own space. For example, you might have one file for "Publicity Clips," another for "Booking Agents," another for "Past Music Clients," and so on, and file relevant material alphabetically within its category. (You'll probably find it useful to keep strictly personal material filed separately from your business data.) A good place to start your file system is your soon-to-be-bulging clip file. Set up a separate folder for "News Stories," "Feature Stories," "Reviews," "Ads," "Calendar," and so on. Remember: no matter what filing system you choose, it won't help you if you don't use it.

6. *A good typewriter* (or access to one). Some things *must be typed;* in many cases handwriting is just not acceptable. If you don't type, think about learning. It's not difficult, and you'll save time and money by not needing to deal with typists and secretaries.

7. *A computer.* If you have one, you already know the advantages for writing, filing, and mailing. Since prices have dropped on some excellent models, you may find that an affordable computer will become indispensable to you—but don't buy one unless your business justifies it. In the beginning, especially, a computer is more a luxury than a necessity. (When you shop for a computer, be sure to check for available music programs. Why limit yourself to word processing when the same machine will compose and print music and interface with your synthesizer?)

8. *An answering machine or service.* As you publicize yourself and build a network of contacts, it will be increasingly important for you to be available and accessible. This does not mean, of course, that you have to wear a beeper and be on call twenty-four hours a day, but if a newspaper reporter needs to check a story detail with you, it will help immensely if you're reachable.

You need to tell the world about your music. Audiences—paying audiences—are everywhere; it's your job to find them and let them know what you do. Start by getting the right people to notice you.

CHAPTER 2
Target Your Audience

ADVERTISING AGENCIES SPEND FORTUNES doing market research to locate their intended audiences—and they choose the media that reach those targets. Thus, sugar-coated cereals and toys are advertised on Saturday morning TV, and pop record albums are promoted on rock-oriented radio stations. The product suits the audience.

You should do the same thing. In your community there are thousands of people who don't really need to know about you. But there are many—tens, hundreds, maybe even thousands—who *do* need to know what you do. These will be the targets of your publicity.

So, before you start your publicity program let's define your target audiences. Public relations professionals call them *affect communities*—meaning those groups that you want to reach, to affect, with your publicity.

Thus, if yours is a top-forty band you probably won't need to reach the elegant gourmet restaurateurs in your area. But if you're a classical pianist, or a harpist, these would be important audiences for your publicity efforts.

Or, if your band plays nothing but authentic country music, there's probably no need to tell the local community orchestra director what you do. But, if you're a double-reed player, the orchestra could provide work—and a chance to enter the classical-music network that naturally leads to such related opportunities as teaching, recording, or chamber-music concerts.

Your goal is to match the audience with your music. Let's say you're in a rock band. The groups you'll want to reach will include

Booking agents
Club owners
Fraternities and sororities
Fair and festival promoters
Rock radio station personalities
Young (18-27) people, primarily singles

That's a good start for a target market list. But keep brainstorming and you'll come up with more categories that match your music. Ask, "Who has parties? Who buys rock records?"

Think, for example, about where your young audience shops and lives, and add those businesses to your list. They all hold grand openings, open houses, special sales, and other kinds of parties that could use your music. Your list continues:

Record stores
Young-fashion clothing stores, boutiques
Dating services
Health clubs, spas
Singles-oriented apartment complexes

You'll add more as your publicity plans develop; the target market list will continue to grow as your career expands, markets change, and your community grows.

Let's take another example. Perhaps you're the beginning piano teacher mentioned in the first chapter. To establish a publicity plan you first brainstorm ideas for target audiences—all the groups that need to know about your services. You come up with

Parents of elementary schoolchildren
Other private music teachers (who could give referrals)
School music teachers
Music stores

This is a start, but it's a small group, and your goal is to be known by everyone in town who could need piano lessons. As you think further about your image, however, you realize that you not only want to teach, but also want to be known as a dedicated arts leader, someone who is active in all areas of classical music. So you add community *opinion makers* to your list—people who might not be directly interested in piano lessons, but who need to know about you nonetheless. This list includes

Community orchestras
College music departments
City arts council members
Neighborhood associations
Arts editors and reviewers for radio, TV, newspapers
Civic clubs
Amateur theatrical groups

You realize that your name must be widely known, that your network of contacts should grow, and that even unlikely groups (like civic clubs) could be productive sources of good publicity for you. Maybe the American Legion needs a program of patriotic music performed by your students, for instance. As you learn to think like a publicity expert, you'll add other possibilities to your list.

Is that all? No, of course not. As this music teacher's career grows, she'll think of new names to add to her publicity network—more people who should know about her abilities. Perhaps the local news radio station should have her on file as a classical music expert, or a teaching expert, to answer questions about issues involving those subjects. Maybe the newspaper needs freelance classical music reviewers. The possibilities go on and on for the musician who is aware of publicity potential.

An interesting thing about publicity is that you never know what results to expect—or when to look for them. Many of your efforts will be like seed, taking time to germinate and grow, but producing excellent results weeks—or months—later. If your students play that program of patriotic songs for the American Legion, it's quite possible that one of the members will remember you when his children need piano lessons. Or perhaps the local college radio station will ask you to host a weekly show about great pianists. Or maybe your town's TV station will decide to do a profile on your innovative teaching techniques.

One thing is certain. If they don't know about you, they won't think of you when they need a teacher, a radio personality, or a subject for their TV show.

Publicity Practice

Knowing your audiences will help you plan your publicity, because you'll know whom you're talking to, whom you're trying to reach. You'll be able to focus your efforts more precisely.

Start a *target audience* list of those who need to know about your music. Include both specific potential clients and those who may never hire you but should know what you do—the opinion makers and style leaders in your community. Since you'll be making lots of lists, and developing other publicity material, you may find it useful to keep everything together in a notebook or a file folder.

Who needs your music? Who would enjoy it? Who would pay you to perform? Make your list as broad as you can, and write down every individual, group, and category you can imagine. Should the mayor know what you do? Is he or she involved in planning civic celebrations and neighborhood festivals? If so, add him to the list. What about the power structure of your community—the rich and influential people who give frequent parties and are mentioned weekly in the society pages of the paper? Include them. And writers, photographers, and recording studios should be part of your referral network, too, so add them to your list. Maybe they'll never recommend you—but perhaps they will. Keep adding names. In fact, this list will remain active as long as you're in the music business, so make it a habit to add names to your *target audience* list as your career expands. As long as you perform you'll need audiences.

DEFINE YOUR PUBLICITY GOAL

Now you have an idea of the image you want to project and your target audience. It's time to define your goal, to think about what publicity can do for you.

If you don't have a goal, a precise destination, you won't make the best use of your time and energy. Without a goal, any road will do; without a destination you'll never know when you've arrived.

What's your objective as you work on your publicity program? What, exactly, are you trying to do? How can publicity help? Consider the following possibilities:

- Publicity can *get you noticed by the right people*. Whether it's concert promoters or church organists, your audience must be aware of you before they can use your talents.
- Publicity can *raise your profile*. Shouldn't all the party-givers in your community know you're the best piano player around? If your name is well-known among this group, they'll automatically think of you when they plan a party. Publicity can also make you a local celebrity. Do you want to be recognized by the strangers you meet? Continuing publicity will help.
- Publicity can *prove your professional competence*. If they've heard your name from lots of sources and read about you in the paper, how can your potential clients doubt your ability to do a great job?
- Publicity *builds on itself*. Each time you're on a talk show or have an article written about you, you can use that material in your future publicity projects. Each item will validate your

accomplishments that much more, and provide more articles, reviews, or TV clips for use in further publicity projects.

• Publicity *increases public acceptance of causes.* If you play jazz, bluegrass, or classical music, your community may need to be educated about that particular style. Publicity can help raise the jazz, bluegrass, or classical consciousness of potential audiences.

• The bottom line, really, is that *good, well-planned publicity can get you more work,* and make you more money.

Are you convinced? Then do the next activity and you'll be on your way.

Publicity Practice

Write down, in one paragraph, what your publicity goal is. If you can, simplify it to one sentence. Start by writing, "I want my publicity to . . ." and finish the sentence. Be specific. Don't say, "I want my publicity to make me rich and famous." Try something more like, "I want my publicity to convince people that my band is the best, most danceable pop group in town for private parties. When people think of a good time, I want them to think of Joe's Band. I want to book an average of three jobs a week."

Or, "I want my publicity to make my name widely known among educators and school people, so I can book more elementary school concerts for my jazz ensemble. I also want educators and parents to know that I teach privately."

Or, "I want to be seen as the most dynamic, up-and-coming Broadway-style singer around. I want to book my cabaret show into clubs, restaurants, conventions, and other outlets, and to lay the groundwork for a move to the West Coast. I want to collect as many positive reviews and press clippings as I can to build an impressive media kit."

Be as specific as you can. One way to do this is to think about money, and set a precise financial goal. Perhaps you want to have fifty regular students who pay ten dollars a week. Or maybe you'd like to make three hundred dollars a show. Your financial goal could be to make $30,000 a year, or five hundred dollars a week. It will help you reach that goal if you actually write it down, think about it regularly, and assess your progress toward it. If you don't get specific, you'll have no way to judge your progress.

Refine Your Publicity Goal

As you read further in *Getting Noticed*, you'll probably revise your publicity goal. That's the way it should be, because publicity isn't a one-time thing; it's a new way of thinking that will become part of your career.

Goals are important—in fact, they're crucial. But they should be realistic, too. If you try to jump from a beginning guitar player to a rock star you'll just fool yourself, and you'll certainly get discouraged. A better approach is to set yearly goals, in achievable steps. This year, for example, work on your individual playing, next year join a band, and in three years plan to have an album finished. That way you can see the path, and it's not overwhelming.

Read inspirational or "positive thinking" books, and notice the emphasis they place on goals. If you have a clear goal that's written down, you'll know where you are in your career. If you don't, you're just floating along, and probably wasting lots of time. Decide on a path, a road to follow, and do it.

THE BIG HOOK

"All this talk about publicizing my music sounds good," you say. "I'd like to be a household name and see my name in the newspaper and on TV. But—how?"

Later chapters discuss specific techniques, but one fundamental idea is so important that we'll work with it throughout this book. It's known in the public relations world as *the hook*.

You're familiar with popular music so you know what the hook is to songwriters—it's the heart of the song, the simple phrase that sums up its interest and appeal. And if you like to fish you obviously know what a hook is. It's the device that snares your prey, even against its will.

In publicity, the hook is a combination of the songwriter's and the fisherman's tools. The *publicity hook* is the item of interest that makes your music or your personality appealing to broad audiences. The hook snares their attention, catches them off guard, and forces them to become interested enough to find out about you.

So, as you develop publicity ideas, think about your music in terms that will appeal to lots of people. Watch the media to see how other people do it. You probably won't resort to burning guitars or killing chickens on stage to generate interest, but you may have to do more than simply perform your music.

Most publicity doesn't just happen. Someone has an interesting idea—and follows through. We'll talk a lot more about creating and using publicity hooks later, but for now, start noticing the publicity around you—study the *media university*. What is it that makes a story interesting? Why did the TV station bother to do a profile on that particular person? What is the focus, the slant of the magazine piece on another musician? Study the examples in your clip file. Watch out for the hooks. They're always there. And you can use them, too.

Closet Music Conductors Going Legit

Associated Press

ST. PAUL, Minn. — Closet conductors, music lovers who secretly gesticulate to their favorite scores with finger, pencil or chopstick now can upgrade their equipment.

The Portable Maestro Complete Conductor Kit, $19.95, includes a cassette tape of "eminently conductable baroque music," instructions, a diploma from the North American School of the Artsy and Somewhat Musically Inclined, and a cork-handled wooden baton.

"I insisted on the cork handle because, after all, if you're going to conduct Handel's 'Water Music' in the bathtub, you've got to have one that floats," said Nicholas Nash.

Nash, an educator, public radio programmer and operator of a classical music store in St. Paul, said he's been a closet conductor since he was a child.

As he grew older, he decided he wanted a baton that was "the real thing, but I was too embarrassed to go into a music store and buy one."

He thought there might be others who'd have more fun with a real baton than a No. 2 pencil, so in 1985 he created a smaller version of the kit to be sold as a promotion by public radio stations around the country.

"We sold about 4,000 or 5,000 without making a lot of effort. It had enough of a positive reaction that I thought, let's develop this one step further," Nash said.

He added the cassette, enlisted Twin Cities conductor Philip Brunelle for help in writing instructions, and created the mythical conducting school in the basement of his home.

Degrees issued by Nash's school note that it's a "Diploma Mill" and all recipients receive a "Master of Music in Conducting (Magna Cum Loud)."

The degree program ran afoul of guidelines set by the Minnesota Higher Education Coordinating Board, which asked Nash to change the degree to "Maestro of Music" because the supposed school isn't certified.

Phil Lewenstein, director of communications and legislation for the board, explained that private institutions must be registered and licensed to offer programs in Minnesota and must have approval to use certain academic terms.

Nash says his school has four requirements for graduation.

"You have to listen to the tape, you've got to read the brochure, you have to like music and you have to pay the tuition in full. No exceptions," he said.

A wire-service story may appear in hundreds of newspapers around the country—and can result in free nationwide publicity. Here, the target audience is frustrated would-be conductors, and the hook is the idea of a do-it-yourself conductor's kit and a fake degree. Humor is difficult to use in feature stories—but it can be very effective.

CHAPTER 3

Your Publicity Plan

YOU'RE READY NOW TO WORK on your own publicity program, so clients, audiences, booking agents, and other musicians will start noticing you. What should you do? Randomly contact media people, visit photographers, hire printers and artists in a frenzy of activity?

No. Before you spend any time and money you should work on developing a *consistent, coherent, individual* approach that will make your publicity material work hard for you. You want a "look" that will make each piece relate to everything else in your program. You need an overall plan, a concept to tie everything together.

Look at the packages in a supermarket—packages that commonly cost $50,000 to $100,000 to design. All the cereal boxes, say, or soup cans, or salad dressing bottles from one company have a similar "look" that says "General Foods," or "Campbell's," or "Kraft." You don't even have to read the label; just a quick glance identifies the product through color, typography, and shape.

You want to do the same thing with your publicity material. You want your cards, tape labels, brochures, even photographs to instantly say "Joe's Band"—or whatever your name is. And you don't want it to look like everybody else's material, either.

Where do you begin to develop such an overall concept? Start with the framework—your logo.

DEVELOPING A LOGO

A logo is a symbol, a graphic sign that tells people at a glance that they are reading about *you*. A logo may be as simple as your initials set in a distinctive typeface, or it may be a complex design incorporating elements of your music, your name or personality, even a slogan.

The logo is a shorthand way of identifying yourself—just as, at a glance, you recognize PBS, CBS, or NBC from their corporate symbols. Since this logo will be used on all your publicity materials, and you'll use it for years, spend enough time and money to be sure it represents you as well as possible.

Your logo need not be complicated, but it should be special to you. After all, you're better than your competition—aren't you? Your promotional material should show it. Make it classy, if that's what your music is like, or make it exuberant, or exciting, or dynamic. Just don't make it average.

If you need inspiration, your library probably has several award-winning commercial art collections that will give you ideas. Such magazines as *Print* and *Communication Arts,* and *Upper and Lower Case,* a free newsletter, frequently run articles about logo design. There are several books devoted to logos and trademarks listed in the Bibliography. Look at how others sum up their activities in a logo and you'll get lots of good ideas.

Here are considerations that will help you design a logo that's right for you and your music.

1. *A good logo is simple.* IBM uses only initials in a particular typestyle and a special shade of blue to identify itself. Coca-Cola uses its stylized script-like name in a particular shade of red. American Motors is known by the three letters, "AMC." The simpler your logo is, the more memorable it will be and the more it will stand apart from all others.

Your goal is to devise an emblem, a symbol that will be recognized at a glance on your envelopes, business cards, perhaps even T-shirts and stickers for instrument cases, so resist the temptation to add extraneous details, elaborate curlicues, or complex designs. Stay away from typefaces that are hard to read, no matter how "creative" they are. People won't take time to figure out illegible script that says "New Orleans Baroque String Ensemble."

Creating a clean, simple design isn't easy. Keep working at it, leaving out as much as possible, paring your idea down to its basic components. The simpler your design, the more versatile it will be.

2. *Does your name give you ideas?* Many logos are nothing more than a name, presented in a particular way. If you're a classical player, an elegant typestyle and your full—even formal—name may be quite appropriate. "J. Alfred Hogenbooth, Flutist" may be sufficient, or "Ann Marie Smythe, Pianist."

MARC ARAMIAN
ANOTHER GREAT COMPOSER

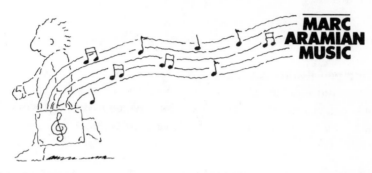

Marc wanted a letterhead that would be memorable to advertising and music production clients, so he worked with a design firm to create these ideas. "I told them that I wanted something that was both whimsical and classy," he says, "and they presented about forty sketches before the 'briefcase full of notes' came along. The 'composer's bust' idea was done by a cartoonist friend of mine."

Think about the parts of your name. Would just a first, or last, name do? It worked for Elvis, and it's effective for Engelbert, Dion, and Pavarotti. Most Johns or Susans, however, will have to look further.

What about using just your initials? That's certainly simple, and, with the right graphic touch, it might provide a memorable logo. It worked for JFK and LBJ.

If you're in a band with an already established name, you still need to work on developing a logo. For a rock band's material, you'll probably want a more energetic, hip, trendy, perhaps even iconoclastic, approach. Use your image sheet and brainstorm as a group to come up with ideas that will graphically reflect your musical personality. You'll work with the group's image rather than individual ones to devise an appropriate logo—and a group identity can be difficult to pin down. Work on this until you're satisfied that your logo design represents the spirit of your band.

3. *Music is filled with strong graphic elements,* and if you can find one that accurately reflects your own performance, make it part of your

logo. Consider the graphic possibilities of keyboards, the music staff, notation, and the shapes of most instruments—perhaps the gentle curved lines of a guitar, string bass, or violin will suggest a design for your logo. A close-up view of part of a flute, trumpet, or almost any instrument reveals interesting graphic possibilities.

4. *Avoid prefab logos.* Every printer and mail-order office supply house offers standard logos that they'll stick on your printing for a small fee—or even free. If you let them use that out-dated, mediocre set of drums on your card, you'll look just as mediocre as the thousands of other drummers who've used the same symbol. Don't take the quick and easy way when you're working on your logo. Spend the time (and money, if necessary), to get something that reflects *you* and your music.

Publicity Practice

Use a pad and pencil and your imagination to brainstorm the idea of a symbol for you and your music. It doesn't matter at all whether you're adept at sketching—you're after concepts, ideas, and images that might work. Don't be concerned with details—simply try for several interesting designs.

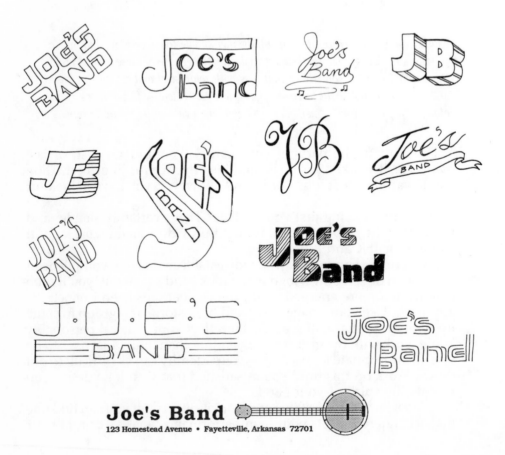

Also, don't worry now about the actual steps in producing the logo. Later, when we discuss typesetting, art, layout, and pasteup you'll learn how to do it yourself or find professional help.

Whether or not you plan to actually produce the artwork yourself, you need a clear idea of what you want. Even a commercial artist will need your input. So brainstorm the logo idea until you've exhausted your creative ability.

Work on your logo design until you're really pleased with it. Then put it aside. Come back in a week or so and take a fresh look. If you still like it go ahead and produce it, but if the perspective of a week has made your design look flat, mediocre, or junky, go back to the drawing board. You are special and your music is unique. Your logo should show it.

YOUR PRINTED TOOLS

When you start designing your printed materials, you'll be amazed at the available possibilities. Hundreds—even thousands—of type styles, paper and ink colors, and graphic elements are readily available. Computer typesetting machines produce an array of different typefaces, and every town has at least one quick-copy center that will inexpensively print everything you'll need. Also, several companies make press-down lettering or press type that's available in hundreds of different type styles and sizes. Though it can be tedious to use, such press type brings almost infinite design possibilities within everyone's reach.

Quick-copy printers are a little like glorified photocopy machines. All you have to do is provide clean *camera-ready art*, and they'll print it in any color, on any kind of paper, in any size you need. (*Camera-ready art* simply refers to the material that you want to have printed, presented to the printer exactly as you want it. "Art" in this case does not mean illustrations—it simply means whatever you want printed.)

Later we'll discuss standard sizes and formats for each of these printed pieces. First, though, here's an overview of what you'll need to be fully equipped for all your publicity projects.

Your own stationery is the first step for any professional. This doesn't mean going to the printer and selecting a standard letterhead from the sample book. Use the same creative process as with developing your logo—in fact the logo should be part of all your printed material.

You'll need letterhead-sized paper and matching envelopes. You might want half-sized, or smaller, note paper, and perhaps a separate format for thank-you notes. All your correspondence should say at a glance,

"This is from a professional who cares about appearance and detail." To make such quality obvious, you'll want to use a paper with a high rag or cotton content—and you may even choose a colored paper.

Business cards are small and simple, but are an important part of your publicity program. Businesspeople often have elaborate filing systems for business cards, and your card should be standard size to match their systems. Everyone uses, and expects to receive, business cards, so you should develop a striking design that will work for years. Use your logo, of course, to reinforce the image you're building. My card features a simple, large keyboard design, with nothing else on it but name and phone number, and people have remembered it for years. That's the kind of recall you're after—but your card has to earn such attention.

Joe Girard, who bills himself as "the world's greatest automobile salesman," throws handfuls of his cards into the air at football games. While you may not need to do that, always have cards with you, and hand them out freely. Clip one to every letter, invoice, and thank-you note you mail. Leave stacks of them with anyone who volunteers to recommend you—club owners, photographers, concert halls.

When you aren't around, that little 2 by 3½-inch piece of cardboard is you. Make it count.

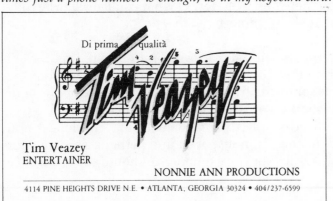

Design can be simple or complex—both can be effective. Sometimes just a phone number is enough, as in my keyboard card.

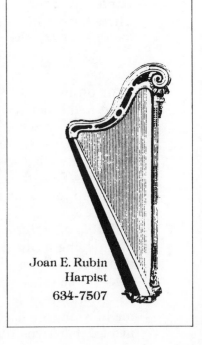

*The first impression is often the strongest, and a well-done mailing label says
"I'm a professional" even before the envelope is opened. "Bands Atlanta's" label
uses strong, easy-to-read type, and a simple design, and it's a standard size that
all printers have.*

Mailing labels are easy to produce, and add a professional touch to
your correspondence and packages. You'll need them for sending demo
tapes and other publicity material, and every printer will have a variety of
standard sizes in the "crack and peel" format. You might also have custom
audio cassette labels printed to give your demo tapes a finished appearance—your printer will have precut stock that fits any standard cassette.
You can even have small stickers made, in any color or shape, bearing your
logo or a sales message, for use on envelopes, instrument cases, photos,
or wherever you wish. (This doesn't include bumper stickers, which will
be screen-printed by someone other than your quick-copy printer. They'll
be discussed later.)

A few standard forms will enhance your professional image. Once
you have the artwork for your letterhead, it's a simple matter to use it also
on invoices and contracts.
Many clients prefer to be billed, and you'll often be paid more quickly
if you send a standard invoice. Custom-designed invoices are preferable
to the stock forms available at office supply stores, but your own design
will cost a little more.

A printed contract form or confirmation agreement will also save lots of time. Why bother to write a letter to each client, when you can quickly fill in the blanks and have a simpler, easier-to-understand, document as well? (We'll discuss contracts in Chapter Fourteen.)

Most performers will benefit by using the items listed above. We all have to write letters, send bills, and use contracts, and we all need business cards and mailing labels.

Many musicians, however, won't need all the items discussed below. If there's a chance that they'll help you get noticed, however, go ahead and prepare them. It's much easier to plan ahead and have a current resume, for example, than to stay up all night frantically trying to get one ready for an unexpected interview.

Resumes are standard throughout the world of work. They simply show, in easy-to-comprehend format, who you are, where you were educated, what you've done, and what you'd like to do. Resumes should be short and to the point, and there are several standard styles. If your only performances are with a country band at the Elks club on Saturday nights you probably won't need one, but if you're going after a teaching job, a scholarship or grant, a recording contract, or a classical music position, your up-to-date resume will be a major part of your information package. And, an impressive resume will quickly show high-society and big-business clients that your background and experience make you the perfect entertainer for their needs.

Bio sheets simply set forth the important biographical facts about you, preferably including a few interesting anecdotes. If you're preparing a full-scale publicity blitz, with a large packet of material for the press, a bio sheet would be useful, and you'll need one if you send demos to record companies. It might be unnecessary—and a little presumptuous—for a guitarist/singer to present a bio sheet to the bar owner who's hiring him, but a violinist who travels the country performing with major symphonies will certainly need one.

Brochures are hardworking pieces and we'll discuss them fully in Chapter Five. Most brochures are really just one piece of paper, folded one, two, or even three times to create several "pages" or "panels." Your brochure will be a sales tool, telling audiences about you, giving references, and quoting past clients and reviews. It may include a picture of you or your group and will feature well-written text. There are dozens of different brochure styles and formats: you'll choose one that matches your music and personal style.

Flyers are single sheets of paper, printed on one side with an advertising message—"Joe's Band will perform at the Moonvalley Saloon Saturday, October 5th at 8:00 p.m. Tickets at the door." Flyers are really small posters for specific events, and can be quickly produced and distributed around neighborhoods, on bulletin boards, on cars in parking lots, and on telephone poles.

Tune lists sometimes come in handy. Even if they've heard you, clients invariably ask, "What kind of music do you play?" A printed sample tune list will answer many of their questions, and isn't hard to produce or update. For many pop and dance bands, a tune list is essential.

Client lists may be useful for some musicians. If you have an impressive file of satisfied clients, you may want to prepare a sheet that demonstrates your experience and association with successful organizations. If you've only worked in two country clubs in your musical life don't prepare a client list, but if you've played for fifty major corporations and associations, why not use their prestige to improve yours? As always, however, don't lie and don't exaggerate.

Press releases are like little news stories about your activities. You'll use them to pique the interest of the local media and publicize upcoming events and musical activities. Press releases follow a standard format and aren't difficult to write; you won't even need to deal with a printer because press releases are typed. A good press release will interest an editor, who will often assign a writer to do an article on your activities. Or, the editor may decide to print your release exactly as you've written it. Either way, it does the job and gets your story noticed. Chapter Eleven covers this important tool in detail.

Newspaper and magazine articles about you, your group, or a current music-related issue can enhance your name and give you status as an "opinion leader." You aren't a writer? It really doesn't matter. If your band has played for 500 weddings, or if your songwriting is aided by a computer that prints out the notes you play, or if you offer free trumpet lessons to ghetto children, you will find plenty of space available for your story. You can write it yourself (as explained in Chapter Twelve) or work with a writer from a newspaper or magazine.

The press kit contains most of the material listed above, plus current photos, in a folder. Often, of course, you'll use the individual items independently, but for big projects, and to make a strong impression, you'll put everything together in the press kit. The folders can come from the office supply store, or be custom-designed and printed just for you.

A well-done press kit is a very useful piece. Even though it's just a folder, it says, "This person cares enough about her image to put together an entire packet of information about her musical activities. She's proud of her profession." A press kit is not only useful, it's impressive. We'll discuss them further in Chapter Eleven.

Newsletters are exactly what the name implies—a letter bringing news, and they're a simple way to keep clients and audiences regularly informed about your activities. If you're part of a large organization—a recording studio, college music department, or community orchestra, for example—a newsletter spotlights activities of the group and individual members. It gives detailed information about upcoming events and keeps your name before those who should know.

If your band, of whatever size, is active, you can use the newsletter to update club owners, agents, and your local fans about developments in your group—new tunes, equipment, dates booked, personnel changes, interesting anecdotes, and so on. In Chapter Twelve, we'll discuss getting your music publicized in newsletters published by other people and organizations.

Miscellaneous printed material includes all kinds of easily produced items. Remember, printing is available everywhere, is surprisingly inexpensive in standard formats, and produces high-quality, professional material that keeps your name before the right audiences and gets you noticed. Once you learn the simple techniques of layout and pasteup, you'll use your local printer the way you now use a copy machine. Consider the following possibilities:

> • *Post cards* are useful for keeping your regular clients, subscribers, followers, or fans updated on news of interest. "Susan Bennett brings her dazzling piano stylings to the El Cordoba cafe on Saturday nights. Present this card for a 10 percent discount on a meal for two."
> • *Rolodex cards* preprinted with your name, address, and phone number will put you directly into lots of "who's who" networks.
> • *Reprints of articles and reviews about you* make impressive additions to your publicity mailings. You can even make a useful promo piece from a collage of thank-you letters you've received (you do save them all, don't you?).
> • *Other miscellaneous printed items*—album covers, cassette J-cards (cardboard inserts for plastic cassette cases), posters, or banners—help reach your audience and aren't difficult to produce.

Picture Perfect

Photos are a standard part of any publicity program. Keep your image ideas in mind when you shop for a photographer because your photos, like everything else, must convey the feeling you want to create. The impact of your head shot can be changed dramatically by expression, pose, lighting, background, clothes, and photographic technique.

You'll want a stock of up-to-date head shots and group pictures, and maybe even photos of newsworthy and interesting activities of your group. You may even choose to have different photos for the different aspects of your professional life—a posed studio shot for publicity about your teaching work, and an informal, perhaps outdoor shot, for your rock band.

Photography is discussed in detail in Chapter Seven.

DEMONSTRATE YOUR ABILITY

Your product is music—ineffable, spontaneous, and probably indescribable. How can you sell a client on your band if he doesn't hear it? Do you tell him you play in tune, with a danceable beat? Do you tell him that your vocals blend so well they'll send chills up his spine? Do you tell him that your drummer never plays too loud or rushes, or that your synthesizer has a really terrific clavinet sound that's perfect for early Stevie Wonder tunes?

If you tell him any of that, he probably won't have any idea what you're talking about. Music just doesn't lend itself to translation into words, and most audiences don't share your vocabulary and concerns. Your client probably doesn't know (or care) what a clavinet is. He doesn't know that vocals should blend, and he hasn't had the piano at home tuned in ten years.

He needs to hear your music—and he won't judge it on narrow, technical grounds, either. He'll just compare it to the records and tapes he owns—the ones produced at vast expense in the best studios in New York and Los Angeles, with the world's best players. You'll have no trouble meeting that standard. Right?

Your first commitment, in planning demo tapes, must be to quality. Sure, it's easy to take a four-track machine to the job and produce a quick, inexpensive tape. But that's not good enough when you consider what you're really up against.

Remember, a tape won't capture all the excitement, the charisma, the interplay that's part of your performance, so compensate by going for top quality. In a live performance the audience often won't notice a little intonation problem, or that the bass overpowers the keyboard. On tape, such lapses are painfully obvious.

(If you're making a pro-quality demo to sell a song or group to a record company, then quality and cost requirements will be even higher. A finished "record quality" demo may cost several thousand dollars for one tune.)

Look at Me—I'm on TV

With the popularity of MTV, the idea of music video has become an established part of the business. But before you paint your face and rush out to do bizarre things on camera, ask, "Do I *need* a video?"

The standard of "quality first" is even more important with video than with audio demos. Why? Because today's audiences are sophisticated—they're "video literate" from years of watching TV, and they aren't easily pleased. Again, the standard for TV quality is the thirty- or sixty-second commercial that is often produced without budget limitations, and often uses the best, newest, most innovative video production techniques.

Unless your band has access to quality production facilities, lots of backing money, and a TV outlet, you probably don't need a "music video." Think carefully about how you'd use such a one-tune product, and remember that in 1986 the low-end cost for a music video was $25,000.

On the other hand, if your performance is unique, and lends itself to video, you'll probably benefit from a video *demo* tape. Be sure the medium is really appropriate, that you have something visual to convey, and that you won't be just a "singing head" (or worse yet, a "playing head"). Television can be cruel, and even if your dance band is the best in town it may be boring to watch you standing there playing "In the Mood." In fact, it could be deadly.

If you're a singer with an act, a comedian, a speaker, a soloist, or you do a show, then you may need a video demo. For many entertainers, as opposed to musicians, the video demo is the centerpiece of their publicity programs.

Think carefully about whether you really need a video, and then plan it carefully and produce it well. You must be committed to quality. Chapter Eight covers videotape production.

Publicity Practice

As you work on your publicity, start a file for samples of other people's publicity pieces. Don't limit this idea file to music, but keep samples of any good brochures, letterheads, cards, and stationery you see. Be alert for good group photos—from magazines or album covers. Listen for unique demo tapes, and watch TV for video techniques that you could use.

Take good ideas wherever you find them—if you like the layout and "look" of a hotel's brochure, why not adapt the same graphic design for your use? You won't copy directly, of course, but that graphic framework, when meshed with your copy, might produce an excellent piece.

HOW MUCH WILL IT COST?

If you choose to do all the publicity chores described in this book, your entire publicity campaign can cost very little—mostly materials, printing, and postage expenses. You can use press type rather than a typesetter for some projects, do your own photography, and even record your own demos if you have time, equipment, and knowledge. It's very possible to do an effective job of publicizing your music for little more than the cost of film, recording tape, and art materials.

Realistically, however, you'll probably use professionals for some publicity chores, so you'll need to devise a budget in advance. If you're a band or part of a musical group, you'll also have to decide how to pay the publicity bills. In most bands, individual members provide their own instruments and equipment, and the band may own little or nothing in common. However, since your publicity will benefit everyone, you may decide that everyone should share a fair portion of these expenses.

Once you devise a budget, perhaps each band member should contribute a percentage. If your group shares income equally, then you'll probably divide publicity expenses equally. If, on the other hand, the group's leader makes more money than the sidemen, he should certainly contribute proportionately more.

To share these expenses, and to be sure all the group members are happy, you'll need a budget. And to devise a budget, you'll have to do a little research. You'll need to decide what publicity items you'll need and whether you can produce them yourself. Then you'll need to decide what quantity you want—a hundred copies, or a thousand? Finally, you'll need to carefully figure the costs of doing it yourself, and get *several quotes* from the professionals you choose to help you.

Reading *Getting Noticed* will give you plenty of information on how to produce what you'll need. But prices vary so widely that you'll have to check with local artists, photographers, printers, even public relations counselors, to produce a budget that will reflect your needs.

Perhaps you decide that you need a letterhead, a brochure, a tune list, business cards, a group photo, and a well-produced audio demo tape. You'll write the brochure copy, but that's all you plan to do—the rest will be professional help. Here's how your budget might look:

Typesetting and printing for 250 letterheads
and 250 envelopes. $72.00
Artist's fee (including typesetting) for laying out
8½ × 11 brochure and business-card design. 175.00
Printer's cost for 500 copies of brochure, printed both
sides, with two folds, on coated paper (one color ink only). 70.00
Printer's charge for business cards. 30.00
Photography session, including two rolls, contact prints,
and three finished black-and-white 8 × 10's 80.00

```
Mass-photo house, 500 prints with band's name
    added at bottom.......................................65.00
Recording studio fee for producing eighteen-minute
    demo master........................................700.00
50 duplicate cassette tapes...............................100.00
Total cost...........................................$1292.00
```

This isn't a complete publicity kit—it's just a few of the most necessary items, and it still costs over a thousand dollars. You could, of course, lay out and design your own brochure, you might be able to shoot your own photo, and you could probably make duplicate cassettes for less than two dollars each, but you'd still have to pay the printer, photo duplication service, and recording studio. Be sure that, as you read this book, you prepare a written budget that includes everything you'll need. That way, you won't get any unpleasant financial surprises later.

Publicity Practice

Take your pad and pencil and look back at the list of publicity tools on pages 23-29. Think about your image, your career, your business. Decide which tools you'll need—letterhead stationery, invoices, demo tapes—and write each item down. If you've had experience doing layout and pasteup, you already know whether you can do it yourself. Otherwise, you may need to read Chapter Six before you decide.

Perhaps you'd like to write your own flyers and brochures, but don't think you could do a good job of design, layout, and pasteup. You'll be your own writer, but will need a commercial artist's help with production. Or, maybe you can write and do layout yourself so you'll only need to find a typesetter. Do you have a terrific idea for your logo—but you can't quite get it down on paper? You need an artist. So, using the list of publicity tools as a guide, and thinking about your musical goals, list all the items you'll need. Then decide what you can realistically produce yourself. You'll probably need professional help for the rest. Chapter Nine explains how to find—and work with—artists, writers, and photographers.

Looking Good

Publicity tools expand your presence and allow you to be remembered when you aren't there. Your material should be distinctive and good; it should alert people that you're a professional, that you care about your image. Before you even meet a client, prepare her by sending your press kit, demo tapes, and a well-written cover letter. She'll think you're terrific, and when she meets you, or hears you, she'll already be convinced that you're a pro. That's what good publicity material can do.

CHAPTER 4

Writing Basics for Performers

HOW'S YOUR WRITING? "It's pretty good," you reply. "I do an occasional lead sheet, a few chord charts for the band, and I'm working on a really big project—full arrangements for a public TV special on the history of bagpipes in Colonial Massachusetts. My music on that TV show will really get me noticed."

Maybe it will, but another kind of writing is just as essential to your career. It's not music at all—it's writing words and it will appeal to people who don't know a quarter note from a quarter horse.

"Oh, no," you think, "not English composition again. I didn't learn about gerunds the first time around and I'm not about to do it now."

Good writing will help your publicity program as much as anything you'll do, and you don't have to know about gerunds. It will require some care and attention, true, but it's no harder than learning the pentatonic scale.

WHY WRITE?

If you're a musician, you've probably spent hundreds of hours writing and reading music. Why should you worry about writing English, since you already speak it?

Look back at the list of publicity tools in Chapter Three. You need most of them, and someone's got to write them. It might as well be you.

But whoever writes your publicity material, it must be good, because: when you're not around, your writing represents you. Will your letters and brochures make a positive impression? Or will clients think you're sloppy and careless—or ignorant?

Also, your audience is barraged daily by nearly *three thousand* messages—all kinds of ads, brochures, magazines, newspapers, commercials, and direct-mail solicitations. Those bits of writing have been worked over, planned, checked and double-checked by legions of copywriters, editors, artists, photographers, and public-relations pros until they're perfect. Your printed pieces must reach that standard or they'll look amateurish.

You have to tell people what you do, who you are, why they should hire you, why your show is interesting, how you can entertain them, and why you'll do a better job than the band next door. To do this, you'll write letters, bio sheets, resumes, brochures, flyers, and press releases. You might even write feature stories about your band, and, as mentioned earlier, you could produce a newsletter.

Actually, you'll find that doing your own writing isn't too difficult. Most of what you'll write will follow standard formats, so much of your task will be simply "filling in the blanks." We'll discuss specific aspects of writing brochures, letters, and press releases in Part Two, but the ideas in this chapter apply to everything you write.

What Is Good Writing?

Good writing is any writing that does its job. Good writing communicates clearly. Good writing tells the audience exactly what you mean, leaving no room for doubt or mistakes. Good writing is direct and simple.

Good, effective writing needn't be complicated. It can be as simple as the announcement, "Joe's Band will perform Friday, June 18, at 8:00 p.m. at the Moonvalley Saloon. Tickets at the door—$5.00." There's nothing fancy here, but the message is clear and unmistakable.

Many writers—professional and amateur alike—get very serious and stiff when they sit down to write. They use big words to sound formal, dignified, erudite, educated. They devise complex ways of saying simple things, often using several words when one would do. They end up sounding pompous and silly, and the message is often lost beneath the inflated language.

As you prepare your publicity material, remember that good writing is direct, forthright, and conversational. You aren't writing the Great American Novel—or if you are, this is the wrong guidebook to use. Your intent is to communicate—not impress. Try to make your writing so transparent that it does the job without being noticed.

Good publicity writing is also informal, so avoid pomposity, complexity, and inflated vocabulary. Try to write in a conversational tone, much as you speak. Use contractions. Don't seek out big words just because you're writing—you're communicating, not building your ego. When the Atlanta Transit Authority calls elevators "vertical circulation elements," that doesn't impress anyone—it just sounds ridiculous.

Good writing is honest; it doesn't pretend to be something it's not. Lots of entertainers exaggerate shamelessly—but you shouldn't be among them. Most readers have a good sense of what's true and what's not, and if your publicity sounds unbelievable it won't be read. When you write, "Joe's Band performs regularly on 'The Tonight Show,' " be sure it's true, because someone will check. If you claim, "Susan's songs have been recorded by several Nashville stars," tell which stars and which albums. Remember, if you exaggerate or lie outright you'll get caught. Once your credibility is questioned, it's difficult to reestablish trust.

Good writing will be understood by the target audience. You'll know a lot more about your subject—music—than your audience will, but don't flaunt it. If you need to impress people do it musically, not verbally; don't try to awe the reader with your education and expertise. Musical jargon and technical terms only belong in writing that's intended for other musicians.

When your band is performing a difficult work that incorporates several time signatures, is modal, changes tempo every other bar, and quotes extensively from the literature of both African folk music and Norwegian sailing tunes, you've got to be careful in writing a press release. Ask yourself, "What will my audience understand about this?" and write simply enough to be clear.

Most of all, good writing is interesting. This is where the *hook* enters the picture. Of course your music is interesting to you, or you wouldn't be doing it. The task in creating publicity items is to make it appealing to your audience. Put yourself in the readers' place. Try to imagine what will grab, and hold, their attention.

Don't tell them the details of programming your DX-7—because they don't care about algorithms. They really don't. They may be fascinated, however, by the idea that a thirty-seven-pound synthesizer can sound like hundreds of different instruments, a space ship, a train, and a tugboat whistle, at the push of a button. Or they may be interested in the fact that Michael Jackson's "Victory Tour" used fourteen DX-7s on the stage—and that you have the very same instrument in your band. Or, they may be interested in the cost of state-of-the-art synthesizers, and the fact that prices are falling. You can be sure, however, that the only readers interested in details of synthesizer programming are other synthesizer owners.

Your job, as a person seeking publicity, and as a writer, is to find out what's interesting to your readers, and use it to help your writing hold the audience. If you can do that you're a good writer, whether or not you'd recognize a gerund on the street.

HOW TO WRITE—THE BASICS

What do you do when you sit down facing that blank sheet of paper? Do you agonize over each word, strive to make it perfect the first time, worry about spelling, search desperately for the exact phrases you need? If you approach writing that way, you'll be frustrated—and you may even get a full-sized case of writer's block.

Whether you're writing a simple letter of introduction or a story about your choir's elaborate Christmas concert, here are ten basic steps to follow that will make it easier to write anything.

1. *Know what you're trying to do.* The clearer you are about what you need to write, the easier it will be to produce it. If you're writing a business letter, look at Chapter Fourteen for more details; if you're preparing a brochure, read Chapter Five. Each item has its own customary form, and you should know what you're trying to create. Public relations writing is not free-form artistic expression.

2. *Decide what you want to say, and in what order.* First, just list everything you want to say. Write down all the subjects you need to cover. Make it simple—you're not writing a story now, just a list. When you have all the ideas on paper, arrange them in order of importance. Decide what is most crucial, most interesting, and put that first. Then move down the scale of importance on your list.

3. *Write it.* Go ahead and do your first draft. Most of the time, you'll have to revise it later; sometimes you'll even change everything. The important thing now is to get something down on paper.

Use your list of facts from step 2, and start at the beginning. Don't worry about style, mechanics, repetition, and so on. You'll clean all that up and fix the problems later. First, just *write it.*

4. *Revise it.* Wait a day, if possible, and then reread what you've written. Does it make sense? It should, of course. Is it logical—do the facts follow each other in correct sequence? If not, rework it.

When you write anything, ask yourself, "Did I say what I meant?" "Did I say it as well as I could?" "Will anyone else find it interesting?"

You may have to do several drafts to get the main points straight, and to make you ideas understandable. That's okay. Professional writers usually rewrite a piece many times. Writing is a process, not a one-time explosion of creativity; you should expect to rewrite, revise, and repair until you're satisfied. If you're using a word processor, revising is much easier, but however you work you must expect to rewrite. And rewrite. And, probably, rewrite some more.

5. *Fine tune it.* Now work on the smaller things. Try reading your effort out loud and see if you notice any problems. Look for repeated words and phrases, clichés. If you catch yourself repeating the same word—"music," "band," or "keyboard," for example—find another word, or rephrase the entire sentence. A thesaurus is handy to jog your memory, but don't use unusual, pretentious, or odd words. For

"piano," you could substitute "keyboard," "baby grand," "spinet," or "upright." Or, you could refer to the instrument as a "Steinway," or a "Fender Rhodes." It would probably be inappropriate, however, to call it a "pianoforte"—unless that's exactly what you intended.

Choosing the precise word you need is crucial to good writing— and the English language confronts you with overwhelming choices. Somewhere, you'll find just what you need, but don't go over- board—it's better to repeat "piano," than to make it obvious that you're searching for a synonym.

Often the ear will alert you to errors in composition and usage. Are your sentences too long? Too short? Too monotonous? If you read your work aloud, you'll know. Good word choice and varied sen- tence length make writing more interesting. You'll be surprised what you'll *hear* that you didn't *see* in rereading. Your musical background should help your writing's rhythm, pace, and flow.

6. *Check for active verbs.* Verb phrases that use *is, are,* or *were* are *inac- tive,* and make for lethargic writing. Relying on weak verbs is like playing every chord in the root position—it may work, but it's bor- ing.

You'll have to read very carefully to find these tired verbs, but *is, are,* and *were* are warning signs. Replace such weak phrases with stronger single verbs that add zest, spice, and movement to your writing.

Look at the difference here:

"The Druid Hills Band is holding auditions this Saturday morning. All students who are interested are invited to try out. It is necessary to bring your own music, and students are urged to be on time."

What's wrong with that? Nothing crucial, to be sure, but we can save several words, and make the announcement stronger *just by changing the verbs.* Notice the difference:

"The Druid Hills Band holds auditions this Saturday morning and encourages all interested students to try out. Bring your own music and be on time."

The first example has thirty-six words; the second gets the same message across with twenty-five. What did we lose by chopping out those extra eleven words? Nothing. What did we gain? A tighter, eas- ier-to-read, easier-to-understand announcement.

Nothing earthshaking, you say. True, those weak phrases and verbs didn't ruin the original announcement, but if you replace weak verbs with strong ones your writing will be more powerful, more fun to read—and more likely to be read.

7. *Simplify, cut, reduce, pare, whittle down, eliminate.* Step seven is dif- ficult, but very important. Go back over your piece again, and see if every word is really working for you. Almost every bit of writing can be improved by pruning. Just as too many notes obscure an elegant melody, too many words will encrust your writing—and make it deadly reading.

Here's an example from a pop band's brochure:

"You'll find that when you hire the Falcon Band your parties will be livelier, and that people will dance and have a good time. As the evening goes on, the band is capable of picking up the tempo, and moving from quiet music to today's rock and roll hits. We know hundreds of songs to suit all your moods."

Not bad, but it's not tight, energetic writing. Let's pare it down and see if we can improve that paragraph by making a few deletions and changes. When you read carefully, you'll find lots of improvements can be made.

Here's the rewritten, tighter version:

"Want a lively party? Like music that makes you dance? Then you need the Falcon Band! We'll start easy, with ballads and bossa novas, and pick up the pace when people are ready to rock and roll. From "Stardust" to "Shout"—we know them all."

Making changes and cutting words isn't easy, and if writing the first draft was difficult, you're going to resist cutting those hard-won words and phrases. But it has to be done. Your writing won't really suffer—it will be improved by taking out extra words, phrases, even paragraphs. Simple is often best.

8. *Use transitional words* to smooth the flow of your writing and lead the reader easily from thought to thought. You wouldn't always go from the key of F to C without the transition of a C7 chord, would you? Such words as "however," "also," "further," and "thus" do the same thing in your writing. Think of them as "dominant seventh transition aids."

Transitions improve paragraphs and sentences. Without them, your writing will seem to be a string of unrelated words and thoughts. Again, reading aloud shows where transitions are needed.

9. *Correct spelling errors.* You say, "How can I correct them if I don't recognize them as mistakes?" First, trust your instincts—if a word *looks suspicious* to you, check the spelling. Often your first impression is right—if a word looks wrong, it probably is. You can use a dictionary, of course, but you may save time by buying a little spelling dictionary that's really just a long list of correctly spelled words.

If you're using a word processor or a new electronic typewriter you may have access to a spelling program. Use it. Finally, have someone else read your work to check for spelling (and other) errors. You probably have a friend who excels in English who'll spot the mistakes you don't recognize.

Correct spelling is just as important as playing a melody precisely as it's written. Get it right, or you'll look careless. There's a big difference in a half note and a dotted quarter; there's a similar difference between "capitol" and "capital."

10. *Is your writing in style?* Writing *style* refers to all the little elements that give writing its look, feel, texture. Each piece should be consistent within itself, and with the image you want to convey. If your band is on the avant-garde edge, you'll avoid formal, studied language and try instead for a hip contemporary tone. If your band is a middle-of-the-road group trying for country-club bookings, your

style should match that audience and be responsible, factual, not too trendy. Read over what you've written, and ask, "Does this sound right for my music, my personality? Will it appeal to my audience? Will they find it appropriate? Will they read it?"

Small details are also important elements of writing style. There are several different approaches to what is "right" and there isn't room to cover them here. If, however, you plan to do lots of writing, buy a style book and use it consistently. Your local paper may even give you one if you plan to send them frequent press releases.

For example, the correct treatment of time (one o'clock, or 1:00?), addresses (25 Main St., or twenty-five Main Street), money ($1250.00, or twelve hundred and fifty dollars?), and numbers (twenty-seven years old, or 27 years old?) can be difficult, and are usually arbitrarily decided. Since such details can vary greatly from style-book to stylebook, the best approach is to learn one system and be consistent with it. You'll find several excellent style books listed in the Bibliography, and they aren't difficult to use—treat them like dictionaries, and look up specific questions. It's not necessary to read and memorize the entire book—just use it as a reference while you write.

Before we leave the discussion of style, there is one area that causes so many problems for so many writers that we'll discuss it. The problem is with apostrophes. The apostrophe has two uses. One, it indicates possession—"Anne's flute." Apostrophes are also used in contractions to replace the missing letter. Thus, "it's" means "it is." "She'll" means "she will." Avoiding contractions sounds too formal and pretentious. Don't freeze up just because you're writing.

The single most common error in writing, according to four college English professors I polled, is confusion about "its" and "it's." "It's" is a contraction, meaning "it is." "Its," *without the apostrophe in this case,* is possessive—it refers to something that belongs to "it."

When you're writing about a musical group, for example, say "Its music is so exciting that it's likely to be a sold-out concert."

The Write Stuff

When your writing is finished, revised, edited, corrected, and as good as you can make it, have someone else read it for you. Once you've spent hours on a project, you'll be too close to it to judge accurately. You know what you wanted to say, so you can't really tell whether you've succeeded. Be sure, though, that your test reader knows what you're trying to do and understands who your audience is, for an accurate critique.

You're going to have to write in order to get noticed. These ten considerations will help get you started. Like music, writing gets easier the more you do it, and like music, practice makes perfect.

CHAPTER 5

Preparing Written Publicity Pieces

YOU'VE JUST REVIEWED SOME IMPORTANT fundamentals of good writing. Now start putting them into action by preparing important publicity pieces—resumes, bio sheets, and brochures. We'll discuss both content and format—because both are important. More detail about preparing written material to be printed—design, typesetting, layout, and pasteup—is in the next chapter.

RESUMES

Not every musician will need a resume but you may be surprised at how helpful one can be. If you're the leader of a country band looking for work at county fairs, a standard resume might not help you book the job—but it might. If you're a composer seeking funding from the community arts council, a resume is essential. And some clients—large corporations, booking agents, and record companies—need the information a resume provides.

Resumes set forth, in one page if possible, your employment goal and the principal facts about you—background, education, relevant work experience, qualifications for the job you're seeking. A most important feature of the resume is its *brevity*; the reader gets a quick sense of who you are and what you've done.

To achieve this conciseness, resumes follow fairly standard forms.

We'll demonstrate one here, and your library will have books on resumes that go into more detail. There's no need to pay to have your resume prepared. Do it yourself, since you know the subject better than anyone else.

What should you include in a resume to give yourself the best chance?

- List relevant *higher educational achievements*. Don't tell about grammar school unless you were the boy soprano with the symphony; emphasize recent accomplishments, including college work.
- Include *private teachers* if they are well-known specialists. "1979-81—Studied tympani with Dr. Finn Bille, with special emphasis on crescendos." Or, "1985-present—Took monthly performance seminar with Dr. Jane St. Clair at her Carnegie Hall studio."
- Include all your *music awards*. If you were first chair flutist in high school and college, say so. If you were in All-State Band each year, mention it. If you received a full scholarship to the Cincinnati Conservatory of Music, list it in your resume.
- Include important *special performances* you've given. Were you invited to perform for the governor? Did you play "Rhapsody in Blue" with your community orchestra when you were fifteen? Have you been featured on a PBS "Young Performers" series?
- List any *special repertoire* you've mastered. This only applies to very difficult show pieces—don't list everything you know. You'll provide more detail on your tune list.
- Include, with dates, a list of *relevant jobs* you've held but don't give addresses and boss's names in the resume—there isn't space. Do you play with a local semiprofessional orchestra? Do you teach privately? Have you been a substitute music teacher in public schools? Did you play the "Classical Music" night at the local country club for years? Or did you host a weekly choral music show on the college FM station?

Aim your work experience listings toward the kind of job you now want. (If you don't have any work experience, leave this category out, and concentrate on your other accomplishments.)

Publicity Practice

Before you begin work on the resume itself, make a list of the important events and dates in your educational, performing, and working life. List any awards or scholarships you've received. Note special accomplishments that relate to the music job you want.

Keep your goal in mind, whether it's teaching school music, a chair in the symphony, or an on-stage performing position at Opryland. Slant your accomplishments that way. If you change your mind next year and decide to go into banking you'll need a different resume anyway, so aim this one at music.

You're selling yourself with a resume, so emphasize the good and leave out the bad. If you were kicked out of Berklee for playing the trumpet out of tune, there's no need to mention that here, though you should include the dates you attended. Such careful editing of your accomplishments, however, doesn't give you license to lie or exaggerate. Every employer will check your references and claims; carelessness with the truth will guarantee that you won't get the job.

Try to limit your resume to one page, two at the most. Edit carefully to leave out unnecessary items. Only include the most relevant, most impressive, strongest accomplishments that will help you get *this* job.

BIO

A *bio* is simply a short biography of you. Again, not every musician will need one, but if you're a guest artist, visiting teacher, workshop director, featured soloist, or a star performer you probably will. To an extent, the bio is an expanded resume with emphasis on what's interesting and important in your life. Your bio will usually be used by writers who are looking for an angle, a slant to enliven their stories, so include anecdotes and humorous events. If you've worked at Christmas as a strolling flutist, dressed as an elf in the toy department of a department store, mention it. Or if you performed for years at the corner of Main Street and First Avenue, use that unusual information in your lead-in paragraph.

Once again, start by listing important dates and accomplishments in your life. Then write the bio in chronological order or with the most recent accomplishments first. Write in the *third person*—that is, say "John Brown studied at the University of Southern North Dakota," not, "I studied at the University of Southern North Dakota."

You've got to toot your own horn here even if that's difficult. Try pretending that you're writing about someone else. You aren't after puffery and you aren't writing advertising for yourself, but the bio must be interesting enough to be read. Keep it light and fill it with the most interesting things you've done. "John Brown spent his apprenticeship playing the banjo at the corner of Main Street and First Avenue. 'The police were my most important critics,' he says ruefully. 'If they didn't like what I was playing—or where I was playing it—they'd arrest me. Believe me, I learned every officer's favorite tunes.' "

RICHARD H. LOGAN
123 Elm Street
Anytown, Anystate
(212)123-4567

OBJECTIVE

Band director's position at small college or university, with emphasis on stage band, improvisation, brass instruction

EDUCATION

M.F.A. Music Performance (Trumpet), University of Miami, 1986
B.A. Music Education, Boston University, 1984

HONORS

First Chair of America Award (1982, 1983); Full music scholarship to University of Miami (1984-86); *South Florida Band Director* magazine's "Student Instrumentalist of the Year" award (1985); Wolftrap Summer Composition Contest—Honorable Mention for "Trumpet Tune Number Three" (1986)

WORK EXPERIENCE

Practice teaching, Battlescar Heights High School, Boston (1983); private brass instructor, Midway Music Center, Boston (1981-84); private instruction, twenty-five students, Miami (1984-86); first trumpet with "The Forties Review" road show, summers from 1983 to 1986; work with small jazz and pop combos, Boston and Miami (1980-86).

PERFORMANCE INFORMATION

Featured soloist with The Miami Symphony, "Aratunian Trumpet Concerto," May, 1985; soloist with Charleston (S. C.) Symphony (at Spoleto Festival), Verne Reynolds' "Concertare Number II," (1986); soloist at Orange Bowl Halftime Show, with University of Miami band, "Bugler's Holiday" (1987)

EXTRACURRICULAR ACTIVITIES

Staff music reviewer, the *Daily Boston Student;* captain, Boston University Music Department's bowling team; bass soloist, All Saints Episcopal Church Choir (Miami)

PERSONAL INFORMATION

Born August 28, 1963. Single. Excellent health. Interests include computers, electronic music, photography, writing, bowling, singing, reading.

MAC FRAMPTON

Biography

"I can't recall a time in my life when I didn't know exactly what I wanted to do," says MAC FRAMPTON. A look at his early years confirms that fact. Born the son of a Presbyterian minister, he had lots of chances to test the piano playing waters: entertaining for church suppers, subbing for Sunday services, improvising "Here Comes the Bride" for a home wedding, playing the Sunday School hymns on creaky old uprights. Quite an exciting lifestyle for a boy of eight!

Today, MAC FRAMPTON carries his musical electricity to audiences around the world. He has traveled from the snows of the Northwest Territory to the sands of Saudi Arabia. He's shared the stage with the likes of Bill Cosby, Roberta Flack, Sha Na Na, John Davidson, Victor Borge, Louis Nye, John Gary, and Merv Griffin. Orchestras from Boston to Cincinnati to Atlanta to Oakland to Milwaukee have given him center stage. But through it all, the memories of childhood linger as some of the sweetest.

"I remember my first combo. Two clarinets, trombone, and piano! I wrote the arrangements and we played at a church men's supper. My little sister came on stage to sing the finale, and when we finished the audience started throwing things at us. It made us nervous until we realized they were throwing money!" The piano lessons he had been taking since the age of five were invested with a renewed dedication. After high school MAC continued his musical education at Erskine College in his home state of South Carolina and at the renowned Cincinnati Conservatory, where he received his master's and doctoral degrees. Recognition with a special medal at the Van Cliburn Competition followed, establishing him as a classical pianist with legitimate credentials.

It was at the Cliburn Competition that MAC began to seriously consider an alternative to a classical career. "I was at a farewell reception and some of the contestants who knew I improvised pop and jazz asked me to play a few tunes. I had just started when Van Cliburn himself walked in. He told me he was impressed with my arrangements and that I should consider doing them professionally. With that kind of endorsement, I had to think seriously about going into the pop arena. I went home and started booking myself with a backup group and found I really loved it."

The style MAC developed during the early years of pop concerts has proved durable. Based on classical technique but drawing liberally from jazz, folk, and rock idioms, the MAC FRAMPTON sound continues to build a wider audience with each of the more than 1500 concerts he and his group have performed for community, college, and convention audiences. His success has spawned ten record albums, a motion picture soundtrack, and unprecedented numbers of return engagements. When he is not performing, he spends much of his time recording, arranging, and composing. MAC and his wife Nancy live in Atlanta and are the proud parents of two sons, Eric and Will.

A typewritten bio sheet gives writers and promoters information about you for use in preparing programs and stories. Anecdotes add interest—for example, Mac's early church appearances and Van Cliburn's encouragement. The bio is best when it's short.

Emphasize your performance training and experience. Be factual, but not dry. Present yourself in the best possible light, but don't lie. If you have performed your "Early Rock and Roll" show to college audiences in thirty states, mention it. "Joe's 'History of Early Rock 'n Roll' show has been warmly received by student union audiences in thirty states, including the University of Georgia, Yale, and SMU." Be positive, but don't stretch the truth.

Include enough personal information to give writers the facts they need, but don't drag in all your family. "Joe is married and has five children, two of whom play the piano—and three baseball." Most audiences will be interested to learn of the five children, but won't care about their names, ages, and accomplishments.

If you can keep your bio to one page, that's great. If it must be longer, limit it to two pages at the most. Anything longer would seem egotistical.

Bio sheets can be typed or typeset, and should be single-spaced so all the information will fit on one page.

TUNE LISTS AND FACT SHEETS

Two other kinds of useful publicity material can easily be prepared by typing them on your letterhead and having them inexpensively printed or photocopied.

Tune lists help you answer the eternal question from prospects: "What kind of music do you play?" *Fact sheets* simply give the who, what, where, when, and, perhaps, why of your group and your music. Both can be quickly updated, and provide, at a glance, a lot of information.

To devise your tune list, first decide what categories of music are important to your clients, and what categories you've mastered. Since you probably won't have enough space to list every song you know, pick the best, most requested, most representative, and most recent tunes for your list. If you specialize in top-forty music, you'll frequently update the list—nothing is as outdated as last month's number one song. On the other hand, if you're a classical harpist, your repertoire won't change very often, so your tune list will last a long time.

The fact sheet should simply give a quick overview of you and your music. Make it easy to read—use short paragraphs or even a list format. Don't go into detail but stick to the most important facts you want to tell. How large is your group? How long have you been together? Where have you worked? Any special honors? Do you have a record? A show? A following? A video that's available upon request? The fact sheet is like an outline—more detail is provided by the bio, resume, brochure, and tune list.

BILL CLARY'S CREDITS:

MAJOR MOTION PICTURES

"STROKER ACE" WITH BURT REYNOLDS, LONI ANDERSON, NED BEATTY, JIM NABORS

TELEVISION AND COMMERCIALS

"FEED THE HUNGRY TELETHON" (C.B.N., ATLANTA, COM—MERCIAL)
"A.M. ROCHESTER": WROC, ABC, ROCHESTER, NEW YORK)
"NIFTY NINE": (WTVC, ABC, CHATTANOOGA, 34 CONTINUOUS WEEKS)
"THE GOOD TIME GANG": (CBN, WANX, ATLANTA, GUEST ENTER-TAINER)
"UNITED NEGRO COLLEGE FUND": (WXIA, 11 ALIVE, GUEST ENTER-TAINER)
"THE MAGIC OF BILL CLARY": ("SPECIAL", CTV, ROME)
"THE MAGIC OF BILL CLARY": ("SPECIAL", ETV, GEORGIA)
"GUEST ENTERTAINER": (KREM TV, SPOKANE)

ENTERTAINING WITH THE STARS

OPENING ACT FOR:
MARC WEINER ("SATURDAY NIGHT LIVE")
CHARLIE CALLIS ("SWITCH")
EDDIE ARNOLD
BOOTS RANDOLPH
DIZZY GILLESPIE ("JAZZ")
TOMMY SANDS
RAQUEL WELCH
CAROL CHANNING
ART CARNEY ("HONEYMOONERS")
JOHN CALVERT ("THE FALCON")
"ELI" (ROCK GROUP)
PAT McQUINN (NATIONAL RECORDING ARTIST)
PERFORMANCES FOR:
LATE PRESIDENT LYNDON B. JOHNSON
LATE DAN BLOCKER ("BONANZA")
MAYOR AND MRS. ANDREW YOUNG, ATLANTA

AWARDS

"OUTSTANDING ACHIEVEMENT IN THE MAGICAL ARTS AWARD" (SOCIETY OF AMERICAN MAGICIANS)
"CLOSE UP MAGIC AWARD WINNER" (SOUTHEASTERN ASSOCIATION OF MAGICIANS) 1982
"STAGE AWARD WINNER" (SOUTHEASTERN ASSOCIATION OF MAGICIANS) 1982
"CITIZEN OF THE WEEK AWARD" (NEW YORK)
"DRAMATICS AWARD" (NEW YORK)
"BOYS LIFE TALENT AWARD" (PENNSYLVANIA)
"HONORABLE MENTION" (MUSIC CITY SONG FEST, NASHVILLE 1982)

PLAYS

"REBEL WITHOUT A CAUSE" (LEAD ROLE, JIM STARK, NEW YORK)
"BENCH 18" (LEAD ROLE, OFFICER, NEW YORK)
"DRACULA" (DIRECTOR OF SPECIAL EFFECTS, GEORGIA)
"CAPTAIN COMPETENCY" (WRITER, LEAD ROLE, PRODUCER, GEORGIA)

SOCIETIES

"INTERNATIONAL BROTHERHOOD OF MAGICIANS" (MEMBER, PAST OFFICER, 10 YEARS)
"SOCIETY OF AMERICAN MAGICIANS" (MEMBER, PAST OFFICER, 10 YEARS)
"MAGIC INNER CIRCLE" (MEMBER 8 YEARS)
"THE GEORGIA COUNCIL FOR THE ARTS AND HUMANITIES"
"CREATIVE ARTS GUILD"
"BOARD OF ADVISORS," LEES McRAE COLLEGE, NORTH CAROLINA

WRITINGS

"MAGIC, UNITY, MIGHT MAGAZINE" NUMEROUS ARTICLES, SOCIETY OF AMERICAN MAGICIANS
"THE LINKING RING" (NUMEROUS ARTICLS, INTERNATIONAL BROTHER-HOOD OF MAGICIANS)
"MAGIC FOR CHILDREN" (AUTHOR)
"BILL CLARY, 1980 MAGIC LECTURE" (AUTHOR, LECTURER, NASHVILLE, NEW YORK, PENNSYLVANIA, CHATTANOOGA, ATLANTA, AUGUSTA, MACON, BIRMINGHAM)
"ARTIST AND LECTURE SERIES" (LECTURE ON STRESS AND STRESS MANAGEMENT VIA RELAXATION AT 95 COLLEGES AND SEVERAL BUSI-NESSES IN PAST 2 YEARS)

EDUCATION

FORMAL:
CATO-MERIDIAN CENTRAL SCHOOL, NEW YORK
MONROE COMMUNITY COLLEGE, NEW YORK
AUBURN COMMUNITY COLLEGE, NEW YORK
OTTAWA UNIVERSITY, KANSAS — MAJOR, RELIGION
COLLEGE OF CLINICAL HYPNOSIS (GRAD. 1982 (HAWAII)
MIME:
LENNY ZORCONE (MIME WORKSHOP) NEW YORK
MAGIC:
KEITH WALKER, LONDON
DIA VERNON, HOLLYWOOD
THE SYLVESTERS, AUSTRIA
PHIL GOLDSTEIN, MASS.
JAN TORELL, WEST GERMANY
GEOFFERY BUCKINGHAM, LONDON
EUGENE ALCORN, NEW YORK
DARWIN ORTIZ, NEW YORK
PETER KERSTEN, EAST GERMANY
MUSIC:
BEN JOHNSON, ATLANTA (BANJO)
NITE DRISCOLL, ATLANTA (GUITAR)
DREW FRECH, NEW YORK (BANJO)
OWEN GRISE, RICHMOND (GUITAR)
MARK CHAMBERS, OKLAHOMA (GUITAR)
HYPNOSIS:
JIM MILLS, NEW YORK
T.X. BARBER, Ph.D., MASS.
BOBBY McGEE, Ph.D. HAWAII (HOLISTIC HEALTH)
MARK STEVENS, Ph.D., HAWAII (HYPNOSIS, STRESS MANAGEMENT)
DR. RICHARD DEL LA FONTE, OKLA. (STAGE, BEHAVIOR MODIFI-CATION)

When you have an impressive list of credits, combine them in one page for maximum impact. Bill Clary is a multitalented performer, so his credit sheet spans the entertainment spectrum. If you've accumulated lots of honors, clients, and awards, and if you've made albums, videos, movies, or written books and articles, they should be listed to promote your career.

BROCHURES

One of the hardest-working tools in your publicity kit will be the brochure. It gives the facts about your music and your group. It quotes testimonial letters. It mentions your past successes, and lists prominent clients. It may include a picture of your band. It *sells you*. It does all this—but it's really only one piece of paper.

A well-done brochure tells your story briefly, and might be used for years. It isn't really difficult to produce, but it adds a finished, professional touch to your publicity material. The next chapter discusses details of typesetting and putting the pieces together; we'll discuss content and form here.

Now, what goes into your brochure? Depending on the final design you use, you'll need a cover, headline, body copy, and illustrations or photos.

You aren't writing a book. Don't tell everything you know about yourself and your music, and for goodness sake stay away from the history of your group. Clients don't want to know who had the idea to form your band, or that it fulfills a dream you've had since childhood. You must rigorously apply the *who cares?* test to everything you write.

Let's take the elements one at a time.

Cover

Your brochure will probably be one piece of paper, possibly folded twice to fit a standard business envelope. The front panel could feature a strong photo of your group, your logo, a relevant illustration, a catchy headline, or a combination of these elements. Inside, you'll tell your story in a way that makes your music seem irresistible. What you're doing, after all, is writing an ad.

Write a strong headline for the front panel of your brochure. Brainstorm ideas. Look for puns, perhaps a line from a well-known song that applies. Maybe, "We play the songs that make the whole world dance." Or, "For a good time, call—Joe's Band." Or, simply, "Try Joe's Band—We Specialize in 'People Music.' "

Sometimes a question forces the reader to open the brochure to find the answer. Pose a question on the cover, and answer it inside the brochure. "What's the most important part of any party?" Or, "Who has helped one president, three senators, five mayors, a hundred major corporations, and five hundred brides and grooms dance the night away?"

Maybe you have a quote from a very satisfied client that you can use to grab the reader's attention. "Your band absolutely *made* our party. We can't thank you enough for the great music."

I saw an effective cover that was nothing more than hundreds of song titles, in small print, covering (in fact, running off the edges) the front of a brochure, with the headline inside, "We Play Them All—and More."

Whatever you choose for the front of your brochure, remember that you have just a second or two to arouse the clients' curiosity and make them want to read further. If the cover is bland, unappealing, or amateurish it will be ignored—and you won't get the job. Spend some time working on the front panel of your brochure and get an artist's help if your own designs don't look good. (See Chapter Nine for advice on how to find and work with an artist.)

Here's an excellent, professionally produced brochure that uses clever graphics and clean design to build interest. Notice how the vertical black-and-white design (which is repeated on each panel) suggests formality and unifies the brochure's design. And rather than fill up every inch with unnecessary copy, the designer has used black and white space for emphasis and impact. This brochure says, "We're the best, and our publicity material shows how much we care."

Headline

Advertising people write books about headlines, and they agonize over them daily. Look at the headlines in newspaper and magazine ads to see how they attract attention. They appeal to your *needs and desires* through questions or emotional ploys, don't they? You should do the same.

What are most clients likely to need from your music? That's what you should stress. Do they want a rip-roaring good time? Should you promise to fill the club? Will your name attract standing-room only for a concert? Will the bride and groom swoon over your wedding music? Whatever it is, emphasize it in your headline.

And work to be sure that every word is strong, and exactly right. Edit, pare it down, think about each word. If you're a wedding band, perhaps something like, "Two Hundred Brides Can't Be Wrong!" would work. Or, if your band specializes in Fifties and Sixties music, try "Joe's Band Makes You Twist and Shout!"

The headline has to grab the reader's attention—and it must do it quickly.

Copy

Copy refers to the text of any written piece. So now that you have their attention, what do you say about your music that will make them hire you? Follow the old advertising adage to "sell the sizzle, not the steak." Tell about the benefits, the excitement, the results of your music; don't concentrate too much on the music itself because the client won't understand.

Here's a most important idea for selling your music: *potential clients don't care about you. They care about themselves.* They really don't care that you're a terrific musician or that your band is first-rate. They especially don't care whether you need the money. What they're concerned about is how you can help them.

Tell how your music brings people together—grandfather dancing with granddaughter. Emphasize that your repertoire lets you play whatever the crowd wants, whether it's Richard Rodgers' "Dancing on the Ceiling" or Lionel Ritchie's "Dancing on the Ceiling." If yours is a big band, point out that your music recreates the elegance of the Thirties and Forties. If you're trying for lounge engagements, show how you work with club owners to fill the room and mention special promotions you'll do; let them know that you understand the importance of the bottom line.

Here are some ideas of what music can do for your clients, taken from *How You Can Make $30,000 a Year As a Musician Without a Record Contract* (see the Bibliography for publication data). These are just samples to get you started—you should devise your own list, based on your own kind of music.

Music creates an appropriate atmosphere for any function.
Music demonstrates affluence.
Music entertains.
Music breaks the ice, encourages mixing, partying.
Music brings people together.
Music sells.
Music inspires.
Music makes people feel good.
Music attracts crowds.
Music recalls nostalgic memories.

It's important to "think like a client" when you're writing the brochure so you can stress the benefits that come with your music. If you really understand this fact about human nature you'll write copy that will get results. Here's how to do it.

Publicity Practice

Get out the old brainstorming pad and pencil and start a new list. This one will cover all the ways your music benefits clients. Forget about what it does for you. What does it do, or what *could* it do, for them? Brainstorm as many ways as you can that your music will fulfill their needs. Like this:

For *pop musicians*, music creates excitement and helps clients party, mix, mingle; it also can attract crowds, fill the club, help clients make money.

Teachers can promote music as a valued educational experience, an enjoyable and relaxing hobby, a happy group activity. It can make students "the life of the party"; it could help them become more popular. And if they're good, they might even be able to make money at it.

For *classical musicians*, music helps the audience connect with the profound experiences of musical genius; thus it uplifts, inspires, relaxes, soothes, and educates.

These are just a few of many ideas you should develop.

Next, list everything you'd like to say about your band, or your music. Remember—you want to fill the *clients'* needs. Include the outline of what you do, how large your band is, the kind of music you play (with examples), but emphasize what your music will do for the client (from your brainstorming list), testimonial quotes from past clients, a list of past clients, and selections from your tune list. Think about the kind of photos you'd like to include.

Now write your copy. Start with a catchy lead paragraph that asks a question or promises a benefit.

"What's the most important part of a really memorable party? Flowers? Food? Decorations? We think it's the music. Here's why."

"If you're hiring a band for your company party—watch out! You've got to please your president—and the stock-room clerks. What band can do both?"

"Why did Bob Hope call us 'my favorite opening act'?"

Once you have their attention, tell how you can help them.

"Joe's Band is Little Rock's most popular party band for one very good reason—we play the kind of 'people music' that everybody likes. Our five-piece group will read your crowd perfectly and pace the music to match the mood."

"The San Diego Baroque Ensemble is perfect for formal occasions where elegance, history, and culture are important. Our impeccable presentation of hits from the sixteenth and seventeenth centuries will give your gathering the special atmosphere you want, with the added excitement of four virtuoso performers playing just for you."

"Bob Hope said, 'I always look forward to sharing the stage with Joe's Band because their enthusiasm is contagious and their music is exciting. Not only are they a great opening act, but I like their music—and they don't tell jokes.' "

When you discuss your music, and your group, keep it short and don't tell too much. Be as specific as you can. Rather than "we play all kinds of music," try "we play polkas, big band tunes, and lots of rock and roll." Actual titles often help. Remember, your clients aren't musicians, and may not really know what constitutes "early rock and roll" unless you tell them.

Be careful if you start writing too much about you, your music, your art, your need for self-expression, or your creativity. Read your first draft, and count the number of times you've written "I," "we," "us," or "our." Then count the number of times you've used "you." Keep the emphasis on the client—not yourself.

Also resist the urge to write about your equipment. You're proud of your instruments and accessories, of course, but remember that it's *very, very rare* for a client to care about brands of amps, speakers, microphones, keyboards, or guitars. He couldn't care less whether you use Shure, Electro-Voice, or Brand X equipment. Don't tell them more than they want to know.

Your copy need not be long, but it should be to the point and lively. Use short sentences and snappy words. Don't feel that you have to fill up the entire page, either. Blank, white space is an effective element of design, and uncluttered, uncrowded copy is easier to read—and more likely to be read. Testimonials work. If you have letters of thanks from past clients, quote from them or print the entire letter. Include a list of past clients, which is a kind of testimonial.

Emphasize your experience, your professionalism, your willingness to work with clients to make your music meet *their* needs.

Should you include your address and phone number in the brochure?

Not if you book through agencies or other third-party employers who don't want clients to have direct access to you. Instead, simply leave a blank area on the back panel for an agent (or you) to rubber-stamp an address, or affix a sticker. If you're booking directly, just staple your business card to the brochure.

When you've finished the first draft, put it aside for several days. Come back and read it over. Have a friend or two read it, to see if it conveys what you intend. When you're sure it does, check it carefully for correctness.

Prices

Should you include prices in your brochure? Usually not. The brochure is a long-term publicity piece, and you don't want to be locked into today's prices if you're still using the brochure next year. Also, there are times when you need to be flexible, to have bargaining room. And, if you book through agents, they'll quote their own prices, which may be much higher than yours. Try to get your client interested in your music before you discuss the price. Use the brochure to *sell*, and save details such as cost for later discussion. When it's time to talk about money, describe your price structure in a cover letter or a separate printed price list that can easily be updated.

Photos and Illustrations

Since the photo is only a part of the brochure, it will probably be quite small. Be sure, then, that it's a close-up that clearly shows your face, and that your expression matches the tone of your brochure. If you're planning a brochure for a band, it's even more important to use a good photo, since your faces will necessarily be smaller. (Chapters Six and Seven explain what kind of photo will reproduce best.)

Photos are important, but don't use a poor one. And don't lock yourself into just one image if your style changes from booking to booking. Photos are a bit like price lists—you can easily send a supplemental one along with your brochure, and tailor the picture to the kind of client you're approaching.

Line art—illustrations that are just black and white with no intermediate gray tones—can be printed directly without the halftone screening process and add no extra cost. So if you have a really good drawing of yourself, or perhaps a caricature, consider using it. Or perhaps an illustration is appropriate—an old-fashioned woodcut or steel engraving, for example. You can use clip-art from sources listed in the Appendix, but don't use an inappropriate illustration just because it's available.

Books of copyright-free music engravings are available from Dover Publications (see Bibliography) and other publishers. Art supply stores also carry books of clip-art that can simply be pasted into your layout. As long as there are no real grays—only black and white—the art won't have to be screened, and can be treated as line art. Old-fashioned engravings such as these could promote a historical festival or be used humorously with other publicity projects.

Format

Brochures can be simple or very elaborate. We'll only discuss the simplest form here; you can expand these ideas into a booklet if needed.

Most of the time a single sheet, perhaps folded a time or two, will provide plenty of space—and the look of a brochure—with just one trip through the printing press for each side. Look at the illustrations on page 54 of different formats for single-sheet brochures, and different ways to arrange the type. You can treat each folded section as a separate page, or panel, or you can treat the brochure as essentially two pages—front and back.

You can leave one outside-facing panel blank for address and stamp, and turn the brochure into a *self-mailer.* You may even find that a single sheet, unfolded, with a strong photograph on one side and headline and copy on the back, will suffice. This format is in effect a flyer—but with a brochure's content and impact. If well done, this simplest of all "brochures" works well. Look at the samples on pages 60 and 216 to see what a top-quality job a single sheet can do.

Whichever format you choose, try several rough drafts of different

CAN BE
VERTICAL
OR
HORIZONTAL

ONE PAGE, TWO FOLDS
(8½ × 11) – OFFERS FOUR
PANELS FOR COPY,
PLUS COVER, AND
BLANK ADDRESS PANEL.
FITS #10 ENVELOPES

ONE PAGE, ONE FOLD
(8½ × 7¼) – OFFERS
TWO PANELS FOR
COPY, PLUS COVER
AND ADDRESS.
FITS #10 ENVELOPE

ONE PAGE, ONE FOLD
(8½ × 11)
OPENS TO FULL PAGE
SIZE. REQUIRES
6 × 9 ENVELOPE.

TWO PAGES, ONE FOLD
EACH, COLLATED,
PROVIDE EIGHT
PANELS, EACH 5½ × 8½
WHEN YOU HAVE
LOTS OF INFORMATION.

BROCHURE FORMATS

There are as many brochure designs as there are ways to fold a piece of paper.
Here are some common, easy ways to turn one or two pieces of paper into effec-
tive, professional-looking brochures.

designs. Should you run the copy vertically in columns, with a photo in
the middle? Should you put the photo on the front and print the copy hori-
zontally? Work with your typesetter, artist (if you're using one), and print-

er, and use your clip file for inspiration.

Tell potential clients and audiences what they need to know, quickly and directly, and demonstrate that you're interested in pleasing them with your performance.

Once you start using printed material, you'll find that it's not intimidating, or especially difficult, to write and produce everything you need. If you need to update a resume to go after a particular job—no problem. If you need to prepare a current tune list to conform with your new band's orientation—it's easy. And, if you need to create new printed pieces that aren't discussed here, it's no problem either, because you have the skills, knowledge, and confidence to prepare good-looking publicity material that will work hard for you long after you've forgotten how hard you worked to create it.

THE PRESS KIT

While you're designing material, why not prepare a unique press kit to hold everything? Of course you can just visit any office-supply store and buy stock folders off the shelf, but think how much better a custom folder will look.

Check with your printer for his size limitations: many quick-copy printers cannot handle a full-size folder (which is printed flat and made into a folder later). Your printer, however, can probably subcontract the job to a "commercial" printer with a larger press, or tell you where to get the work done. A one-color print run of 250 folders will cost at least $250; 500 folders would probably cost eighty cents each, so a custom folder is a big investment.

Design the folder as you would any printed material. Use your logo or your name in an attractive type style, perhaps even in a very large size. Remember that the press kit is like an advertisement—it must be so attractive that the client will want to look inside. If you can't afford a custom-printed folder, visit a large office-supply store and choose a plain folder in a finish and color you like. Use your mailing label to personalize it, or have stickers made with your logo or name to affix to each one.

What goes into the press kit? Everything! It's a handy way to show off your brochure, photo, tune lists, resumes, and anything else that's appropriate. If you've collected lots of reviews and articles, include appropriate photocopies for each client.

The press kit goes to "the press," of course, but it's also the best way to present your material to interested clients, agents, and anyone else who expresses an interest in your music. Package your material as well as you can, and it will make a positive, professional impression.

Atlanta Metropolitan Orchestra
Ronald Mendola, Conductor

ATLANTA HAS SOMETHING TO CELEBRATE

The Atlanta Metropolitan Orchestra, under the direction of Ronald Mendola, is the newest addition to Atlanta's musical family. This 35 piece ensemble has the professional credentials to play ballet one night, accompany a name act the next and do a stand-alone pops or formal chamber concert the following evening.

The founder and musical director of the orchestra, Ronald Mendola, is nationally respected as an accomplished classical and commercial trumpet player and conductor. Four years ago IBM recognized his ability and appointed him musical director for its National Marketing Division. They put his talents to work on directing, contracting and arranging its multimillion dollar musical production each year. Mendola has also conducted nationally known acts on the road with stars such as Bob Hope, Rich Little, Flip Wilson, and Charlie Callas.

Ironically, these travels served to intensify Mendola's strong commitment to create something more with the wealth of local talent in his "hometown" Atlanta.

"I've always known what we've had here potentially," Mendola explains. "After conducting in most major cities in the country, I was anxious to return to Atlanta and hand pick an orchestra comfortable in

both classical and popular literature; an orchestra comprised enthusiastic, polished professionals. I'm happy to say my colleag surpassed my expectations from the first rehearsals."

The key to Mendola's musical success has always been conci directing, a perceptive view of the best way to serve his client interests, and perhaps most importantly, the respect and inspiration h gives his musicians and they return to him. Ron's vision for the Atlanta Metropolitan Orchestra reflects his twenty years of musica experience in its bold and expansive goals.

"Long term" he states, "I see a chance to recreate the triumphs of other cities alive in the arts...a season like that of the St. Paul Chamber Orchestra or a festival modeled on the Mostly Mozart Series in New York to balance an active popular schedule. The sophistication of Atlanta's audience demands it, and I want to be there when it happens."

Join in the celebration. Contact Ron Mendola for more information on how easily--and professionally--your entertainment needs can be arranged.

For more information: write 1385 Oxford Road, Suite 115, Atlanta, Georgia 30307 or call (404) 351-0817.

* * *

"We've got something to Celebrate!" is Atlanta Metropolitan Orchestra's press kit. This well-done package was targeted to large producers and corporate clients who might need a full-scale orchestra for major productions and concerts. The folder includes information on the conductor, the orchestra itself, and suggested soloists. The first teaser mailing was a small box, containing only an announcement card, a party noisemaker, and some colorful confetti. Subsequent mailings included the full press kit, with the confetti/celebration theme continued; the letterhead even has colored flecks of "confetti" printed on it. This is part of an expensive, professionally produced campaign.

RONALD MENDOLA
MUSICAL DIRECTOR

MENDOLA & ASSOCIATES
1385 Oxford Road / Suite 115 / Atlanta , Georgia 30307   404 351-0817

FROM THOSE WHO KNOW..

"Your support and quality 'touch' at our recognition events over the years have created many special memories."

> **L.W. Gray, President**
> **South West Marketing Division**
> **IBM Corporation**

"Ron Mendola is a consummate professional, always totally concentrating on his client's project."

> **Erik Magnuson**
> **Magnum Production Services**

"Our annual awards program could not have been more successful. Much of this success is due to Ron and his orchestra. Their music provided a most enjoyable evening for both the formal program and for the dancing pleasure of our guests."

> **J. David Chatham, Past President**
> **Home Builders Association**
> **Metropolitan Atlanta**

"Ron not only proved himself a capable arranger and conductor -- he solved production problems before they got to me. We'll be working with him again, and soon."

> **Dick Anderson, President**
> **Trilogy Productions**

"Your performance was simply outstanding.....so excellent that the King Center family have named your group our "House Band."

> **Coretta Scott King**
> **The Martin Luther King, Jr. Center**

"As providers of Ron's sound support services, we were most impressed that not only was Ron always available, he always had the answers."

> **Robert Jones**
> **Staging Techniques, Inc.**

"I've found his approach to both conducting and playing to be one of total professionalism and commitment to his art. He is truly a first rate musician."

> **Mac Frampton**
> **Concert Artist**

RONALD MENDOLA
Biography

EDUCATION

Master of Fine Arts in Performance 1980
State University of New York at Buffalo

PROFESSIONAL EXPERIENCE

1986 - Present	Director, Atlanta Metropolitan Orchestra A 34 piece pops / light classical orchestra
1985 - Present	Composer / Conductor / Contractor Home Builders Association of Metropolitan Atlanta Awards Show
1983 - Present	Music Director / Contractor IBM South West Marketing Division Recognition Events with duties as arranger / composer / coordinator with choreographer, other writers, arrangers and composers
	Conductor for shows including Mary Welch, Mac Frampton, TBS Emmy Awards, and Theodore Bickel
	Contractor for Jack Jones, Mitzi Gaynor, Tony Bennett and others
	Member of Spoleto Brass Quintet
1981	Featured Soloist with Tommy Dorsey Orchestra
1979	Guest Soloist with Atlanta Chamber Orchestra
1976 - 1977	Performer / Conductor, Center for Creative and Performing Arts at Buffalo, New York
1974 - Present	Live performances with artists including Perry Como, Tony Bennett, Nancy Wilson, Johnny Mathis, Rita Moreno, Jack Jones, The Fifth Dimension, Ella Fitzgerald, Burt Bacharach and Carol Bayer Sager Recording dates with Isaac Hayes, Curtis Mayfield, as well as many TV / Radio themes and jingles

CHAPTER 6

Producing Printed Materials

NOW YOU KNOW WHAT MATERIALS you need—letterhead, brochure, bio sheet, invoices, business cards, and so on—and you've reviewed basic writing techniques. If you're going to produce these items
yourself, this chapter will show you how to transform handwritten or
typed pages into handsome, hardworking publicity pieces.

First, you'll come up with a pleasing design, and have the material
typeset to give it a professional look. Then you'll lay it out and paste it in
position for the printer.

BY DESIGN

Books have been written on layout and design, and commercial artists
work for years to develop good design skills. However, with your clip file
for inspiration and a little practice, you can design publicity material yourself.

Look for samples of whatever format you're working on, both for inspiration and to see what the standards are. Standards, particularly for
size, exist in every area, and your material should meet them unless
there's a good reason to go your own way. Thus, letterheads should be 8½
by 11 inches, and business cards should be 1½ by 3. As mentioned earlier,
to design a business card in an odd size would be counterproductive, since
wallets and card files accept only the standard.

Use your clip file for ideas. If you see a good design, why not copy it? Always watch for interesting brochures, letterheads, business cards, photographs, and other publicity material that looks good. Incorporate the elements you like into your own material; by the time you've changed the typeface, copy, and illustrations it won't be an imitation anymore.

Regardless of what you're designing, apply these principles:

- Simple is better than cluttered. White space is a design element too, and lots of clear space will highlight your message. Study advertisements to see how professionals do it.
- Try for balance among the different elements. If you use a block of type on the left side of a brochure, balance it with a photo, or some smaller blocks of type on the right. Let your eye be the guide; layouts can be top-heavy, side-heavy, or bottom-heavy.
- Work to create a visual path through the piece. Use headlines, subheads, white space, and graphic elements to lead the reader. Large blocks of type are deadly in promotional material, so break up your copy. Don't let your material look like a textbook.
- Your logo should be an important part of most of your publicity items. A printer can make *stats* of it in different sizes for use in your layouts. (A *stat* is like a very good photocopy that can be printed with no loss in quality.) You may want illustrations, and your art store will probably have several books of "copyright-free" illustrations that you can use, or you can order a catalog of such "clip art" from Dover Press (see the Bibliography).
- Photos must be *sized* and *screened* before printing. A good photo can add impact, but it must be excellent to begin with. The printing process often degrades image quality. When you're doing the actual layout, just leave the spaces blank where photos will go, and work with the printer to be sure the pictures reproduce well.

Publicity Practice

First, brainstorm for design ideas. The elements you'll use are headlines, subheads, body copy (that's set in paragraphs), illustrations, photographs, and design elements such as boxes, dots (called "bullets"), ruled lines, and so on. These are like the pieces of a puzzle—the solution is a pleasing, coherent design.

Try several ideas for each project. Do as many rough drafts of your design as you can. Let them sit for a few days, look them over again, and continue working on the ones you still like. Try lots of combinations before you settle on a final design.

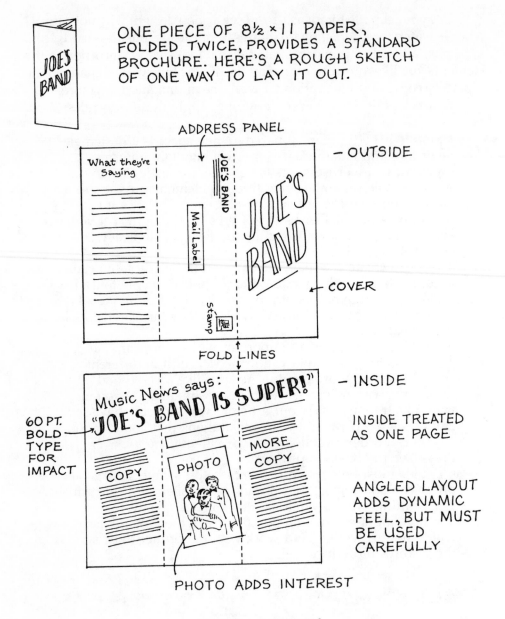

ONE PIECE OF 8½ × 11 PAPER, FOLDED TWICE, PROVIDES A STANDARD BROCHURE. HERE'S A ROUGH SKETCH OF ONE WAY TO LAY IT OUT.

ADDRESS PANEL

— OUTSIDE

What they're saying

JOE'S BAND

Mail Label

JOE'S BAND

Stamp

← COVER

FOLD LINES

— INSIDE

Music News says: "JOE'S BAND IS SUPER!"

60 PT. BOLD TYPE FOR IMPACT

COPY

PHOTO

MORE COPY

INSIDE TREATED AS ONE PAGE

ANGLED LAYOUT ADDS DYNAMIC FEEL, BUT MUST BE USED CAREFULLY

PHOTO ADDS INTEREST

ROUGH LAYOUT

Designing a brochure is like solving a puzzle: move the graphic elements around until they fit. Here, the design is on an angle to add a dynamic "feel" to the brochure, and a photo is used. If Joe's Band were more stately or sophisticated, the brochure would probably be more formal, but here the exciting design matches Joe's music.

To repeat, quality is the goal. If you find that you can't get the pieces of your project to fit together in a pleasing way, find an artist to help you. You don't *have* to do everything yourself. (See Chapter Nine for details.)

TYPESETTING

Your first question may be, "What's wrong with typewritten work? Why bother with typesetting?"

```
True, typewriters can produce beautiful results.
But typewritten copy doesn't look as good as type-
set work because typewriters space each letter, word,
and line the same. Typeset copy doesn't--it micro-
spaces to adjust the space required to justify the
right margin--or make it even. This paragraph is
typewritten: notice the difference.
```

What needs to be typeset? Almost any printed material except letters, tune lists, and press releases. Your typesetter will set your name and address in interesting type, and in the exact size you will need, for use on cards, letterheads, envelopes, and invoices. And he will produce finished, professional-looking copy for brochures, flyers, and information sheets.

Finding a good typesetter can be important to all your publicity projects, then, so interview several prospects before deciding to work with one. Look in the Yellow Pages and ask your printer for suggestions. To find moonlighting freelancers, call the art or publication departments of large companies or government offices. Prices will vary, and so will service. Tell the prospect about what you're doing, and let her know that you'll need advice and help. Choose someone, even if her prices aren't the lowest, who will work with you, because that help will be very valuable. Often the small, one-person shops will be the best choices, both for service and price.

Typesetting also lets you choose from many different type styles, called *faces,* in varied sizes, densities, and spacing. Most of your printing will use a few well-known typefaces because they're easy to read, but sometimes an unusual one is appropriate.

People won't work to read your material, so choose a typeface that's legible. Advertising agency research shows that type with *serifs*—the little lines that decorate the tops and bottoms of letters—is easiest to read. *Sans-serif* typefaces don't have those lines, and look cleaner and more modern, but they aren't quite as legible. Both styles, however, are popular. Good serif typeface selections for general use include Times Roman, Bookman, Cheltenham, Schoolbook, and Bodoni. Common sans-serif faces include Univers, Megaron, Helvetica, and Franklin Gothic. This book is set in Palatino.

Match the typeface you choose with your music and personal style. Different types have different connotations—symbolic and emotional values—and you should carefully assess what they are before choosing one.

Helvetica Outline **Beton Extra Bold**

Horace Light Bodoni Book

Horace Medium *Bodoni Book Italic*

Horace Bold **Bodoni Bold**

A press-type catalog (see the Bibliography for addresses) will surprise you with the incredible variety of typefaces that's easily available. You'll find a type style that exactly matches your ideas and that will promote the image you want to project.

Some faces look traditional, conservative, or formal. Others seem futuristic, avant-garde, unrestrained. In fact, some typefaces evoke specific feelings: Gold Rush would be appropriate for a Country Western band, Broadway for a show band, for example.

To show you what's available and illustrate different faces, most typesetters provide a sample book of available sizes, fonts, and weights. You won't be expected to speak the language (picas, points, leading, ems), but you can use the sample book to show what you want. Your typesetter may also be able to offer valuable advice on what you should choose.

Show him a sketch of your layout so he'll know what you're trying to do. Get his ideas on type sizes for your headlines, subheads, and body copy. If you're doing your own layout for the first time, you'll rely on your typesetter's advice and knowledge, particularly about spacing and type size. With experience, you'll develop a "feel" for using type, but the following guidelines will help you in the meantime:

- Your finished material must be legible, and type that's too small to read will be ignored. Type is measured in *points,* a technical term; for most purposes ten- or twelve-point type will be the right size for text use. Eight points is too small, and fourteen- to eighteen-point will be used for subheads. Larger sizes are useful for headlines, titles, and even poster copy.
- Don't combine different typefaces in the same piece—the result will look confused and cluttered. In fact, try to choose a style of type that you can use on all your printed pieces; it will become your "look" and each printed piece will reinforce your image. You can, however, use different forms of the same typeface for variety—make headlines bold, or extra bold, for example. Your typesetter will offer suggestions.
- Don't use all capital letters, except in very short headlines; words set in upper case are harder to read. And white letters

A – 10pt.

A – 12pt.

A – 14pt.

A – 16pt.

A – 18pt.

A – 20pt.

A – 24pt.

A – 30pt.

A – 36pt.

A – 42pt.

Type that's too small can't—and won't—be read. Type that's too big won't fit the page. Your typesetter will help you select the size and style that match your needs. Ten point type is commonly used for text, and larger sizes for subheads, headlines, and even posters or bumper sticker design.

on black background (called *reverse type*) are usually more difficult to read, again except for short headlines.

• Resist the urge to be graphically "creative." There are so many exciting, unusual, and "different" typefaces that you might decide to choose a style no one else uses. Such typefaces as Prisma, Sunshine, or Magnificat have specific applications in advertising and audiovisual production, for example, but would be a poor choice for your printing. Don't worry that using a common typeface will make your work look average. Being graphically unusual for its own sake may lead to illegible designs, and your aim is to make it easy for the reader.

Working with the Typesetter

For the best possible results, it's important to realize the typesetter is *not an editor*—his only job is to set into type the material you give him. If the copy you provide contains misspelled words and grammatical errors, you'll probably receive beautiful, typeset work that includes misspelled words and grammatical errors.

So make your copy clean, clear and legible. Don't waste your typesetter's time (and your money) by providing poor-quality originals with lots of crossed-out lines and minuscule scribbling in the margins. Write on one side of the page only, and double space between lines. Leave wide margins all around for technical typesetting notes.

Also check and double-check all copy for accuracy. All typesetters will correct their own typing errors free, but will probably charge extra for any changes, called *author's alterations* or *aa's*, that you make later. Read your material carefully, watching for all kinds of errors—spelling, grammar, usage. Double-check names, addresses, telephone numbers, times, and dates. Some people read backwards to make errors stand out, or you could have someone else carefully check your copy. If you let it sit a day or two, it will be fresh when you come back to it, and you'll spot problems that you'd overlooked. Try very hard to catch mistakes *before they are set into type*. Remember, it's really difficult to see your own errors.

Know in advance what the typesetter's charges will be. Typesetters usually charge by the page, and complicated formats will cost more. Prices vary enormously—one person may charge seven dollars a page, while another may charge thirty. Always shop around, and get a firm cost estimate. You're after a top-quality, professional job, and typesetting can do more per dollar for your image than anything else. Many typesetters actually do many commercial art tasks, and can help with page layout, brochure design, and even logo production. When you find a typesetter who's easy to work with, who will give you advice, whose work is nearly error-free, and whose price is reasonable, strive for a good relationship. You'll benefit for a long time.

Many print shops have their own typesetters, but you may find freelancers to be less expensive. Frequently, typesetters who work for large companies will do extra work on the side, and you'll probably be able to find several freelancers nearby who have Compugraphic, or similar machines, at home.

A typesetting machine, which may cost $20,000, is not the same as a personal computer, though both have keyboards and screens. Some personal computers, however, with laser printers and the right programs (called *desktop publishing programs*) can produce copy that's about as good as typeset work; but always compare their quality with professional typesetting.

Alternatives to Typesetting

Typesetting is the standard way of giving your words a finished, professional look. There are, however, at least four alternatives to typesetting—transfer type, calligraphy, typing, and computer printers. Each has its use.

Transfer Type. There may be times when your typesetter doesn't have exactly the type style you need. Perhaps you're designing a poster, and you need something outrageous and unusual. Or maybe you want the headline on your brochure to be in a startling typeface. In these situations, you can use *transfer,* or *press type,* which come in hundreds of different styles and sizes.

Transfer type is easy to use, but it can quickly become a tedious and time-consuming job. Only use it for doing a few words at a time—a headline, a poster, or your letterhead, for example. You wouldn't want to spend the time required to use press-down letters for the actual copy of your printed pieces—it would take forever, would cost more than typesetting, and would probably look bad. Transfer type is best for applications where large letters, few words, or unusual typefaces are needed.

The most common brand of press type is *Letraset.* Any art-supply store will have a good selection of these typefaces and sizes, and you can easily order what the store doesn't have. Depending on the size you buy, you'll get a large sheet that contains dozens of letters, arranged alphabetically, for between five and ten dollars.

Most transfer type comes with an instruction sheet, but also ask at the art supply store for a demonstration of how to use the brand you buy. Put simply, to use transfer type, draw a guideline with a nonreproducing blue pencil and rub the letters one at a time from the backing sheet to your layout surface. Some brands use a clip-and-paste (rubber cement) method instead.

With care and a little practice you can produce as many headlines, posters, and signs as you need. You can pick just the type style you want for your letterhead, for example, and produce it yourself. Glance through a press type catalog and you'll be excited by the possibilities for enhancing your image through creative use of type.

Graphic elements are also available in transfer form. You'll be astounded at the variety of borders, boxes, lines, decorations, and even illustrations, that can easily add professional design elements to your publicity material.

Calligraphy. If your music is formal, calligraphy might be a good way to prepare invitations, letterheads, even business cards. If so, find an experienced calligrapher, and be sure that what she produces is legible, neat, clear, and straight. Also, if you choose to use calligraphy or other handwritten forms, the original art should be done in black ink on white paper for best reproduction.

While calligraphy looks good for certain formal invitations, an entire handwritten brochure would probably be too much of a good thing. Remember, your goal is to be read; don't make it difficult by using an unusual handwritten style.

To find a calligrapher, ask at art-supply stores and college art departments. In large cities the Yellow Pages include a "Calligraphers" listing. Interestingly, the mayor's or governor's office could probably recommend one, because many government offices use calligraphers to prepare formal declarations and proclamations. Some calligraphers charge by the line—two dollars per line is a rough standard—whereas others charge by the hour or by the job. Charges may vary according to the complexity of your copy, so discuss exactly what you're planning with the calligrapher to get current fees.

Typewritten Material. There will be times when you'll simply use your typewriter to prepare material for publicity projects. Press releases and letters, for example, are always typed, not typeset. When typing a finished piece that will be read by your audience or clients, use a standard typeface. Even though daisy wheel and ball-type machines offer inexpensive variety, stick to a standard typeface that looks like a typewriter—since that's what you're using. *Never* use script—it looks amateurish and tacky, and is hard to read.

Use a new black carbon ribbon—never a colored one. And keep the machine clean. Use a toothbrush and a little solvent to keep the *o*'s, *e*'s, and other letters clear. (If you don't have cleaning solvent, you can use a little *wood* alcohol on the brush. Don't use rubbing alcohol because it contains minute amounts of oil.)

Sometimes typewritten copy looks better when it is reduced slightly before printing. If you're having copies run off at a print shop, ask the printer about a very slight reduction—it won't cost you any more, and it could improve the appearance of your material.

Desktop Printing with Personal Computers. Personal computer technology is changing so fast that you may have to read a computer magazine each month to keep up. Many personal computers with the appropriate program and a laser printer can produce perfect typeset-quality material. These combinations require top-of-the-line machines, and are expensive, but they are creating a revolution in the communications industry.

Such "print shop" programs not only produce typeset-quality output, but can do design chores as well. You can create forms, charts, graphs, and even complete newsletters right on the computer screen and dispense with layout and pasteup entirely.

Such programs are much more complex, however, than the commonly available word-processing programs. It's true that almost any printer gives access to lots of typefaces, and all word processors can justify your type (make each margin even), but word processing and print-shop-style programs are two entirely different things.

At this writing, the Apple MacIntosh is the most used desktop publishing computer, but the IBM AT and others will do similar tasks. However, special programs, such as Aldus Page Maker or Ventura Publisher are required. These computers and programs are expensive and laser printers are also costly. Such programs doubtlessly will soon be available for other popular personal computers; if you're interested in producing lots of top-quality printed materials yourself, you'll need to keep up with *desktop publishing*.

(Of course, any computer with a good word-processing program will make your *writing* chores easier, but most computers can't run the "print shop" programs that produce typeset-quality work.)

Finally, be careful about using dot-matrix printers for anything except rough drafts. Even with programs that produce different typefaces, these printers still rely on tiny dots, and their quality usually isn't good enough for most publicity material. If you have one of the superior dot-matrix printers that produces "near letter quality" type, you can use it for press releases, but be sure that the dots aren't visible. Your goal, as always, is to make it easy for the reader.

LAYOUT AND PASTEUP

Once you have your finished copy—typeset or press type—you're ready to lay it out and paste it up. You're going to turn those good-looking strips of typeset copy into finished publicity pieces.

Layout is simply the task of arranging, and rearranging, all the pieces of your graphic puzzle until they look right. Pasteup is, of course, the process of pasting them down.

You'll need a few special tools.

1. *A clean, clear place to work* is essential. Layout produces lots of tiny bits of paper, some of which are important. A cluttered workplace will insure disaster, so find a large, clean table or countertop with good lighting. Avoid the kitchen if possible—one spill can undo hours of work.

2. *Sharp scissors, and a special "mat knife."* Your art supply store will have several brands of inexpensive knives—get the pencil-sized one.

3. *A metal ruler and a square or triangle.* The ruler is for measuring and to use in cutting straight lines. The square and triangle help get everything straight, at exactly right angles.

4. *A bottle of opaquing liquid ("white out") and white masking tape* can be used to clean up any mistakes. Also get a blue "nonreproducing" pencil that won't be "seen" by the printer's camera, and several fine black pencils or pens.

5. *A light box* is handy because layout is easier if you can see through the material you're working on. Commercial lightboxes are expensive to buy, but you can easily make one yourself. Get a two-by-four-foot scrap of frosted glass or Plexiglas from a commercial plastics store and build a box with six- or eight-inch sides to support it. Paint the inside of the box white and add a couple of fluorescent "light sticks" from the hardware store.

6. *Layout board or bristol.* You'll actually lay your material out on a special board or bristol. Get the kind that has a light blue grid printed on it and get a size that's larger than the project you're working on. If you're preparing an 8½-by 11-inch letterhead, for example, be sure

your layout board is at least fourteen by seventeen inches.

7. *Adhesive.* Finally, you need some way of sticking your pieces to the layout board. The standard adhesive for this kind of work is rubber cement, a liquid that's applied with a brush. It's messy, and leaves residue that has to be cleaned up, but it's easy to use and is inexpensive.

Another approach is to use hot wax to stick down the pieces. A handheld waxer about the size of a hair dryer melts wax and applies it to the back of your material. It isn't messy, and isn't permanent, so your layout decisions aren't final. A waxer costs about forty dollars.

Don't use regular glue or glue sticks in pasteup because they'll cause wrinkles and air bubbles.

Publicity Practice

Now you're ready to lay out your camera-ready art. *Always practice with photocopies.* Never use your original typeset copy until you're sure of what you're doing and have practiced it a couple of times.

First, tape the layout board to your lightbox or table top; a small piece of tape at each corner is sufficient. Then use the nonrepro blue pencil to draw an exact outline of the outside boundaries of the piece you're working on. If it's a letterhead, it's probably 8½ by 11 inches. If it's a business card, it's probably 1½ by 3. Mark the center with the blue pencil, and make guide marks outside each corner with your black pen.

Using photocopies for practice, cut apart the pieces of material you'll be working with. If you're doing a letterhead, for example, separate your name, address, and phone number, and any design elements you're planning to use.

Now follow the rough draft ideas you've sketched out. Try different positions for each element of your design. When you've found a combination that's pleasing and balanced, mark the position carefully with your blue pencil.

To paste the pieces in place, use cement or wax on the back of the small pieces only—not on the layout board. Carefully put the pieces in position, making sure they're straight and square with the edge line. Use the grid on the layout board, and double-check with your triangle and ruler to be sure everything is precisely in position. This is tedious, but it's very important; crooked lines will ruin your work.

To check the layout, use a photocopy machine. Often you can't really judge the original because of the confused jumble of edge lines, the blue grid, and your own markings. A copy will show how the printed version will look; if you don't like what you see, now is the time to redo it.

When you've finished and are satisfied with the practice version, repeat the process using the original typeset material.

When everything is in place, roll it flat; use a roller from the art store or a smooth glass jar or can. Start from the center and work toward the edges, pressing firmly to squeeze out any bubbles or wrinkles.

Repeat this step with all the pieces. When you're finished, clean up the copy; use a rubber cement pick-up from the art store to "erase" little blobs of cement. The printer's camera will "see" everything except white and light blue, so get rid of bits of rubber cement, flecks of ink, and other imperfections. Use opaquing liquid freely.

When you like the way your layout looks, and have checked it on a photocopy machine, it's ready to be printed. Protect your valuable original by taping a flap of clean white paper over it, and storing it carefully in a clearly marked envelope.

PRINTING IT

With finished pasteup in hand, you're ready to print hundreds—or thousands—of copies so clients and prospects can really start noticing you. The printer will help you with those final decisions about paper, ink, and other services.

Finding a printer isn't hard—quick-copy franchises are in every city and town—but finding a reliable printer who will give you advice and work with you may take a bit of shopping around.

Avoid the really big printing firms—the ones that print catalogs and four-color brochures for large companies. You don't need their facilities because virtually all of your printing needs can be met by a neighborhood offset print shop.

As with other professionals, printing costs vary a lot. When you're comparing prices, be sure that you are talking about the same paper, the same number of copies, and the same extras—such as folding and punching.

Look carefully at the samples your printer offers, to check for quality. Is the density uniform throughout? Are edges straight? Is everything precise and square? Do photographs look crisp or muddy? Does the printer seem to deliver work on time? Ask around to find out. (Many printers traditionally have difficulty with deadlines.)

Will your printer take the time to show you paper samples and discuss colors and weights with you? Will he advise you on your layout projects?

Choosing paper is more complicated than you'd expect. There are hundreds of different weights, textures, finishes, and colors. There is newsprint, book, cover, and coated paper—and all kinds of special deals. Look at lots of samples from different companies. Ask if the same paper is still likely to be available next year when you reorder.

Pick a paper that's good enough for your job, but not too good. Twenty-pound bond is an inexpensive standard, similar to photocopy paper, without a watermark, and without much texture. It's fine for flyers, and maybe for your tune lists and so on, but it's not good enough for your letterhead. Nicer papers have higher cotton, or "rag" content, and a heavier "weight." Keep your budget in mind, however, and don't get the most expensive paper in the catalog. Leave that for stockbrokers and investment bankers.

Paper "weight" is a complex concept that's different for different types of paper. Basically, the heavier the stated weight, the nicer the "heft" or "feel" of the paper, but a twenty-pound bond is not the same as a twenty-pound cover or book stock. There's no need to try to understand this maze, just look at different samples to match your different projects.

Paper color is equally complicated. You can use pastels, earth tones, "brights," and many different shades of white. Again, remember that your goal is communication, so don't choose a color that will make the piece hard to read; white and the lighter shades are safest for most material, though bright colors are effective for posters and flyers.

Try to match your letterhead color with a standard correction fluid color. This is more important than it may seem; if you choose an unusual paper color how will you correct the inevitable errors you'll make in typing? If your paper is a standard color, mistakes aren't a problem.

Be sure the exact same color is available in sheets, envelopes, and business card stock so your stationery will have a uniform look. Ask the printer if this color is established, doesn't fluctuate over time, and is always available for reorders.

These ideas, too, will make your printing easier—and maybe save money:

- Double-check your material before leaving it with the printer. Her job is to print what you give her—*exactly as it appears*. She might notice a corner of your pasteup that comes unglued, or a line that is really crooked—but she might not; most printers are too rushed to spend time double-checking your work. Before you leave material with her, look it over one last time for cleanliness. Be sure that all the pieces are still glued firmly in place and that no smudges have appeared.

- Don't be seduced into ordering more than you need just because quantity prices are cheaper. Sure, the second thousand costs much less than the first thousand, but do you really need that many? If you move, and get a new address and phone number, what happens to all that expensive letterhead stationery? It becomes expensive scratch paper. Don't overorder.

- Printers offer other services that can make life easier. If you

have several pages in a set, the printer can *collate* them for you. She can also fold, punch, and even bind your work. She can *score* a line that is to be folded or cut, and can cut material to any size you need. Why spend your time folding a thousand letters in a mass mailing when, for a few dollars, the printer's folding machine will do a perfect job?
• Most jobs call for black ink, but a variety of colors is available. As with paper color, don't get carried away by the creative possibilities—your aim is communication, and light green ink on brown paper won't help. Printers charge more for colored ink—for the time required to reink the press and clean up after printing your job. Black ink will suffice for most of your printing needs, but the combination of a colored ink with your paper stock might provide just the graphic touch that really sets your promotional material apart.

Beyond Black and White

If you're interested in going beyond simple black-and-white printing, the use of colored ink on colored paper stock offers unlimited possibilities. You can devise powerful combinations that look colorful and expensive for a fraction of the cost of four-color work. Look at lots of samples as you think about paper and ink.

What if you do want to have a brochure printed, including photos, in full color? It can be done, of course, but it is so expensive that you'll need to carefully weigh the advantages against the cost. Printing in color requires mostly "color separations," and four trips through the press. If you want to use color you'll almost certainly need to work with a professional designer. Though costs vary, here's a rough guide to *four-color*—which means full color, versus *one-color*—which usually means black-and-white printing. If it will cost about eighty dollars to print 500 one-color brochures on excellent coated paper, the same brochure in a four-color version would probably cost at least 500 dollars. Maybe more.

Standard sizes always cost less than unusual ones. Try to design your letterhead, card, brochure, and invoice to the accepted stock sizes. You'll save lots of money that way.

PRINTING PHOTOS

If you plan to use pictures in your brochure, remember that although most printers are capable of printing photos, some will do a better job than others. If you understand the process, you'll be sure that your printer will produce the high quality you need.

A printing press can only put ink on paper—black on white (or colors, of course). But black-and-white photos contain a broad range of grays, from dark to light, that offset printing can't directly reproduce. To overcome this difficulty, printers rephotograph your picture through a screen that breaks it down into thousands of tiny dots. These dots print as solid specks of black, of course, but they can give the illusion of any shade of gray.

How? In a dark section of a picture there will be many black dots, which are perceived as a solid black area; in a light gray area of the photo, there will be far fewer dots, so the area looks gray. Look at the photographs reproduced in newspapers; it's easy to see the dots. *Screening* a photo this way turns it into a *halftone*, and this is the method your printer will use.

Two factors, aside from picture quality (which we'll discuss in Chapter Seven), affect how well your photos reproduce when they're printed. The first is paper quality. Rough paper, such as newsprint, can't handle the minute detail required for excellent photographic reproduction; so ask your printer specifically about printing photos on the paper you've chosen. High quality coated papers are the best choice for excellent photographic reproduction.

The second factor influencing the quality of reproduced photos is the size of the screen the printer uses—finer screens produce more dots, which produce smoother tone gradations and more detail. Ask your printer what kind of screen she uses—the range is from 85 to 150 dots per inch. More dots (finer screens) produce better pictures.

Many quick-copy printers use automatic equipment that requires a relatively coarse screen, often eighty-five dots. They can, however, send your photos out to be made into metal plates by a subcontractor. Though this may add to the cost, it could be worthwhile if excellent photographic reproduction is important to you.

Always ask to see samples of printed photos *using the kind of screen your printer suggests*. If they don't look crisp and clear, insist on a finer screen. Of course, the printed version of your picture can't be better than the original, so be sure to start with an excellent photo.

Printing turns your words and graphic ideas into hardworking sales tools that tell clients about you and your music. If you give the printer what she needs—clear instructions and clean camera-ready copy—she'll present you with a box of professional-looking material that will enhance your image.

Typesetting, layout, and printing are important steps in creating publicity tools. Since many potential clients haven't met you or heard your music, they'll judge you by the appearance of your publicity material.

Work hard, then, to create the best material possible, so when a prospective client sees your brochure and your business card he knows immediately that you're a professional who cares about detail. With such a good start, you'll be one step ahead.

CHAPTER 7

Focus on Photography

CLIENTS AND PROSPECTS NOT ONLY WANT to *hear* you, they want to *see* you as well. It's not that they expect you to be overwhelmingly handsome or beautiful—though that never hurts, of course—but they need to know what you look like, to be able to put a face with your name.

And, of course, photographs are such a standard, expected part of every performer's equipment that you must have a current one or they'll think you're an amateur or a beginner.

Keeping a stock of current photos takes work. You change, your group changes, and new photos must be made. You can't use that old one, no matter how good it was, if you've shaved your beard, or the blonde singer isn't with the band anymore.

So decide what you need and look at what you already have to see if it meets your new standards for publicity material. You know that the "head shot" is the staple of the entertainment industry—but do you have a good one available right now? And do you have a sparkling, up-to-date photo of your group? Further, do you have action shots of all your different musical activities? You'll need them to accompany feature stories.

You'll use this supply of photos to accompany press releases and to leave behind when you call on clients. Since your public wants to know what you look like, a good professional photograph will enhance your image. On the other hand, a shoddy, third-rate picture, or one that was obviously made ten years ago, will do more harm than good.

BLACK AND WHITE OR COLOR?

Most of the time you'll only need black-and-white pictures. Not only are they cheaper, they're needed more often. While national magazines and newspapers often use color pictures, the local publications that will be your publicity outlets usually want black and white. The eight-by-ten black-and-white glossy is the standard of the entertainment industry, and is expected by the media, agents, and clients. Black-and-white materials are less expensive for the photographer, and less expensive to reproduce. You can get either photographic or printed (lithograhed) copies of your black-and-white photos made for a fraction of what color would cost. For example, a thousand *photographic* reproductions might cost about eighty dollars from a reproduction house, while the same number of color prints would cost nearly $800. Even if you choose the less expensive lithography (as opposed to photographic reproduction) the cost for color is still several times that for black and white.

It's also easier to get good quality in black and white. Creating a good color photograph is more challenging for the photographer, and reproducing it is more difficult for printers. Stick with black and white for the easiest route to a perfect print.

What You'll Need

Here are the kinds of photographs you may need.

Head shots. Everybody in the entertainment business has one, and it's exactly what it sounds like. The head shot is a closeup of your face, and your expression is important. So are the posing, lighting, and other technical factors that we'll discuss below. If you're a solo performer, a teacher, or are working for individual publicity, you'll need a good head shot. And if you're the spokesperson for your band, or make speeches, or do something newsworthy (like get a scholarship or award), you'll need a head shot to send with your press release.

Group shots. If you're part of a musical or entertainment group you'll need a photo of the entire organization. A good group shot is more difficult to make, because the photographer must come up with a dynamic composition that suits your music and image. And it's not easy to get four or five people to have similar expressions at the same time.

Many contemporary pop bands prefer rigorously unposed, candid, photos. If this is the kind of picture your music inspires, you'll still need to be sure it's technically excellent—in focus, and with a printable range of tones. Many of the album covers that look like they were made by the singer's four-year-old child are actually professional photos—designed to look spontaneous.

SUSAN BENNETT

A good head shot is essential for every performer, and a head shot should be just that—a tightly cropped photo that shows your face and little else. Susan Bennett's photo is lithographed on paper that can be printed on both sides. By reproducing her credits on the back, her head shot works twice as hard. This won't work with photographically produced prints.

By combining two photos on one sheet, David Pengelly makes his photos work harder, and the action shots give a sense of performance style.

Many people come and go
Wherever I play and sing
But you made this year special
So I send my warmest greetings

Merry Christmas and Happy New Year.
Carol Albert

A postcard with your picture on it is a simple and effective way of publicizing your music. If you have a good head shot (a screen will cost only a few dollars more) use it; the photo adds lots of personal interest. If you maintain a band fan mailing list, such cards quickly and inexpensively tell your friends and clients where you're appearing now. Or you could do a mailing just to wish them "Happy Holidays."

SHARON STALEY

Hope you'll come by and see me.
I am currently singing at:

Omni International Hotel
Lobby Bar

Tuesday through Saturday
from 8 p.m. until midnight
Through June

Action shots. When you start working on feature stories about your music, you'll need shots of you or your group in action. Maybe it's your marching band performing in the rain. Perhaps it's you composing with your computer/synthesizer. Maybe it's your free concert at a community center. Get pictures of anything you do that's worthy of notice.

If you're adept at photography, you can make these photos yourself, using the camera's timer or perhaps a long cable release. It's easier though to work with a photographically inclined friend, or even hire a photographer to make these shots—though a pro would be quite expensive. Here's where your own photographic ability can be very useful in building a photo file that covers all your musical activities. Needless to say, whenever your events are covered by a newspaper photographer, be sure to get a set of prints for yourself.

Record shots. This is the kind of photo that simply records an event. If you're named "musician of the year," get a photo of the plaque being presented. If you give a speech to the local Lions club, get a shot of you at the podium. If your string quartet lands a grant from an arts foundation, get a picture of the check being awarded. While these photos often aren't creative, they are grist for the publicity mill, and will often be the kind of picture that newspapers print.

THE PHOTO SESSION

There are, of course, several ways you can get your photo done. You can hire a professional photographer, have a friend take them, or you can shoot them yourself. There are advantages each way; the photographer has experience and can guarantee excellent results, while shooting it yourself or having a friend do it will save money. We'll discuss each approach.

If you decide to use professional help, follow the guidelines for finding a photographer in Chapter Nine. Check around, discuss prices, and look at several portfolios. When you've found a photographer you like, how can you be sure that you get the kind of photograph you need?

First, *know exactly what you want.* What's the image you want to project? Sincerity? Excitement? Youthful energy? Formality? Have a clear idea of the kind of clothes, hair style, makeup, and pose that will contribute to the right "look" for your photo.

Here's an important concept for dealing with photographers: *you must be in control of the photo session.* The photographer, regardless of how good he is, will be inclined to make the kind of pictures he likes, that are his "trademark." If his portfolio contains only formal, posed portraits, don't expect him to be avant-garde with your group. Or if she specializes in high-fashion, trendy, experimental work, that's what you should expect. If you know what you want, and know that the photographer can produce that kind of shot, you're a step ahead.

One way to get the kind of photos you need is to have samples of what you want. Use your clip file, and look for pictures that match your ideas. *Show* them to the photographer—don't just tell him—because one picture really can be worth a thousand words.

Indoor shots, usually in the studio, are the standard, and are the easiest to control. You'll get the formal head or group shots you need inside, and the photographer can arrange backgrounds, poses, and lights as she likes.

White, or light, backgrounds are probably best for most entertainers. Light colors reproduce better, without the danger of your hair blending in with a dark background, and they usually look more cheerful. A photo with a light background and light-colored clothes is called *high key*, and conveys a pleasant, upbeat feeling. The opposite, with dark background and clothes, is called *low key*, and seems more serious, even somber— though well-done low-key portraits can be dramatic. Discuss these options with your photographer, and get her input on the best background for your image and her style of picture. However, avoid totally white or black backgrounds because they reproduce poorly in newspapers and magazines.

Outdoor shots, taken on location, can be useful, too. You've seen photos of rock groups standing in alleys, of string quartets posed at the concert hall, or of country bands sitting on split-rail fences. If a location is important or evocative of your kind of music, don't hesitate to use it. If you need to spend time scouting for a location, or pay a bit more to get just the shot you want, go ahead and do it—you may use the photo for a long time, and it should be as good, and as "right" for you, as possible.

Be sure she shoots enough film to assure plenty of choices. In photography, film is the least of your expenses, so don't skimp. If you have an idea for a pose, a clothing change, a different background, or whatever, don't hesitate to try it because if you don't get what you want from this session you'll have to come back and start over. Magazine photographers commonly shoot several rolls to get one shot, and you should keep shooting until you feel that you've gotten the picture you want.

When the film has been processed, you'll usually get *contact sheets* from the photographer—eight-by-tens with an entire roll per sheet. Use a magnifying glass, or a *loupe* (a special magnifier designed for photographic viewing), to make your choices. Choose shots that are technically good (sharp, well-lit, no scratches or flaws), and well-posed (eyes open, similar expressions, good design), to have enlarged.

Posing

This is the area that separates the really good photographers from the average ones. Devising dynamic, interesting poses is not easy, but it's crucial for your group shots, and even for head shots. You don't want a static, boring line-up type picture, and you don't want your head shot to be exactly like every other portrait the photographer has made.

Of course you'll follow the photographer's directions, but you can make suggestions, too. For head shots, remember that a straight-on, frontal photo with your shoulders square to the camera is bad—it looks like the pictures on the post-office wall. You'll usually get better results if you sit at an angle to the camera, and look back at the camera. Generally, head shots are taken with the camera close to your eye level, and with you looking into the lens.

There are as many clichés in photography as in music; avoid them if possible. Coy poses with your chin resting in your palm, for example, have been done so often that they look stilted—even if they aren't. Go back to your file for inspiration.

What kind of expression is appropriate for your publicity photos? It depends on your music. You may need a cheerful, happy smile, or a warm inviting look. Or you may choose a defiant, belligerent, nasty expression. You may need to use makeup, with a little Blistex on your lips—or you may not shave the day of your session so you'll look appropriately macho. Your photographer will advise about what makeup, if any, you should use. Let your picture match your music.

Group posing can be difficult. Look at the sketches of dynamic group designs on page 82. These are only suggestions, of course, and there are many other pleasing arrangements. Study the good group pictures in your clip file and on album covers, and notice the arrangement of bodies, heads, hands, and accessories. Usually the heads, which are the center of interest, are arranged in an S-curve, or triangle pattern, so that the viewer's eye follows a visual line from one to the next.

The worst arrangement for your band picture is the line-up shot in which you simply stand shoulder to shoulder, with everybody's heads on the same level. Of course there are exceptions, and many rock groups use this arrangement because it looks unposed, and very natural. If this is the look you want, use it—you can rely on clothes, expressions, and posing to add interest to the static design. For most entertainers, though, a more interesting composition will result in a more interesting picture.

What about photos with your instruments? Sometimes this is an effective approach, but it requires careful planning to work well because adding all those elements complicates the composition. You don't want a jumble of instruments piled together, so look for similar photos and work with your photographer to devise an interesting arrangement.

Sometimes solo performers include a bit of their instrument in a three-quarter-length pose, or even a head shot. With dramatic lighting and a good photographer, including a wind or string instrument can add interest, and class, to your photos.

If your clip file hasn't grown to include good examples of the photos

Here's a high-key shot—light background and predominantly light-colored clothes and accessories. Though most of the tones are black and white, this is a color photo, and the subtle use of color makes the picture more stylish and effective.

This popular band conveys its spirit through its photos. Animation and facial expressions tell the story; an evening with Dr. Bop looks like fun.

The design possibilities with five people are almost endless. Kid Glove's photo uses two diagonal lines of interest to give the photo a dynamic look. Again, white on white is used effectively to create an upbeat feel.

Here's an effective action shot. Note the symmetrical arrangement of the performers, and that the pose is repeated on a giant video screen in the background. If you have a dynamic act and use interesting sets or backgrounds, an action shot may be more useful than a posed studio photo.

ANGLE   ANGLE   ANGLE

TRIANGLE   90° DROP   SINGLE LINE

"S" CURVE   "T" FORMATION   FOREGROUND

PHOTO COMPOSITION

Look at the good group shots you see in magazines and on album covers. Usually, there is a dynamic design that leads the viewer's eye through the picture. Here are some suggested poses; you'll come up with more, depending on the size of your group. The old-style line-up shot can work, of course, but a strong composition makes it easier to get a good photo.

you need, look at record albums and music magazines. *Rolling Stone*, for example, publishes a giant year-end issue that's filled with contemporary album ads and feature photos that will give you lots of ideas. Or, you'll get ideas from any issue of *Spin, Melody Maker, New Music Express*, and—if jazz is your style—*Down Beat* and *Jazziz*. Photographic styles change, and current magazines will keep you up to date on what's hot.

For classical musicians looking for graphic ideas, an excellent source is the annual edition of *Musical America*, which features lots of slick, well-done head and group shots. Other sources for terrific photographic inspiration are *Clavier* and *The Instrumentalist* magazines.

Remember, though, that the style, look, and "feel" of your pictures should match your music. Just because Bruce Springsteen is photographed in a white undershirt doesn't mean that you should do the same. Neither does it mean you shouldn't.

Some photographers, like some musicians, work too hard at avoiding clichés. A head shot, after all, is pretty standard, and there's little room for excessive creativity. Don't resort to outlandish hair styles, unusual photographic techniques, or weird backgrounds, just to be different.

If you have a good idea of the kind of picture that suits your music, and you find a photographer who can produce such shots, you'll be able to supply your clients with high-quality photos that enhance your image and help you book jobs.

SHOOT IT YOURSELF

What if you don't want to work with a professional photographer? Maybe you can't afford the rates, or perhaps photography is your hobby. You or a photographically knowledgeable friend can probably make the pictures you need. Today's cameras are so sophisticated that you can produce near-professional results without knowing an f-stop from an f sharp.

To shoot yourself, you'll have to be quick, but it can be done. Most cameras have *self-timers* that trip the shutter ten to twenty seconds after they're activated. You can probably run from the camera to your position in the picture in that time, but it's not easy. A similar approach is to use a long cable release that you can hold behind your back, and trip the shutter remotely.

It might be easier to work with a friend who can actually operate the camera for you. If you're the photographer in the group, you can set the camera, plan the composition, and just have your friends make the picture and advance the film. Shoot extra pictures in these situations, however, because they can't be carefully controlled.

Here's how to photograph yourself or your group without getting in to trouble.

1. *Use a suitable camera.* To some extent, the quality of your picture depends on the size of the negative; avoid tiny formats like 110; 35mm is the smallest negative size you should use, and sophisticated 35's are very popular. You, or a friend, probably have a good camera and a couple of lenses.

What about Polaroids? Unless you choose the black-and-white Polaroid film that also produces negatives (55PN), you'll find that these instant pictures won't provide what you need. Prints are too small, and reproduction is cumbersome.

Generally, a good 35mm camera with a 50mm lens is good for group photos. For head shots, lenses of 100mm or so are better.

2. *Know how to operate the equipment.* This isn't a photographic textbook, but your library can provide lots of good ones (see the Bibliography). If you've decided to make your own pictures, be sure you're familiar with the camera. Know how to set it for the film you've chosen, and how to accurately load the film. Don't laugh—every photographer has horror stories of the great shots he missed because the film wasn't properly advancing in the camera.

3. *Use the right film.* You'll probably need black-and-white pictures, so use black-and-white film. Choose the slowest film possible, because slower films producer finer grain and sharper prints. It's fine to use Tri-X for available-light work inside, but use Plus-X or Panatomic-X (or an equivalent) for studio or outdoor shooting.

4. *Shoot lots of film.* Don't limit your choices by being stingy. If you've gone to the trouble of dressing up, finding the right location, rounding up the necessary equipment, and so on, don't skimp on film. To repeat: film is the cheapest part of your photographic endeavors. Use enough to be sure you have the shot you want. You may get only one good shot per roll—or only one good shot per several rolls. That's okay—professionals don't expect each frame to be a winner, either.

5. *Be careful with exposure.* Sure, the camera has automatic exposure control, but its meter can be fooled by bright or dark backgrounds, so use a camera with manual exposure override if you can. And be careful to hold the camera still—use a tripod if at all possible. Focus carefully, and remember that longer focal lengths—telephoto lenses—require more critical focusing than do normal or wide-angle lenses. And generally, photos for professional publicity uses require more care in shooting than family snapshots.

6. *Plan your composition carefully.* Know in advance how you're going to pose the group. Scan that clip file, take sample pictures with you to the session, and experiment.

Try to use a simple, uncluttered background. Inside, you can use a plain wall, suspend a roll of background paper from the photo store, or even an unwrinkled sheet or blanket. Outside, find a brick or stucco wall, or use the sky. Or you could pose your group in a parking lot and shoot down so that the asphalt provides a plain background. Using a large (low number) f-stop insures that the background will be out of focus and less distracting.

Static pictures look dead. The exact center of a photo is boring; slight offsets to one side are more dynamic. Don't divide the space right down

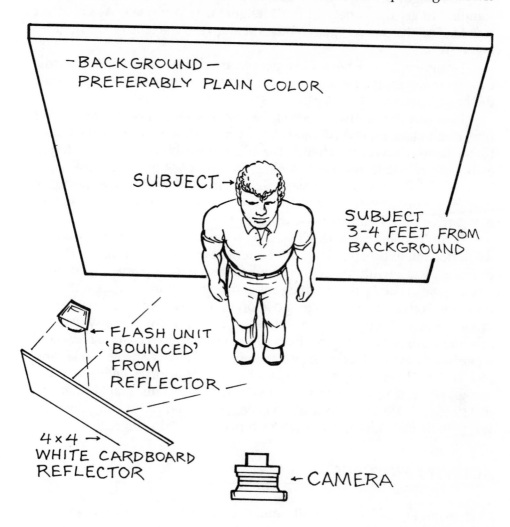

BASIC PORTRAIT LIGHTING SET-UP

If you want to do a studio-style photo yourself, this standard lighting set-up is a good way to start. Use a single, strong, diffused light source to one side and slightly above the subject—it can even be window light. This kind of lighting is the basis for many portraits and provides good, even illumination. It's important that the light source be large; if you're using a small flash unit, bounce it from a reflector to soften and spread the light.

the middle, for the same reason. Use the triangle or S-curve composition discussed above.

You might try having one person seated, one kneeling, and others standing to get the variety of head heights that you need. Again, don't stand facing the camera; place bodies at angles to the lens rather than facing in frontally.

Group shots look best when people are closer together than normal. Check your sample photos—see how the shoulders usually touch, how the heads are close together?

Poses are important. Try several. Even though you're shooting lots of film, don't make exact duplicates. Vary your positions, change the hands, tilt the heads differently, change the angle of the body, and try different expressions. You'll develop a feeling for compositions that look good. Look at the illustrations on page 82 of different posing ideas—notice how the groups are arranged so the viewer's eye will travel around the picture. Strive for dynamic poses; work to avoid those tired, static clichés.

If you're using flash, don't keep it on the camera unless you're after a harsh documentary-style look. It's better to bounce it off a wall or ceiling, or from a large white reflector (a four-foot square of painted cardboard works great). Standard portrait lighting, from time immemorial, is to have the main—often the only—light positioned slightly above and to one side of the subject. It worked for Rembrandt, and it will work for you.

Don't skimp on processing. Find a local lab that does custom black-and-white work; avoid drugstore processing. Get contact sheets made, and look at them with a magnifying glass to make your print selection. Mass-market processing may be fine, but why take risks after you've spent all that time and effort? Custom labs will be more careful with your film, and will usually do a much better job of processing and printing.

ACTIVITY PICTURES

Keep a photographic log of all your musical activities. As you become more expert at public relations, you'll devise lots of events that can be publicized, and you'll need good photos of these events. If you're trying for a feature story in the local paper, your chances will be better if you provide a few top-quality pictures.

First, learn to think like a feature writer. Whatever you do musically that could be interesting to the public should be photographed. Maybe your piano students are giving a recital, costumed like famous composers. You should have pictures of this event—even if you have no immediate publicity plans for them. Cover yourself for future ideas.

When shooting feature photos, cover the entire story—beginning, middle, and end. Perhaps your local paper will run a complete picture story on your activity; in any case, the more pictures you provide, the more choices the editor will have.

Since the most important subjects in most feature photos are people, emphasize the human element. Do closeups of faces, hands, fingers on keys. Get close group shots. Look for dynamic interaction, interesting expressions. If you're doing a story about your collection of early electric guitars, try a picture holding that early Stratocaster—or sitting on the floor surrounded by guitars. Be creative, but not outlandish—editors won't print weird, or poor, photos.

Use your clip file for inspiration and remember that a picture often brings a story to life. If you can do it yourself, great, but hire a photographer if you need to. The pictures will pay for themselves in good publicity for you.

Whenever you get an award, give a speech, are a guest soloist, or play a recital, have photos made. Call the newspaper in advance and ask for a photographer to be sent. If they assign one, ask about buying a few prints. If no photographer has been scheduled, ask a friend to make pictures or hire a photographer yourself. It might seem pushy, but a photo of you getting the "Songwriter of the Year Award" could run in several papers and even a few magazines. Don't miss these photo opportunities.

Such shots won't win any photographic awards, but they are important. If your band is signing a record contract, get a picture—even if it's nothing more than five people crowded around a desk looking at a contract. If you make a speech to the National Association of Jazz Educators, get a picture, even if you have to pay the photographer. Watch your local papers; these are the kinds of photos that get printed by the thousands—because they show people doing important or interesting things.

If you're taking these pictures yourself, or having an amateur photographer do them, keep these ideas in mind: look behind the subject for distractions—avoid busy backgrounds when possible. When a wall is the background, stand three or four feet in front of it, not right against it, to avoid harsh shadows. Try to keep the camera on eye level with the subjects; shooting from below is an unattractive angle. Don't shoot into a mirror or window—your flash will reflect and ruin the picture. If you're using the self-timer to shoot a picture that you'll be in, carefully visualize where you'll stand and be sure that that part of the picture is in focus, and that your head won't be "cut off" because you're so tall.

Be familiar with your camera *before* you try to make important pictures. Shoot a roll or two in different situations for practice. If you're interested in photography, take a course or read a couple of the books listed in the Bibliography. Photography is a great hobby, and when you use it to get noticed in your profession it's a tax-deductible business expense as well!

THE PRINTS YOU'LL NEED

For years, the eight-by-ten glossy has been the standard, and it's still the best size for all-round use. You can send eight-by-tens with press releases, give them to club managers, and include them in your press kit and with material you mail to prospects.

The best way to buy quantity prints is to use a duplication house. Several are listed in the Appendix; check your Yellow Pages for local companies. Have your photographer make one or two excellent prints of each pose you select and send those pictures (not negatives) to the dupe house. They'll add your name at the bottom, in whatever type style you select, and make hundreds—or thousands—of prints for you at a fraction of what your photographer would charge. (This is not unethical—all photographers know that duplication houses are the best route for anyone who needs large numbers of prints—though if you only need a print or two, buy those from your photographer, of course.)

If you're doing a large mailing of press releases, five-by-seven prints will be acceptable and will save money over the larger size.

If you need lots of photos, check into litho prints, which are produced on a printing press rather than in the darkroom. Good quality lithos, on coated stock, look almost as good as photos, and are considerably less expensive.

Using Photos

Once you have a stack of new head shots and a file full of feature photos of your band's activities, how do you distribute them?

First, be sure they're labeled. An editor of a large paper will receive dozens—maybe hundreds—of pictures every day. She won't spend time searching her desktop to find the photos that match your press release. All photos sent out *must be labeled*.

If your head shot has your name printed on the bottom, that's sufficient. For other pictures, type the names (from left to right) and other pertinent data across the bottom of a piece of paper that's as wide as the picture and tape it to the back of the photo. Fold the caption over the bottom of the picture, so that it reads right when it's unfolded. Or you can type the caption and names (left to right) on a self-adhesive label, and stick it to the back of the photo.

Never write on the back of a photo and never use paper clips on a picture. Any indentations will show when the photo is reproduced, and such carelessness may result in the photo being discarded rather than used.

When you're ordering prints to be used in a newspaper or magazine, ask the photographer to make them "flatter," with less contrast than normal, since printing adds contrast. And prints submitted for publication

PAPER TAPED TO
BACK OF PHOTO

TYPE OR PRINT CAPTION TO BE READ
WHEN PAGE IS UNFOLDED.

Be sure all photos you send to editors are identified. Never write on the picture, and don't use paper clips. Instead, tape a sheet of paper to the back of the photo, with the caption written on the bottom. Don't risk having your captionless photos lost on an editor's desk.

need a white border so the editor can make *crop marks* that indicate what part of the photo is to be used.

Photos to be used in your brochure should also be printed *flatter*, if possible, and should be very sharp and clear. You'll probably want to use a close-up, since the picture will be quite small in the brochure. Also, pictures for use in brochures or other publications should have medium gray backgrounds, since pure white and black backgrounds may reproduce poorly when printed.

Mailing Photos

To mail a photograph you must protect it against the rigors of the post office. Use a regular nine-by-twelve envelope with a sheet of cardboard to support the photos. If the pictures are really valuable, sandwich them between two sheets of cardboard and use rubber bands diagonally from corner to corner to hold the material together. Or you could buy special stiffened envelopes, such as the Calumet Self-Mailer (see the Appendix), at office supply or photo stores. These are designed to protect your photos without additional cardboard inserts. Also, though it may be futile, always write or stamp PHOTOS—PLEASE DON'T BEND on the envelope in big red letters.

If you're sending material to an editor for possible use, and you'd like the pictures back, include a self-addressed, stamped envelope (called an *SASE*) and a note asking for their return. Most editors will try to return material to you, but don't send anything you can't afford to lose, because they often get misplaced or damaged in transit. If your pictures run in Thursday's paper, ask about the return of your photos when you make your thank-you call on Friday.

Many papers won't return pictures that are submitted with press releases, so, again, don't send valuable material. If you've submitted a story that's accompanied by pictures, there's a good chance that your material will be returned, but don't bet on it. Editors are swamped with pictures, and their desks are always piled high with manuscripts and photos.

Keep Yourself in the Picture

Australian aborigines are right; photographs do capture your spirit—or at least the image of it. Work to get pictures that depict you as you are, and as you want to be seen. Let pictures show your clients and audiences what you're like. Use them to help tell your story. Photos can help you put your best face forward to clients around the country.

CHAPTER 8

Demo Tapes

THE PROSPECT SAYS, "OKAY. Tell me about your music." How do you reply? Can you really describe your music? Can you explain exactly what you do and how you do it? Can you convey the beauty of your performance—in words?

No, you can't. Music is, simply, a unique art that can't be translated into words. You can talk *about* it, sure, and even write about it—but no matter how hard you try, you can't tell people how your music *sounds*.

Other artists don't have this problem. A potter, photographer, or carpenter can publicize her craft, and there'll be no uncertainty because you can *see* pottery, pictures, and projects made of wood. But when you talk or write about your music, how can you really get the message across?

"Sure, Mr. Jones. We're the best band in town for your party. We play all the top hits. Good? Of course we're good. Talented? Absolutely. Our singer even has perfect pitch. What do you mean, 'What do we sound like?' We sound great."

That's the point. You can't tell anyone what you sound like. You can, however, show them—with demonstration tapes.

If your clients know music—and they rarely will—or if they will take the recommendation of agents or friends—and they rarely will—you won't need demo tapes. In reality, clients will almost always insist on hearing what they're buying, and you can't really blame them. You'd probably do the same thing if you were hiring a band.

Where Can We Hear You?

Have you heard that one before? You've just finished your sales pitch, you've shown your brochure, press clippings, and letters of recommendation. They're an East Lake High School Alumni committee, and they're interested in booking you for the Reunion Dance. They say, "Gee, everything looks great, and your band is highly recommended. But where can we hear you?"

If you're playing in a club, there's no problem. You just invite them in to hear the band. But if your group plays only private parties, or if you're not currently booked in a club, what do you do? You don't want a scraggly committee to come barging into another client's party, do you?

The answer: demo tapes.

Now, there are two different kinds of demo tapes, made for very different purposes. One is the demo that's intended to sell your band, or a song you've written, to a record company. That kind of demo usually requires extensive production, and involves lots of money and time. In essence you're making a recording that meets—or exceeds—industry standards, and you'll need a producer, lots of studio time, and perhaps some extra musicians. Such demos are outside the scope of this book, since they aren't really publicity tools but finished products in themselves. Consult the books in the Bibliography for more information.

The other kind of demo tape is the one you make to demonstrate what your band can do, and to show what you sound like. Such a tape will show the quality of your music, and the variety of your repertoire—and it has to be good. But it doesn't have to be the same finished, ultraexpensive quality as a tape you're sending to Columbia Records. This chapter discusses this second kind of demo—the one that showcases your band, your music, and your wide-ranging performance. It's a sales tool, and a great publicity helper.

Before you start thinking about making a demo, though, think about this: if your demo tape isn't excellent it will do more harm than good. This doesn't just mean that the music must be good. Good production—and even the finished appearance of the tape—are also important. You won't have to hire a string section or extra percussionists—as you might if you were sending the tape to a record company—but you've got to strive for a really good tape anyway.

THE PROS SET THE STANDARD

Everyone today expects excellent, professional-quality recordings because they're accustomed to high-fidelity sound—it's not the exception but the rule. You can buy a portable cassette player for less than fifty dollars that sounds incredibly good, and people are constantly surrounded by well-produced music in cars, homes, offices—even elevators.

Yours has to measure up.

Of course you can use a little cassette recorder to make a demo tape on the job. The drums may be too loud and the vocals will probably be muffled—in fact, the fidelity won't be very good and there'll be noticeable wow and flutter, but it's only a demo tape. Right?

Wrong. When there's well-produced music everywhere, yours has to measure up. Remember, every thirty-second commercial features top-quality players, singers, recording, and engineering.

When people listen to the radio they hear pop records and commercials that cost a fortune to produce. That's the standard, like it or not, and if your demo falls short—even if the music is terrific—it won't get much consideration.

You've heard the saying, "The medium is the message." That's what's happening here. The quality of the recording, mixing, and effects—even the printing of the label—may actually overshadow the musical content. It may not be fair, but that's the way things are. The standards for recorded sound and video are set in the media capitals—New York, Los Angeles, and Nashville—and those standards apply to your demo just as much as to a pop record.

If you're going to make a demo tape, then, you just have to make it a good one—not spectacular, not over-produced, with layer upon layer of strings and background vocals, but good; it's that simple.

Meet the Competition

What are your competitors—other bands or soloists—doing with their demo tapes? If they aren't using demos, or if their tapes are poor quality, you're in a great position. Yours will automatically be better. But if their tapes are excellent, you'll have to at least match them to compete.

Your clients won't understand the intricacies, expense, and effort of spending time in the recording studio. They just know that the demo tape for Band X sounds great, and yours sounds bad. Don't expect them to understand musical or recording ideas or jargon. They won't.

So, for both reasons—industry standards and meeting the competition—you have to commit yourself to producing excellent tapes.

WHAT DO YOU NEED?

Maybe you'll just need a single audio tape to demonstrate your music. Or, you might profit from several specialized tapes, one for each different kind of music you perform.

Perhaps you'll need a video demo to give the full picture. For some performers, a good video will be the most useful publicity tool of all. Broadway-style singers, show bands, conductors, soloists, comedians, and magicians—who are primarily entertainers—need strong video demos.

Videos, though, are more expensive to produce, and require much more planning and care. How do you know if it's worth the expense and effort?

If your performance has a strong visual element, you need a video. If costumes, sets, or action are important, or if choreography and movement are part of your show, you need a video. If, on the other hand, you just play music, an audio tape or two may be all you need.

Audio Pointers

This book is not a technical manual on making demo tapes; you'll probably rely on professional studio engineers to produce your tape, anyway. Whether you plan to produce your own, or work in a studio, however, these considerations will help you get the best possible tape, at the least possible cost.

Target each tape to an exact audience. If you play pop, jazz, country, *and* classical music, your repertoire is exceptionally broad. Will you ever have a client who wants all those different kinds of music? Probably not. When you're in the studio, then, record enough material for as many different tapes as you'll need, and simply package relevant tunes together— pull several tapes, if you need to, from one session.

Don't overestimate a client's flexibility and imagination. If you give her a demo that includes Beethoven when she's looking for Willie Nelson, she'll be suspicious of your country-music abilities. Or, if you include sophisticated jazz when a client is planning a toga party, he'll think you're not the band for his needs—even if you play "Shout" with the best of them. If your musical abilities include different genres, make several tapes. Have a jazz tape, a pop tape, a country demo, and a classical one, if you book jobs in all those areas. (In fact, if your abilities really are that extensive, you'll probably need a completely different publicity kit for each specialty.)

Won't that cost a lot? Yes, but the tapes are ultimately sales tools that will help you book jobs. A good demo tape will pay for itself many times over—so in the long run it won't really cost you anything. It will *produce* money.

Be sure to shop around when looking for a studio. Rates vary enormously, and you may be able to save hundreds, or thousands, of dollars by using a smaller studio, rather than the one that's "hot" in your community at the moment. Don't pay for equipment and expertise that you don't need.

If you're working on a demo tape to sell your songs or group to a record company, you'll probably need to spend lots more money than if you're doing a demo for your band. Where a simple fifteen-minute band demo might cost eight hundred dollars (as my last one did), a complete production, with extra musicians, arrangers, and all post-production work, could easily cost several thousand. (This will be beyond the reach of many groups; if you're aiming for stardom you may find that you need financial backers. Be very careful, however, about going into debt to finance your project. If you don't get a record deal, how will that expensive demo ever pay for itself?)

Plan your tape in advance. Think carefully about selections that would appeal to each target audience. Remember, you're not making an album to showcase the music you like—you're making a sales tool for specific groups of clients.

What tunes are requested most often? Which ones always get a positive response? Shouldn't those tunes be on your demo—even if they aren't your personal favorites? Plan your tapes to include a variety, within the musical type, to show what you can do. Perhaps you'll include a couple of standards, a couple of slow tunes, some new material, and some up-tempo numbers.

You won't be able to update the tapes every time a major hit comes out, so try to pick tunes that will last beyond the usual two-week half-life of most pop tunes. You'll have a feeling for the ones that will survive.

When you've decided what to include, do all your rehearsing *before* you get to the studio. Know exactly how each tune will be structured—intro, solos, ending—so you won't waste expensive studio time making these decisions.

Shop around. Recording studios have sprouted like mushrooms in many communities. *Eight-track*—and even *four-track studios* abound, and many music stores and hi-fi shops claim to have demo facilities. To find the right studio, it's important to know what you need before you start shopping. Your five-piece rock band will have a hard time producing a good demo in a four-track studio, though of course it's possible. On the other hand, a pianist wouldn't need twenty-four tracks to do a solo tape. (If you want to learn more about the recording process, read the books and magazines listed in the Bibliography.)

Call the studios listed in the Yellow Pages to learn the range of features and cost of services in your area. You can also ask other musicians for recommendations. You'll be surprised at the variety you find—in cost, features, and *sound*.

And that's what you're looking for in a studio—a *sound* you like. You shouldn't care whether the studio is trendy cedar, glass, and chrome, or even whether it has produced several hit records. You're after a good sound for *your* tape. That's all. Often a studio will be the "in" place for advertising agencies to produce jingles and commercials, but that doesn't mean it would be the best place to record your demo—and it would probably be very expensive because it's so busy with high-paying ad work.

The best—really the *only*—way to judge a recording studio is by the quality of its products. In searching for a studio listen to similar work they've done. Do the drums sound right? Is the piano tinny, or full-sounding? Do the instruments have the right timbre? Are they balanced? Are vocals full, with a good, natural sound? Listen critically before you schedule a session, because different studios and engineers have different *sounds*. Part of the difference is the physical set-up, and part is in the intangible mixture of skill, equipment, acoustics, and care.

Studios offer a maze of electronic capabilities today, but the same gizmos that can help can also clutter up a take. Be wary of too much equalization, reverb, compression, or stereo separation. You are, after all, making a demo and not a full-fledged album, so don't try to make your four-piece band sound like twelve people. You could have the same problems as some early disco bands whose live performances never matched their recorded work.

So don't overuse, but don't overlook, studio capabilities for augmenting and completing your tape. You can *punch in* to correct mistakes, but don't spend too much time making every single note perfect in every respect. Don't overproduce, in other words, for your audience.

Do you need a full-fledged producer? If you're preparing a demo for a record company, you'll certainly need all the expert help and advice you can get, and a good producer can help with a wide range of decisions, from what tunes to pick to how to mike the drums. If, however, you're doing a demo for your band, your own expertise and a good engineer's knowledge and experience will usually suffice. Talk to the engineer who'll be doing your session in advance to see if you communicate well, and if you have confidence in his abilities.

Get a firm idea of the price of your demo. What's the cost per hour of recording time? Mixing time? Set-up time? How many tapes are included in the price? If the studio runs out of master tape in the middle of a session, who pays while the engineer reequalizes the recording head?

If you're using an acoustic piano, will it be tuned? If other instruments will be provided—synths, amps, drums—will you be comfortable playing them? If you're using your own outboard equipment, is it good enough for studio use—or is that old volume pedal you use at the club too noisy for recording work?

What about duplicate tapes? How much will the studio charge for a hundred? Are there other duping facilities in town that would provide the same quality for a lot less money? (Probably.) Or, could you do the duping you need yourself? (Again, probably, but listen to a homemade dupe on a good system to be sure there's no *audible wow, flutter,* or *distortion.*) Think again about your audience. Would they likely listen to your demo in the car, on a fifty-dollar blaster, or on an expensive home stereo system? If you think your demo will usually be played on medium quality equipment, don't waste money on metal tapes and exquisite reproduction.

Expect the session to take longer than it should: they always do. So, expect to pay more than your original estimate. If you can afford it, go ahead and do it right. After all, a poor tape won't create good publicity or book any jobs.

In fact, a poor tape wastes money. Just a little more time spent in punching in to correct one mistake, or adding one overdub, or remixing one more time, might pay for itself with the first job you book.

Consider using a short spoken introduction to present your message to the listener. There's no need to jump immediately into the music.

"Hello. This is Joe, of Joe's Band. Thanks for listening to this demo tape. We've tried to include a representative sample of the hundreds of tunes we know, and we hope you like them."

Some bands even insert commentary between tunes, but it's easy to talk too much. Prospects might enjoy the music on your demo enough to listen over and over, but they probably wouldn't put up with a continuing sales pitch. Keep any introductory material short.

Finish your demo tapes so they look fully professional. You know by now that appearance is often as important as content, so make your tapes look good by using printed labels and *J-card inserts.*

Of course you can just type a label and stick it on the tape, but that doesn't look like a successful musician, does it? Any quick-copy printer can provide custom printed cassette labels in any color. Just prepare the camera-ready art exactly as you did for your letterhead, and the printer will do the rest.

You'll probably also want cardboard *J-cards* to fit inside the plastic cassette boxes in addition to the labels you've stuck on the tapes. Again, your printer can prepare them for you, and you can do the art work yourself, or have a typesetter prepare it inexpensively. The J-card does the same job for a tape that the album cover does for a record, so make yours look good.

If you work through agents, and most musicians do, don't put your address or phone number on the tapes or J-cards because agents don't want their clients contacting you directly. Your name, logo, and the tape contents are enough. (When booking jobs yourself, simply include your business card.)

Records

Can you use records as demos? It's possible, of course, but it's rarely done because records are expensive in small quantities, they're impossible

The Gibson/Bennett band uses a less expensive, simple-to-produce black-and-white J-card that any printer can provide. (The printer will "score" the cardboard so it will bend in the right places for an exact fit.)

to update, and producing a good-looking album is complicated. Also, records are losing popularity—compact discs and digital audio tape are the future of recorded sound.

If you do shows or concerts, however, you might need records as a back-of-the-room sales item, even though producing a record is a very expensive project (see the Bibliography for further reading). If you choose to do an album, spend plenty of time and money on the cover, both front and back; make it look as good as any record in a store (even though four color photography, design, and printing are very expensive). Remember, the medium is the message and a cheap-looking black-and-white record jacket will be counterproductive.

Flexible *soundsheets* (see the Appendix) are a compromise medium. These plastic sheets can be mailed inexpensively, and sound great. They don't require expensive covers, either, and if you're looking for an unusual medium to publicize your music, and you need lots of copies, soundsheets may be a good investment. However, they're much more expensive to produce than a few dozen cassette tapes.

USING AUDIO TAPES

Your aim is to publicize your music, so don't be stingy with your tapes. If you buy wisely, you can keep the unit costs surprisingly low. Shop around, and order as many tapes as you think you can use. Although budget is a consideration, twenty-five tapes would be a good number to start with.

Demo tapes are like seed. If you put out enough, you'll reap a full crop of bookings. So, why ask for demo tapes to be returned? Encourage people to keep them. "No, Mrs. Jones, we don't need that tape back. We hope you'll keep it in your car and play it for your friends. We know it will remind you of all the fun you had at your company Christmas party."

Keep enough tapes on hand to distribute as requests come in. Mail them out the same day. A stack of demo tapes on your shelf won't do you any good at all.

VIDEO DEMOS

Do you need an MTV-style video? Probably not. (If you do, this isn't the book for you.) Industry estimates on the cost of a "video" start at twenty thousand dollars, and go up to over a hundred. If you can afford that much money for one tune you're already a success.

Maybe you are trying to make it with a record, and you feel a video will insure the record's success. Work with your record company, or backers, to get funding for the video, and search for the right producer.

This chapter, however, is about *demos*, not program-style videos. Do you need a video to promote your music? You do if:

• You produce a *show* that's booked as entertainment.
• There is a strong *visual* element in what you do.
• You are exceptionally *telegenic* and know how to use the medium.
• You are *frequently on television*, and have already acquired impressive clips of your appearances.

Not every musician and band will profit from a video demo. You may not need one if you just play music. If yours is a dance or club band there may not be a strong visual element, telegenic personality, or charisma. (That's not necessarily bad, of course. Many musicians are musicians first, and performers second. They like to play music, and don't think of themselves as "entertainers" at all.)

If your band makes frequent changes in personnel, a video would also be a bad idea. A client can't tell what you look like from an audio demo, but if he *sees* that your singer is blonde and trim, he may be unhappy if the singer on *his* job is brunette and overweight. A video can lock your personnel decisions in place—and clients can be very unhappy, and feel cheated, if they don't get what they've seen.

Obviously, if you don't have the money for a well-produced video demo tape, just rely on your audio tape. A poor video is like a poor violinist—any lack of quality is immediately apparent.

Finding a Producer

Shop around. This is even more important with video than with audio. There's division in the video production world between *commercial* and *consumer quality* video equipment and production. With new equipment and digital techniques, however, this distinction may be less important in the future.

Commercial video producers work mostly for businesses and advertising agencies. They use larger tape—usually ¾ or 1 inch—and better, much more expensive, equipment. They produce video training materials and commercials, and they're often accustomed to big budgets.

If you ask a commercial video producer for a quote on a twelve-minute demo tape, you might be told that a minimum price would be eight thousand dollars. That's a lot of money.

Consumer-level producers are the people you see videotaping weddings. They use essentially the same cameras and equipment that you may have at home, and charge much less for their work. They'll usually work directly in the VHS format. Often, the quality of their work isn't as good as that of commercial producers, and they may not have the same technical capabilities—but these drawbacks may not be relevant.

One new development that may change the video production scene is the use of advanced personal computer programs in video editing. Sophisticated programs give advanced capabilities to home equipment, and if your producer uses this route he may be able to provide superior—perhaps even digital—quality at consumer prices, and with consumer equipment. This field is changing so quickly that you'll have to check out the situation in your area when you start looking for a producer.

For budget reasons, you'll probably work with a *consumer-level* producer, but if you're careful you can still get an excellent video for much less than a commercial producer would have to charge. Use the Yellow Pages; look for someone who's done band demos before, and spend time talking, looking, listening, and asking questions before you make a commitment. Look at the producer's samples very carefully. Notice image quality, color, *video noise* (flecks, spots, bands on the screen). Does the color balance change from shot to shot? Are the fades even? Are the cuts clean—and logical? What kind of lighting does this producer typically use? Direct frontal spotlights that make people look like they're being interrogated? Usually such *light-on-the-camera* techniques are the mark of an amateur.

Find out how he would shoot your group, and pay special attention to his audio technique and equipment. How many mikes would he use?

What kind of mixer? Listen critically to his samples for balance, tone, wow and flutter, and crispness. If possible, listen through a good pair of headphones, or at least on a high-quality stereo system. Don't rely on the built-in speakers in a TV set to make this important judgment. What happens to the soundtrack when the picture changes? Is there distortion or poor balance?

What about the ideas, the logical movement from point to point? Does this producer use enough cameras to do close-ups at the right time in your performance? Is his sense of timing good—or do some shots seem too long and others too short? Are the titles imaginative or staid and boring? Remember, your audience is accustomed to the best.

These are hard questions, but you must be satisfied about them before you start on your own video. You're about to commit a chunk of money, and a lot of time, so be convinced that you'll get a tape that will work hard for you—a useful sales tool that will *make*, not *cost*, money.

Video Bits

Knowing what you'll need will help you decide which producer to hire. To repeat, this isn't a book on producing videos—which is a complex and rapidly changing subject—but these important considerations will help.

Use the free media university we've discussed. Television brings the best output of the best producers and engineers into your home every day. Watch their products closely, because the same techniques that work for them will work for you. You'll write, or at least work on, your own script, so you should know what "works" on TV, and what looks good. If the average time a shot is on the screen is six seconds, don't plan to include a thirty-second one in your script—it will seem catatonic.

Pay particular attention to commercials, because that's where the big production money is spent. A good thirty-second commercial is like a well-done short story and can be a masterpiece of video art. Think of commercials as little demos, and watch how they get their message across.

Keep a written record of the average length of their shots—usually three to five seconds—and the proportion of close-ups to long shots. Watch their titles, and listen to how they use the music. A thirty-second commercial may cost well over fifty thousand dollars to produce, so you can be sure that you're studying the best efforts of the best professionals in the business.

Audio quality is crucial. After all, your video is about music. Most video producers work with voice only, or with prerecorded music, so you'll have to investigate their audio recording capabilities.

A good video demo will require extreme care in recording your

Local group going national with video as contestfinalist

By Gerry Yandel
Staff Writer

The local group Shebang is going national with, well, a shebang.

The four-man band — vocalist Brent Daniel, guitarist Peter Stroud, bass player Neel Daniel and drummer Timothy Gardner — is one of six finalists in Music Television's "Basement Tapes" contest featuring videos of unsigned local acts. The winner of the concert, on MTV at midnight Thursday, will get its video aired for the month of January on the show "120 Minutes" on the video network,which should provide the group with extensive national exposure.

The band recorded its video, "Is This the Top?" at Big Apple Studio in New York and sent it

in to the network two weeks ago.

"A woman at MTV said they bumped another video to use ours because they liked it," Stroud said. "That's a good sign, I guess."

Not a bad sign at all considering that Shebang only got together two years ago.

"I think [Shebang's video] is very well done. It has a good rock sound that's borderline pop with a good hook," said Lisa Berger, clip coordinator for MTV. "Basically, we're looking for quality [when judging]. We don't want something done in a day and just thrown together."

Shebang released it's debut album, "Shebang," last year and recently released a single of "Is This the Top?"/"Waiting for the Magic" which was produced by Stephan Galfas — the producer

for pop star John Waite — on the independent Ivory Tower label. The group has also been an opening act for John Waite, Katrina and the Waves, Bachman Turner Overdrive, Survivor and Johnny Winter.

Ms. Berger said she received about 25 tapes a month and the judges tried to get a diverse mixture of rock, pop and new wave music.

"If we win, I'll be doing flips," said the band's manager Danny Hamilton. "It's good exposure and people need to know about the Georgia groups. There are a lot of good groups from Georgia like the Georgia Satellites that people aren't hearing about. As far as I'm concerned soul started in Georgia, not with British groups."

If you release a video, as the group Shebang *did, be sure to publicize it—don't just assume that it will get noticed on its own. The news peg for this story is that Shebang is a finalist in a national music video contest—and the group is reaping publicity from it. This story ran in* The Atlanta Journal, *a major daily paper, so Shebang's story reached hundreds of thousands of people who might never watch MTV.*

sound. One mike on the camera won't do the job. Neither will two mikes plugged into the tape unit. If you're taping live, work with a full board and as many mikes as you need. Be sure the mix is what you like before it's put on tape, because, depending on the route you choose, you may not have a chance to remix later.

One possibility is to use the audio demo you've already recorded, and lip-synch as you shoot the video. This must done *perfectly*, however, or it will look sloppy—or silly. Adding video to an existing audio tape is possible, but it's tedious and risky.

Shooting live requires a script. Work with the producer to sketch out, or *storyboard,* exactly how each song will be photographed. How many seconds on the keyboard for the introduction? When will he cut to the drums for an elaborate fill? What about fading to the backup singers for their *Do-Wops?* This requires planning and time, and isn't cheap. You should, of course, know as much as possible about what you want going into the project, but you should also work on the script with the producer, and be open to suggestions about flow, pacing, and technical matters. After all, he's the expert.

Learn which video techniques your producer can use, and be familiar with what they mean. *Long shots, close-ups, pans, wipes, freeze-frames, cuts, fades, superimpositions,* and *computer-generated graphics* will give your video a professional look. But they must be planned and coordinated—they won't just happen.

If several cameras are being used, the producer will use the *SMPTE (Society of Motion Picture and Television Engineers)* code to keep all the images and music coordinated. This is a complex procedure that keeps the music and video from each camera and recording device in perfect synch. Small producers may not have this capability—so be sure to view samples of similar work before you sign up.

Titles and artwork are important. Find out what's available, and how much it costs. Look at the computer-generated graphics possibilities, and see what would fit your music. If you're a classical pianist, a high-tech, whirling, phantasmagoric title probably wouldn't be appropriate, no matter how exciting the technique is.

Should you incorporate your logo in the title? Why not? It represents your music and you and should be part of all your publicity material. You can also use collages of print material, closeups of reviews, and other elements to give your demo a "story" feel. Such still shots, however, must be carefully scripted to maintain pace and continuity.

Use TV clips. If you have good clips of previous television appearances, work them into your tape. In fact, if you have several good clips, particularly if you've been on prestigious shows, your demo might include nothing more than those clips strung together.

Each time you perform on TV, get a tape of your appearance. Ask the station for a copy (you provide the tape and make arrangements for copying in advance), and also have a friend record a backup tape off the air. Don't miss such opportunities for free, professionally produced publicity.

Your video can also include clips from concerts, interviews, or even shots from several performances. Do you have a tape of the governor dancing to—or applauding—your music? Do you have a tape of hundreds of people dancing to your band's "Louie, Louie"? Use it. Even if the video isn't perfect, the impact will be strong.

Quality does count. Can't you just use a quick-and-dirty tape that's made at the job, with a consumer-quality camera, and no editing? Can't you just have a friend come in and videotape your band on the spot? Of course. You can use anything—but remember that if the quality of the production is poor, the publicity results will be, too.

Get it in writing. Video producers usually charge by the job. Discuss price in detail, and be sure that you understand exactly what you're getting. To be safe, insist on a written contract with your producer. Spell out exactly what you expect to receive, when it will be finished, and how much it will cost. This doesn't imply that you don't trust him—it can simply avoid unpleasantness and confusion later.

Don't be a copycat. Each time a videotape is copied the quality of the duplicate degenerates considerably. And a copy of a copy—which is what you'll usually give to clients, can suffer from video noise, poor picture quality, inaccurate color, and poor audio. That's one reason professional producers use larger formats—there's more room on the tape for signal, and each copy loses proportionately less quality.

You probably won't be able to make your own video copies, and the ones you buy will cost much more than audio demos. Check with your producer for his per-dupe prices, and call the tape duplication houses in the Yellow Pages for comparison. Insist that the copies you get are as good as they can be and work to attain a tape you'll be proud to watch.

USING VIDEO TAPES

Since videotapes are expensive, you won't blanket the area with them the way you do with audio demos. But, if you've gone to the trouble of producing a good video, be sure that all your prime clients have copies.

All the agents who book your music should certainly have their copies, and you should keep a few available for your own clients to view. It's appropriate, however, to ask that a videotape be returned, and to keep track of who has your tapes. Enclose an SASE to help insure that your copies get back to you. To get the most impact from your video, prepare a client for what the tape contains. If you especially like one aspect, tell the viewer about it before he's seen the tape. "When you watch our demo, Mr. Jones, notice the crowd reaction to our music. We're proud of the way we work with the audience to make a party happen, and this video shows it."

This way, Mr. Jones is alerted to watch for your strong point—you've made the point twice, by telling and then showing, which doesn't hurt your chances. Use videos when you have a message that should be seen as well as heard. Use them wisely, however, and don't be bedazzled with the chance to "be on TV." It won't do you any good to be on the tube if your appearance isn't up to television's standards. If you have an act with a strong visual component and if you can produce a good video demo, however, it could become the most-used publicity tool in your kit.

After all, if video messages sell everything from soap powder to cars, why shouldn't they sell your music?

CHAPTER 9

Finding Professional Help

IN YOUR BATTLE TO GET NOTICED, we've said that you, yourself, can produce almost everything you'll need—and you can. With patience, a few graphic skills, some basic tools, and the nuts-and-bolts information from earlier chapters in this book, you'll have what you need to do it yourself.

But perhaps you don't think you have any artistic ability, or you don't have the patience for tedious layout chores. Maybe you're paralyzed by "writer's block" every time you face a typewriter. Possibly you just don't have time to plan your own publicity. Perhaps you even have enough money to hire all the professional help you need. Actually, you'll probably use professionals for some publicity projects and do other tasks yourself. This chapter will direct you to the expert assistance you need.

In seeking professional help, shop around. Use the guidelines in this chapter, and get several *specific, written* quotes from different people. Prices will vary considerably—but quality can, too. Spend your money wisely, and you'll get extra mileage from each dollar you spend on publicity.

HOW GOOD ARE THEY?

One of the most frustrating aspects of "creative" businesses is that anyone can call himself a professional. Buy a guitar, learn a few chords, and presto! you're a musician. Anyone with a couple of cameras and lights can refer to herself as a professional photographer, and anyone with a drawing board, some rulers, and colored pencils is a commercial artist.

How do you separate the good from the bad? How do you find someone who is technically excellent, understands your needs, is truly creative—and affordable? Should you try to save money by hiring a beginner or part-timer, or use established professionals?

This chapter gives rough ideas of what professionals charge for their services, though rates vary so much that you must check each one in your own area. If an artist would charge $175 to design your brochure, you may decide to learn how to do your own pasteup and layout. If a photographer would charge $100 to shoot two rolls of film, you may decide to spend an afternoon with your own 35mm camera, and do your own pictures.

If you decide to do most of these publicity chores yourself, you'll save money but the quality may not be up to professional standards—and you may take forever to finish a project. However, you are a creative person, so if you have time and patience why not do it yourself? It may take time, and some tasks (layout and pasteup, for example) are tedious and require patience, but with a little practice you can do a good job.

On the other hand, if you get professional assistance you'll pay for it, but you'll have the benefit of the person's training, experience, and creativity. And since you're paying for it, you can insist that it be finished on time.

HOW TO FIND HELP

How do you locate competent artists, writers, and photographers? You could choose at random from the Yellow Pages, but there are better ways to find the right person for you. Start by asking for recommendations. When you see good examples of similar work, find out who produced them. The key word is *similar*. Don't expect an excellent wedding photographer to automatically produce the head shots you need, or a fashion illustrator to be an expert at logo design. Professionals usually specialize.

Also check at local colleges, technical/vocational schools, and private art schools. Students won't have years of experience, but they may have a fresh approach, a lot of enthusiasm—and be reasonably priced.

Freelancers and moonlighting professionals offer excellent possibilities. Often artists, writers, typesetters, and photographers who work during the day for businesses, universities, or government do freelance work on the side. Call the advertising, public relations, or publications departments of these institutions and ask if anyone is available for outside work. Also check at photo stores and print shops.

Full-time, established professionals are always available, and may offer the best value—though they may be more expensive. Again, be sure that their specialties match your needs, because professionals often work in very narrow areas of expertise. Technical writers may not be able to prepare a good press release. Architectural photographers may not know how to light a group photo. The Yellow Pages will direct you to professional help, but don't be awed by a fancy office; look for samples that match your needs.

And don't forget to shop around. Never take the first person who's available, because you have nothing with which to compare his or her skills. Prices vary, and so does creativity. Paying more doesn't automatically guarantee the best quality—but it might.

Once you've found several possibilities, how can you assess the publicity professionals in your area to be sure you get exactly what you need? Consider:

1. *Do you communicate well with the person?* Do you like her? Does she understand what you want? Do you think she'll spend time working with you? Or is she condescending, rushed, perfunctory? Too busy with her own work to take time with your small project?

2. *Look at samples of similar work.* Artists, photographers, and writers all have portfolios of their best work, and they'll be happy to show them to you—you may even get some ideas from what they've done. Compare apples with apples, however; if you're looking for help with layout, be sure to see samples of brochures or letterheads that match your needs. In every area, look for quality, for precision. Does this person take pride in his work?

3. *Ask for written cost estimates,* and be sure everything is included. Don't be afraid to ask or you may be unpleasantly surprised. Does the cost include materials? Are there any hidden expenses such as outside, subcontracted costs that will be extra? Be sure you get the bottom-line total. People who work in advertising often enjoy nearly unlimited budgets so let them know that you're concerned about cost—but don't be petty. It's easy to be too cheap, and end up wasting your money by going second (or third) class.

4. *Will the work be delivered when it's promised?* Can you depend on it? Does this person have a good reputation for reliability? If you're counting on a photographer who only freelances on weekends, are you sure your pictures will be ready when you need them? You usually won't have a contract, so if you're especially concerned about deadlines, ask for, and check with, past references.

5. *Who will own the material that's produced?* Always discuss this point because it can be important. Most photographers will keep the negatives, even though you paid for the materials—that's the custom in photography. On the other hand, artists will usually give you the original artwork, but you should ask to be sure.

If you're like most musicians, you won't have a lot of extra money to spend producing publicity, so do a little research to be sure that the help you get will fit your budget.

The Professionals Are There—If You Need Them

In planning your publicity, here are some of the professionals who are available to help you. You may not need them now, but you might call on them later as your publicity program grows.

Public relations firms are the ultimate professionals in the business of getting noticed, but they're probably too expensive for most musicians. These are the people who produce PR campaigns for businesses, government agencies, and celebrities. Much of their time is spent *networking*. They are responsible for producing press releases, stories, brochures, photographs, and for placing ideas with the media—"getting good press." Public relations firms also plan and produce all kinds of special events to create media attention—new-product introductions, press conferences, parties, contests, and so on.

If you become a star you'll need to retain a *PR* consultant to "pump the press" and keep your name in print, or if you are working on a special project with a sizable budget—a community music week, for example— you might want to work with a pro.

For most musicians, public relations firms would be a good choice for publicizing a special project, such as an album release or a concert series— where a specific budget would be devised. PR people can handle as little, or as much, of your publicity as you can afford.

Public relations professionals commonly charge a weekly or monthly retainer fee—a small PR firm in Atlanta has clients that pay from $500 to $10,000 monthly for public relations services. You'll find these firms in the Yellow Pages under "Public Relations." In smaller towns, advertising agencies often have public relations departments.

Visit a couple of public relations firms—the smaller ones would be the best bet—and explain your publicity goals. Find out what they could do for you, and how much they would charge. If they are even close to your budget, ask for a written proposal in which they'll outline exactly what they would do for you, and what their fee would be. Even if you can't afford their help you'll have the pleasure of knowing what your own publicity efforts are worth in dollars and cents, and you may pick up some good ideas.

Finding a writer to help with your brochures, press releases, and feature stories might be more difficult than you'd think. There are as many different kinds of writing as there are kinds of music, and you need a style that matches your specific publicity projects.

At first, you may think of an English teacher as a writing expert. Actually, freelance copywriters and editors will be more appropriate for your needs because your writing will be closer to advertising than to term papers. Journalism teachers or students, however, might be a resource worth checking.

Call newspapers, magazines, ad agencies, and public relations firms to get leads on good freelance writers. You'll pay by the hour or by the project; again, don't hesitate to talk about money. You don't know how fast a writer will work, and you don't want to owe $200 for a one-page brochure when you were expecting a $50 fee. Writers' fees vary so much that you'll have to research your own area.

Ask to see samples of similar work. Don't assume that just because a writer has excellent command of the English language she'll do a good job on your brochure. You have to make sure that she knows what you want and can produce it.

Artists, like writers, develop narrow specialties. You need a *commercial artist* to help with logo and brochure design and layout chores. Fine art is something else—a great painter may have no idea how to prepare a *mechanical* for the printer, so don't ask your neighbor who paints landscapes to help with your letterhead.

Always examine examples of similar work, and judge it by what you need. Does it look stilted, old fashioned? Are the details correct? Does the piece look fresh, creative, or does it have a tired, institutional appearance? The greatest artist in the world won't help you if he's not appropriate.

You can get names of artists from the same sources that recommend writers, and from print shops and art-supply stores. Commercial art students can produce excellent work, and their rates should be lower to match their lack of experience.

Photographers, like musicians, vary greatly in experience, skill, and competence. Photography can be fine art or a mundane craft, and you'll do best if you can find someone in between these extremes. You don't want avant-garde weirdness (unless you're a weird, avant-garde band), but neither do you want the kind of photographer who "nails his lights to the floor" and shoots each portrait exactly the same way.

Look for someone whose work suits your needs. Ask to see samples of group and head shots. Look for posing—is it natural or stiff? Look at the backgrounds—are they the same in every picture, or does the photographer vary location with each subject? Look at the photos technically—is the focus crisp and sharp? Is there a good tonal range from white to black? Are there spots, flecks, black dots on the picture? In photography, cleanliness is next to Godliness, so look around the studio for signs of carelessness and sloppiness.

Finding the right photographer may be as simple as asking around. Look at brochures and publicity photos used by your competition. In smaller towns, one photographer may really "do it all" as many Yellow Pages ads claim, but in larger cities photographers are highly specialized. Look for a photographer who shoots models and bands and who likes the creative challenge of matching her photos to your image and moods.

Some photographers charge by the hour, not including materials. Others quote a set price for a session, including a certain number of prints. Most will provide you with contact sheets, and you'll select the prints you like for a per-print fee. The best, and most common, procedure is for the photographer to print one or two of the shots you like and have them duplicated inexpensively at a mass production house (see the Appendix). The photographer will expect this, because he can't even buy photographic paper at a price that's competitive with the mass production houses. Remember, though, that photographers retain ownership of the negatives even though you may have paid for the film.

What if you find a terrific graphic artist, but you can't afford her rates? Why not swap your music for her art? *Bartering* can benefit both parties. In bartering, swap value for value, and don't reduce the quality of what you offer or receive. A photographer might swap two photo sessions and ten prints in exchange for your band playing for his party. Or, a writer whose daughter is planning a wedding may write your brochure and several press releases in exchange for your string quartet's playing at the wedding reception. If the idea appeals to you, be sure to ask. You may be surprised at the deals you can make.

All these publicity experts are available to help you. They know their crafts, and can give you the benefit of years of experience. Successful people often delegate specific tasks to others, and you may prefer to have someone else prepare your publicity material to free your time for other projects. All you have to do is ask—and pay.

Remember, even the best writers, photographers, and artists can't read your mind; it's your responsibility to let them know what you want. Show samples, keep clip files of similar work, ask questions, draw sketches. The professional you are hiring wants to please you by providing what you're seeking, so be as clear as you can about what you want and can afford.

Never allow yourself to be awed by technical vocabulary or jargon from another discipline. There is no reason that you should know the language of printing, photography, or professional public relations. Those folks probably don't know music terms either, so ask questions to find out what you need to know. If the person you've hired won't answer your questions clearly, find someone else.

Once more, with feeling: do as much of your own publicity work as possible; after all you're the one who benefits from all this effort. You may be able to produce almost everything, but don't skimp to the point that the quality suffers. Don't "nickel and dime" yourself out of a quality job by insisting on the cheapest everything, every time. A few more rolls of film, a better grade of paper, may add just a little to your overall cost but result in the superior quality that you need.

Once you have your tools in place, remember the professionals who helped you. Good resource people, like good musicians and good clients, are to be treasured.

PART

TWO

Using Your Publicity Tools to Get Noticed

CHAPTER 10

Publicity and the Media

NOW YOU'VE PREPARED THE TOOLS you need—letterheads, business cards, photos, and demo tapes. How do you use them to attract clients and audiences?

We'll explore lots of ways—from special events to T-shirts, but we'll start with the biggest fish in the publicity pond—the *media*. We'll see how individual musicians and unknown performers can catch the media's interest—by using publicity hooks. News stories, feature articles, regular calendar listings, and mention in columns will combine to raise your visibility to new heights.

THE MEDIA

Actually, there is no such thing as *the media*. Instead, there are thousands of different media, large and small, local and national. *The media* includes both CBS and a small-town country music radio station. It includes *Newsweek* and the free shopper's paper distributed at your neighborhood supermarket. It includes *The New York Times* and the weekly *Cooperstown News and Views*.

Still, people speak of the media as though it were an imposing monolith and anyone would be afraid to approach such a powerful institution. Fortunately, the media isn't really overwhelming at all.

To begin, think of the media as being local writers, artists, photogra-

112

phers, technicians, and businesspeople who together make up newspapers, radio and TV stations, magazines, and other communications outlets in your community. When you approach a media person, it won't be Mike Wallace or Dan Rather; it will be someone from your community *who needs your story as much as you need his help.*

Hard to believe? It's true.

Media people need you because they need your ideas. They need news and features to interest their readers and viewers. Every day editors face the same challenge—fill up all that blank space, all that empty air time. If your story ideas are interesting, you'll be welcomed.

But you do have to know the basic principles.

1. First, learn to recognize trends.
2. Learn what makes a good feature story.
3. Learn to think like a publicist who recognizes *news pegs* and *feature hooks* everywhere.
4. Learn to relate your music and performance to broader issues that appeal to the public.
5. Finally, learn to reach media people by using press releases to generate news and feature stories. Your release could simply give them the idea for a story, or you might write and photograph it yourself.

We'll talk about newspapers and broadcast outlets in more detail later, but first—what makes news?

What's News

News tells what's happening in the world that's important and interesting, in the opinion of an editor. This includes, certainly, items of national and international interest, but it also involves local events that are important to you and your career.

Music is not usually a "hard news" area, so most of your media exposure will probably be through feature stories that focus on interesting facets of your performance and life. There will be times, though, when you'll make news, so you should recognize what's newsworthy.

News stories answer the readers' questions and, traditionally, tell "who, what, when, where, why, and how." (This simple formula is called the *five w's and an h* in the news trade, and is a useful way to remember what's important in news stories.)

Every day editors must decide what to cover, to print, or broadcast because there isn't room for everything. To help make these decisions, editors ask:

- Is it important?
- Is it interesting?

- Does it appeal to our audience?
- Does it pass the "who cares?" or "so what?" test?

News stories should be factual, with no opinions expressed. They give just the facts, and deliver them in a particular style, called the *inverted pyramid*. Newswriting is discussed in the next chapter, but basically, a news story always starts with the most important facts and adds explanations and details later.

Watch your local paper for *news* items that affect the music world, and clip them for your file. (This doesn't include "news" stories that were obviously created to keep famous stars' names in the news. You probably won't need to make news by hitting a photographer or suing the *National Enquirer*.)

Often music does tie in with *news stories*. For example:

In a budget-tightening move, the local school board votes to cut funding for music, band, and chorus classes. That's news. You're a band director and your job is at stake. You must use the media to convince the community and school board that music education is important.

The national controversy about rock lyrics has gotten lots of publicity in local papers. You, as a rock musician, write an editorial for the newspaper, appear on a radio talk show, and make a speech to the local PTA advisory board to explain your band's position on this issue. Even if your band isn't directly affected, you have gained some recognition by connecting with a hot media topic.

Your city is going after convention business in a big way, and your songwriter's club holds a contest to choose a theme song for the city's audiovisual sales extravaganza. You get several stories in the paper and TV news and lots of airplay for the winning song. You have taken advantage of the city's interest in economic salesmanship and linked your club directly to it.

Your piano studio is so successful that you are able to design and build a new facility that incorporates a recital hall, private classrooms, a library, and computer teaching aids. You should tie into news stories on teaching (always a popular news issue), entrepreneurs, building design, and computers.

There are dozens of news issues that affect musicians. When you link yourself, your music, or your group to these issues, you automatically expand your influence.

In practice you'll find that there is a continuum—a range of story ideas, with news on one end, and features on the other. Most stories about the arts fall somewhere between the two extremes—there may be an element of news, but focus is usually on a human interest angle. Don't waste time trying to decide whether a story is news or feature—it's probably both.

Feature This

Though you'll try to be newsworthy, you'll probably find it easier to get media attention through *feature stories* that focus on people and interesting activities. Features are written to entertain as well as enlighten, and almost always are in a more interesting, subjective, relaxed style than a news story would be. Sometimes feature articles include interviews, often they incorporate photographs, and they're frequently longer than news stories.

In many newspapers, the first section is devoted mostly to news, but the rest of the paper is filled with features—the local section, lifestyle pages, arts review, business events, and even the sports pages include articles on interesting people and happenings. This is where most of your newspaper exposure will be.

You can't just call an editor and say, "Hi. I'm Joe and I play the guitar in a rock band. How about doing a story on me?" That's not the way it works. You've got to have an *angle*.

What's an angle? It's a mathematical description of a hook. Find an approach that ties your music in with something bigger, that's of interest to lots of people. Link yourself with a trend, a fad, a worthwhile project, or a news story, and try again.

"Hi, Mr. Editor. I'm Joe, and I play guitar in a band that's giving a series of free workshops at inner-city high schools. We're working with young musicians, helping them learn about the music business. Our first session was standing-room-only, and we thought you might like to send a writer and photographer to the next event."

That's a lot better. It's more likely to arouse an editor's curiosity because you're doing something that involves the community. It's really interesting, and the editor knows you have something to offer.

There are *trends* in news and feature stories. From year to year, different subjects catch the attention of the public and of editors. John Naisbett's popular book, *Megatrends*, tells how the amount of newspaper space devoted to different issues changes over time. One month there are lots of articles on smoking and health; another month you'll see lots of pieces on jogging and health instead. News, like everything else, is subject to the pressures of changing fashion.

So learn to recognize trends. Read newspapers and magazines. When you see a new fad emerging—aerobic exercise, for example, or jogging, or walking—figure out how to relate your musical activities to this new interest. Maybe one percent of newspaper readers are interested in the trumpet, while fifty percent of them are interested in health issues. Your challenge as a trumpet player is to find a way to link trumpet playing with the health issues of the day. Can you do it? Of course.

Or perhaps you'd like to tie your music to another subject that interests lots of people—education, say. What if you're not a teacher; can you

Liquor licensing ordinance hits sour note with musicians

By Connie Green
Staff Writer

Atlanta's musicians are furious over a city ordinance that requires them to be fingerprinted and to buy a liquor license each time they perform at a club where alcohol is served.

After police cited a band at the Metroplex club on Aug. 9 for non-compliance of the licensing law, several entertainers appeared before a City Council committee asking that the law be repealed or musicians excluded. The band members were fined for non-compliance.

"It's inherently unfair to use liquor licenses to regulate musicians who work in places they do not own," said Nicholas Pennington, executive secretary of the 1,200-member Atlanta Federation of Musicians. " If you've got four jobs, you have to get fingerprinted four times. I don't think that's what you had in mind when you passed the law."

City Councilman Dozier Smith, chairman of the Public Safety Committee, has scheduled a work session Friday to discuss the ordinance and consider changes.

Smith, who sponsored the ordinance which passed unanimously last April, said he has not deter-mined whether to support a change in the law. "I want to look at it and get the police side of it."

The law states, "No person may be employed by an establishment holding a license for the sale of alcoholic beverages for consumption on the premises or the operation of a bottle house until such person has been fingerprinted by the police department and has been issued a permit ... "

The ordinance also states that any permit issued will expire in 12 months or when the holder changes jobs. Each permit, which includes a photograph of the licensee, costs $10 and is issued at the police department.

However, the provision may be waived by the commissioner of public safety in cases of "celebrities and entertainers of national reputation," an exception that incenses local musicians. Pennington complained that allowing waivers unfairly singles out local performers, from symphony musicians to vocalists, who are only in the business of entertaining, not serving alcohol.

He also questioned how the police bureau determines which entertainers have a national reputation.

"If you've got a police chief who knows about music, maybe he can decide who's nationally known. The bottom line is it's unconstitutional and unfair to treat the well-known and the less well-known musicians in different fashions," he said.

Police began enforcing the ordinance in August, after giving entertainers and club employees four months to get fingerprinted and licensed, said Atlanta Police Lt. D.V. Lee. Though entertainers are not directly responsible for liquor sales, police are concerned about the criminal element attracted to certain entertainment spots, he said.

"People who like to use and sell drugs follow entertainers," Lee said. "I think we could safely say that there have been enough entertainers arrested to say entertainers are involved in drugs. There's a definite need to control the (liquor) industry."

Councilman Bill Campbell, who opposes the law, said he would try to change the ordinance after the Friday work session. "I don't think this is a good law. It is not an equitable provision," Campbell said. "This is a town that prides itself on entertainment. It's not appropriate for entertainers to be fingerprinted."

When the Atlanta City Council passed an ordinance requiring musicians to be fingerprinted each time they performed where alcohol is served, the musical community responded forcefully. Such "hard news" stories aren't as common for musicians as feature ideas are, but events such as this can benefit from wide news coverage. Atlanta musicians worked to publicize this ordinance, and the intensive coverage helped have it repealed.

still link your projects to learning? Of course. Did you enter the computer age so you could MIDI your synthesizer to a computer? Have you developed a unique method of teaching rock guitar that you've successfully used with thirty students? Did you write and record several simple songs that your schoolteacher spouse uses in elementary classes? Did you learn to play the bass, even though you started professional life as a trumpet player, because there's more work for bassists? These ideas all link easily with the idea of learning, education, personal advancement. They could be developed into hooks for stories that would grab readers' attention— about computers, teaching, elementary education, or self-education.

Publicity Practice

Make a list of news and feature themes that are "hot" right now. What fascinates the media this month? Computers? Health? Nutrition? Poverty? Self-development, reaching one's fullest potential? New businesses? Entrepreneurs? Women in new roles? High technology?

First, list subjects that you see over and over on TV features and in newspapers and magazines—call it your *What's Hot* list. Then brainstorm ways your music could relate—even if its only a slight connection. Writers and editors, more than most people, are interested in what captures the public's interest, and if you can tie into a popular issue, you'll find yourself featured.

As usual in brainstorming, be as creative as possible. If your ideas won't work, that's fine—but maybe they will. For example, does the press seem fascinated by smoking and health? How could you relate your music to this issue? A few ideas:

  • If you work in nightclubs, do a story on how you cope with smokiness in the room. Detail how you go outside and do deep-breathing exercises for ten minutes after each job to clear your lungs of smoke. Talk about how you hang your clothes in the garage so your closet won't smell like a nightclub. Discuss what your doctor has told you about breathing that smoke-filled air every night for years—is it equivalent to smoking a pack of cigarettes a day? More? What can nonsmoking nightclub patrons learn from your experience?
  • If you're a band director, invite a lung specialist to speak to your students, demonstrating the loss of lung capacity that comes with smoking. Relate this to wind instrument playing. Perhaps your band could take the lead in a school-wide "stamp out smoking" campaign.
  • If you're a pianist in a bar, try for a feature called "Smoke Gets in My Eyes." Discuss how difficult it is to sing with customers blowing smoke in your face, and how difficult it is to avoid the problem without offending them. Talk about the ever-present cigarette burns on the club's grand piano. Point out the times your clothes have been ruined by careless smokers. Show how smokiness irritates your contact lenses.

Do these ideas seem far-fetched? Perhaps, but this is the kind of thing that editors and writers love—a *peg* on which they can hang their stories, an *angle* that allows them to focus on something that links up with a larger trend. Try it. You'll be surprised at how you can fit your music into a larger issue.

WHAT'S THE ANGLE, WHERE'S THE HOOK?

You see now that the *hook* is important—snares readers' interest. When you start thinking like a publicist you realize that not only do you have to hook the reader, but to reach that reader you first have to hook the editor. It helps to know what editors do and what they like.

Editors are the first step in the story-selection process. They determine what gets covered and how much time or space it gets. They're under immense pressure from all sides and have to decide which stories to run, which ones to leave out. Sometimes they may run a story as a favor to a friend, but usually editors choose stories to interest readers or viewers. Their ultimate aim, of course, is to sell newspapers or attract viewers— and sell more ads.

So, when you call and say, "Hi, Mr. Editor. I'm Joe, I play guitar in a rock band, and we'd like to have a feature story on us," your chances of success are zero. You haven't passed the "so what?" test. The editor doesn't see anything interesting in the fact that you're a guitar player— even a good guitar player. You haven't found a hook.

Musicians gather to savor and study resurgence of jazz

By L. Eric Elie

Staff Writer

Like surgeons after a successful operation, the National Association of Jazz Educators gathered in Atlanta this past weekend, pausing briefly to celebrate the resurgence of interest in jazz, and musing long and hard about how to keep the patient healthy.

In a slew of clinics, workshops and concerts, the players, students, teachers and lovers of jazz agreed that the best prescription for this music is to keep fighting for it by expanding and improving its teaching.

"There has been an enormous struggle in getting jazz to the point that it is today," said Valerie Capers, an associate professor of music at Bronx Community College in New York and panelist for a student rap session. "But what makes me so mad is that many of the colleges still treat jazz as an also-ran."

Veteran bassist Rufus Reid added, "If this truly is an American art form, it should be taught in our schools. And that's not just to make jazz musicians."

But teaching jazz in not an easy task. Jazz has traditionally been taught informally by veteran musicians, not trained professors. Therefore, unlike teachers of classical music, jazz teachers have very little in the way of textbooks and proven methods.

Some of the participants in the conference said that to be successful, jazz education programs must learn to combine this mentoring system of previous eras with academics.

"Count Basie once told me the guys go to school and they play the notes beautifully, but it's all so businesslike," said Ellis Marsalis, who is the father of the celebrated duo of Branford and Wynton Marsalis and who now teaches at Virginia Commonwealth University.

"But I do think we can get the kind of results in a learning situation like a college campus," he said.

Is it a news or feature story? Often an event such as the annual gathering of jazz educators is both. When possible, use the timely news peg to interest an editor; then provide enough background material to turn a short news story into a longer feature-oriented piece.

With musical hands, man signs group's songs

Deaf Atlantan is interpreter for '87 Up With People tour

By Hank Ezell
Staff Writer

When Ross Deadwyler talks, people watch.

Indeed, they tend to watch raptly, since the 19-year-old Deadwyler is something of an artist in his field — interpreting music into sign language for the deaf.

Deadwyler, an Atlantan who has been deaf since birth, has been selected as the first deaf person ever to perform with Up With People. In January he will join one of the group's five performing troupes, which are now in their 18th year of touring the world with elaborate, upbeat song and dance reviews.

"I don't think they could have picked a better person to initiate it," said Tim McCarty, Deadwyler's theater director at Gallaudet University's model high school for the deaf in Washington, D.C. "He takes the stage with tremendous power and energy. He loves what he's doing so much that it just takes the audience with him."

Deadwyler, a June graduate from the school, will become an interpreter in both the linguistic and creative realms. That's because song lyrics don't necessarily translate directly, or gracefully, into American Sign Language.

For example, the "signing" of "The Greatest Love of All," recently recorded by Whitney Houston, involves not just sign language words and letters, but also movements intended to suggest untranslatable concepts. In effect, Deadwyler becomes a dancer from the pectorals up.

His recruitment was something of a surprise, the result of an Up With People performance at Gallaudet two years ago. The visiting troupe performed with Gallaudet students, and at the end Deadwyler and another deaf student did an impromptu sign version of "Summer Nights," from the musical "Grease," as the Up With People performers sang it.

"It was real magic," McCarty recalled. "They said that visit was the No. 1 most uplifting community relations activity they had during that year."

Deadwyler later tried out and was accepted for a 1987 tour. He got a $3,000 scholarship from the program, which as a side benefit will yield 18 hours of college course credits. He is home in Atlanta now, trying to come up with the remainder of the $7,500 fee for the one-year program.

"It's an ideal marriage," McCarty said. "Ross wants to sign songs, and he wants to perform for audiences all over the world, which is what Up With People does."

ANDY SHARP/Staff

Ross Deadwyler, 19, has been selected as the first deaf person ever to perform with Up With People.

Try to link your story with a larger issue that will be interesting to a broad audience. Here, an interpreter for the deaf is the focus of an article on a musical group—expanding the circle of interested readers. An editor might not be interested in "just another story about a musical group," but a unique angle such as this could make the story irresistible.

Return to your clip file to see what kinds of stories newspapers in your area typically run about musicians, artists, and community groups. Are most stories related to concerts and recitals? Or do they frequently run profiles of successful people who have overcome obstacles? Are most of their music-related features community oriented? Do they like new ideas, fads, technology?

Read those stories carefully because yours will take the same approach. Strange as it may seem, writers and editors are quite conservative, and once they find a story formula that works they'll stick with it. You'll improve your chances for coverage if you fit into their story schemes.

Thus, if most articles about musicians in your local paper emphasize their community involvement, go out and get involved—and you'll get noticed. If, on the other hand, the music stories are mostly reviews, invite the reviewer to your next performance, with plenty of material sent to her beforehand to acquaint her with your music. Go with the flow; don't try to start a new media wave by yourself.

PLAN AHEAD

Once your publicity wagon starts rolling, you'll find that it's easier and easier to get noticed. But you have to plan carefully. Newspapers and magazines operate on a rigid deadline schedule that can't be changed just because you didn't know about it—or you forgot. If you're publicizing a big event you'll need to plan months ahead to get all the publicity you need.

Call the publications and broadcast stations you're interested in. Ask about deadlines, including the "Calendar of Events" sections, regular columns, and news and feature stories. Tell them what you're planning and find out who the appropriate editors are, who does theater and music reviews, and whether photographers are available. You may have to talk with several departments, but you'll have the information you need to get your information to the right person, and in time to be used.

To help remember deadlines you could create a master deadline calendar or chart, showing exactly when each media outlet needs certain information. Perhaps a simple list on your bulletin board will suffice: "Monday—midweek newspaper calendar and Sunday feature articles, Wednesday—Saturday Leisure Guide, Thursday—Sunday events directory," and so on. Make it clear, so you won't miss good publicity because you forgot a deadline.

Let's take a really big project—publicity for a community orchestra/theatre's musical comedy production—as an example to see how much free publicity we could produce. In a case like this, you'd have a committee of assistants because there's lots of work involved. (Of course, chances are that you'll never be in charge of publicity for such a theatrical production, but whatever your musical project may be, you can use some of these same techniques. You may only need one or two of these ideas for your band—but you might need them all.)

First, state the publicity goals for yourself, your organization, your committee. Write it down. "Our goals in publicizing this performance of *Money Talks* are to increase the attendance at all three performances, raise community awareness of our theatrical company and orchestra, focus attention on our talent, make fund-raising and ticket-selling jobs easier, and add good publicity clips to our files." Be sure that everyone involved knows the importance of good publicity in reaching these goals.

Use your wall calendar and datebook to sketch out when your main publicity thrusts must happen. Remember, deadlines won't wait and excuses don't count. If your news release doesn't arrive on time, your event won't be mentioned. Even small papers and radio stations are flooded with promotion for worthy events.

Here's a rough sketch of one way to publicize the musical comedy your school or community group is producing. The steps would be much the same, though probably on a smaller scale, for a nightclub band, a concert, recital, or almost any other musical event. Remember, these are just suggestions. You don't have to do them all; in fact, you might not need any of them, so don't feel overwhelmed by the possibilities or the amount of work involved. If your musical activity is a rock band playing the motel circuit, you'll devise a quite different, but still important, list of ways to publicize your group.

1. *The big day.* As soon as the date is chosen, announce it to all your contacts. Write a short press release and send it to all feature editors, reviewers, other theater groups, community leaders, and newsletter publishers who might mention your activity. Early mention should help "claim" the date so there won't be a similar event scheduled by another community theater.

2. *Auditions.* If you're holding open auditions, do another press release. Try for coverage of the audition itself by a feature writer, TV crew, or radio news reporter. Call the editors and suggest an angle—such as the total reliance on community talent, or the mixture of old and young people at the auditions. You could also write a short feature story on audition anxiety or opportunities for beginning actors and musicians. Be sure to notify all calendar editors, in any case.

3. *Use press releases* to announce the audition results. Who was chosen for each major role? Why? What are their qualifications, backgrounds, other interests? The more local the paper or broadcast station, the more important names will be—so list everyone who's involved.

Writers love anecdotes, so include short interesting or humorous ones that relate to the story. Did a young clarinet player do better at the auditions than more experienced musicians, and thus land her first paying job? Did the drummer forget his sticks and have to try out using kitchen knives? If so, include these items in your release or story.

4. *Feature it.* Write a feature story on the composer and/or playwright. Strive, as usual, for a tie-in with a relevant hook or news peg. Maybe the theme of the musical offers insights into modern American life. Maybe its historical perspective presents a critical look at progress. Perhaps you can find a unique local connection.

As the performance date nears, try for a feature story on the set design and construction or other production highlights. Again, look for a current trend that will broaden your appeal. Is the set designer a woman? Great, slant your story that way. Has smoking been banned at rehearsals? Does the entire cast do fifteen minutes of warm-up aerobic exercises before rehearsal? Are the lights controlled by a computer? Find a tie-in that will interest people who don't care about the theater. Then you've hooked a new audience.

5. *Up-to-the-minute promotion.* As the performance dates get closer, shift into high gear and double-check with media people to remind them—and urge them—to cover the big event. Be *sure* all events calendars have the information they need. Try for a slot on all the local

news shows and try to place a cast member or two on some talk shows. Other publicity ideas could be used now, too—posters on telephone poles, flyers on community bulletin boards, banners across the street near the theater, a telephone ticket-sales contest.

6. *Reviews.* Send all reviewers in the area a packet of information that includes previous stories and releases. Be sure they have good seats for the dress rehearsal or first performance, and double-check with them by phone to be sure they've received the tickets, and to urge them to attend. (Don't, however, ask for a good review—the performance must stand on its own merits. Your job is just to be sure the reviewer attends.)

7. *Follow-up promotion.* After the performance, do a wrap-up article. How many hours went into the production? Any injuries? Any adversity overcome? Did the flutist's wife deliver a baby the night of the first performance? Did the standing-room-only crowds buoy the spirits of the producers? Are any cast members turning professional because of their experiences and reception in this performance?

If there is any special social, cultural, or community angle involved, be sure to publicize that, too. Did the composer come down from New York for the premier performance? Was enough money raised to make the down payment on a permanent home for the troupe? Or was the money raised given to a local charity?

Planning publicity this way is a lot of work, and in a project this big you should have a committee to help you. The hard work will pay off, though, when you meet all your goals and see a full audience applauding every performance.

In this example the community theater and orchestra represent a broad segment of people, and are therefore likely to be covered by the media in your area. However, if you are just one musician, or a for-profit band trying to get noticed, you'd follow the same steps. You'd try for strong tie-ins with trends, fads, or newsworthy events to magnify your importance and relate your activities to popular causes.

If you're a pop band, for example, you wouldn't use most of the steps discussed above, but you'd formulate your own plan of action. You could:

• Plan your publicity campaign, map out your goals, and divide responsibility among the group's members.
• Issue a press release to announce opening night, or contract renewal, at the club where you work.
• Devise promotional activities, probably including the club owner, that would include the kind of hooks that would interest the media. Then you'd publicize these activities with press releases, calendar listings, and feature stories. See Chapter Nineteen for ideas of events to publicize.
• Take advantage of the publicity angle of normal changes and events, when possible. If your drummer is leaving the band, why not hold auditions to find a replacement and

publicize the auditions—even make it a contest? (You'll hire the replacement you want, of course, but why not make an event out of it?)

If you do this activity, it won't really be "practice"—it will give you some much-needed information, and will save you time when you're actually publicizing an event.

Look through your clip file, and newspapers and magazines, to find all the local *calendars of events* that you can. Don't overlook tabloids, weeklies, and free *shoppers newspapers*. Also, keep a list of which broadcast stations run *community calendars* that would be relevant to your musical activities.

Then call all the stations and papers. Ask to speak to the community affairs director or calendar editor. Find out when their deadlines are, and how to submit items—on a three-by-five card, in a letter, by phone?

While you're on the phone, find out the same deadline information, and editors' names, for feature articles. Make a chart showing these deadlines. Call it the *contacts/deadline* chart, and include addresses, phone numbers, and names for easy reference. Now you're ready to get listed when you have a concert, show, festival, or anything else that should be publicized.

In even a medium-size city there is so much going on that the weekend calendars are filled with events. The calendar editors aren't going to go looking for you to find out what you're doing. You've got to tell them. And you'll have to tell them over and over. Making the deadline chart will make getting listed easy for you.

IT WORKS BOTH WAYS

Once you've learned to prepare a *press release*, and you know more about the structure of newspapers and broadcast stations, you can jump right in and publicize yourself until you're rich and famous. Remember that *the media need you as much as you need them.*

Your job is to make your ideas interesting, to make them pass the "so what?" test. You have to look outside yourself and your own needs to see how your music would appeal to others. Maybe you'll have to start some new projects that would help your publicity efforts.

The job of the media is to inform and entertain their readers, listeners, and viewers. If you can help editors, writers, photographers, and cameramen by letting them know how interesting your music and performances are, you've really done them a big favor—but they won't know about it unless someone—*probably you*—tells them.

CHAPTER 11

The Press Release

YOU'RE PLANNING THE PUBLICITY for your band's opening at a new club in town, and you've come up with a great idea—a *hook*—that would snare any editor's attention. What do you do now? Do you just call her on the phone? Should you write a letter? How, specifically, do you get the media interested in you and your projects?

You send a *press release*. It's a standard tool that works better than letters and phone calls; it's universally used to publicize people and events. The release is essentially a pared-down news story that presents the outline of your event in a way that will grab an editor's attention.

Why are press releases (also called *news releases*) so popular? Because they tell your story at a glance. An editor can run the release exactly as you wrote it, call you for more details, or send a writer and photographer to cover your event. A good press release is part of virtually every publicity campaign, and yours will be no exception.

You'll send releases to all kinds of people besides those in the media, too. They're an ideal way to reach agents, club owners, your regular clients, and even other musicians. Releases look professional, get attention, tell your story, impress your readers, and get you noticed.

The best part: producing a press release isn't difficult.

What events in your musical life need a press release? After all, you don't want to waste time publicizing the wrong activities.

Anything that's newsworthy should be publicized, and you should define *newsworthy* as creatively as possible. Use your brainstorming lists from previous chapters and study your clip file. Scholarship awards, opening night for your band, formation of a new band, signing a record contract, production of a video, open auditions, and dates for concerts, shows, and recitals are newsworthy, and a press release will help you spread the word.

Often you won't really be trying for *news* coverage—you'll send a release to stimulate interest for a *feature* article—but you'll still use that hook or slant to relate your activities to something else.

A press release will help your musical activity get noticed by the media if:

1. *It's a first.* The first night of your engagement at Coconut Grove, the first all-girl rock band in the history of Graceland County, the first performance you've given since graduating from college, the first time bagpipes have been used in a fusion band—these happenings will benefit from well-written releases.

2. *It's a specific event* that will attract an audience. Concerts, recitals, plays, musicals, workshops, seminars, even speeches can be effectively publicized with press releases. Is your jazz group playing a be-bop concert to commemorate Charlie Parker's birthday? Is your rock band opening for Michael Jackson's Post-Victory Tour?

3. *It's the oldest, newest, largest, most unusual.* If you regularly play a guitar that was made in 1879, if your high-school band is experimenting with prototype drums made of graphite, if your barbershop quartet uses wireless microphones, if your pop band is trying for a *Guiness Book of Records* endurance test—send a release.

4. *It involves a celebrity, noted expert, out-of-town artist, or famous person.* If Ed McMahon visits your school to publicize a talent contest, if Dudley Moore will be featured pianist with your stage band, if Huey Lewis sits in with your lounge group, if Barbra Streisand records a song you wrote—send a press release.

In short, if your music is involved with anything that's likely to be interesting to a broad audience, use a release to publicize it. It may even be an event that's contrived solely for its publicity value, such as the *Guiness Book of Records* stunt, or a legitimate news story. In either case the release is the proper way to tell the editor about it.

News doesn't always just happen. *Much*—some say *most*—of what you read in the papers and see on TV is planned news, carefully orchestrated to publicize someone or some event. You should do the same.

The ideas given above are typical of those that can be profitably publicized. Chapter Nineteen summarizes these and adds more events that can be turned to good publicity for all kinds of musicians. You'll continue to think of many more.

When you've become experienced at generating your own publicity, you'll produce press releases almost without effort. "Oh, yeah," you'll

'World's largest' office bash brings charities holiday cash

By Monte Plott
Staff Writer

It was billed as "the world's largest office party," but the thousands of revelers who packed the Hyatt Regency Hotel in downtown Atlanta Thursday night had anything but office work on their minds.

"You see this many happy people, just having fun, it's great," said Martin Hackley, an Atlanta salesman who was among the throngs that filled three levels of the hotel's lobby and ballroom areas.

The four-hour party, featuring live music, dancing and entertainment by local groups and celebrities, was at heart a charity benefit to raise money for multiple sclerosis and the Scottish Rite Children's Hospital.

Admission was $3, or a donated toy to go to young Scottish Rite patients. Based on the intake of money and toys, Hyatt officials estimated that by 9 p.m. the crowd had surpassed last year's turnout of 4,000 people and had approached 5,000.

"We've got wall-to-wall people. We've extended the party an extra half hour or so (beyond the original 9 p.m. cutoff) so everbody can enjoy it," said Kathleen Schoch, director of public relations for the hotel. The Hyatt Regency was among 77 Hyatt hotels holding charity holiday parties this year, according to officials of the hotel corporation.

Office personnel from downtown skyscrapers mingled with workers who drove in from the suburbs — and further — as Atlanta celebrities helped serve drinks and snacks to the crowd.

Celebrities ranged from 1986 Georgia Watermelon Queen Kendra Tomlinson to professional baseball veteran Phil Niekro, who paused between his duties as a guest bartender to pose for a picture with Sheri Boyle, a Kroger Co. employee who came from her home in Rome, Ga., for the party.

"My brother was named for him (Niekro)," Ms. Boyle said. "My father would kill me if I came home without a picture of him."

The emphasis was on a having a good time, but not overdoing it. Representatives of Arrive Alive Georgia, a community campaign against drunken driving, manned tables where literature was dispensed and where revelers could take a Breathalyzer test if they wished.

The news peg here is the idea of the "world's largest" office party, but the story also deals with fund-raising for worthy charities. The band, "Clutch," got good publicity, even though the story was not about them. They were successfully linked to a larger story with broad community interest.

think. "We're adding an amateur participation night at the club for the next two months to stimulate business. We should send a release to generate some feature articles. Let's see . . . what kind of hook would work best?" That's how a successful publicity seeker operates; everything can be turned to good publicity with the right approach. The release is your standard weapon.

WRITING THE RELEASE

Press releases are like little news stories, and they follow the same *inverted pyramid* form. It's a simple, direct format that gives the most important details first and adds more information as the story goes on. The idea is to give the facts and arouse the readers' interest so they'll read on. The inverted pyramid looks like this:

First comes the summary lead.
Then come more details.
Then more details.
More details.
More.

If an editor chooses to print your release exactly as it's written, this form lets him cut the story to fit the available space without losing the most important facts. And it gives the main idea of your story in the first paragraph. So, to write a release, simply list everything you want to say. Use the old *5 w's and an h* formula as a guide, and fill in the blanks.

What _____
Who _____
Where _____
When _____
Why _____
How _____

Once you have the facts together, organize them with the most important point first. Is this a *when*-oriented event, like a concert? If so, put that first. Or is the *who* more important—Phil Collins, say, visiting your music store to promote a new line of drums?

In writing a press release you're trying for publicity, true, but you're also writing news. All editors recognize puffery and unsupported self-promotion—and they'll reject any blatant attempts to use their media this way. Stick to the facts, but present them as interestingly as possible.

The Lead Paragraph

The first sentence of your release must demand attention. Editors are busy and overworked. They're inundated daily with releases from every organization from the League of Women Voters to the Hog Growers' Association. How can you make your release stand out in this crowd? By using the strongest hook you can think of—in the first sentence.

Several approaches work for the lead:

● *Question.* "When is the last time you heard authentic, acoustic bluegrass music in a relaxing outdoor setting?"
● *Who.* "World-famous bandleader Ron Mendola will conduct the Mid-West College All-Star Jazz Ensemble at. . . ."
● *What.* "Synthesizers, new keyboard instruments that turn anyone into an instant composer, will be demonstrated Saturday, July 4, at. . . ."

• *Where.* "The Stone Mountain Riverboat will be the site of the tenth annual reunion of the Jordan High School band alumni. . . ."
• *Why.* "Because of renewed interest in early Black American music, the Allen Stone Quartet will present an evening of authentic Spirituals and early Blues at. . . ."
• *How.* " 'Proper warm-up exercises for pianists can help avoid cramps and muscle fatigue,' says Dr. Sandra Underwood, well-known sports medicine specialist."

Make that first line interesting and you've won the editor's attention. He'll read on to get the rest of your story, and (we hope) decide to print it. But if that first line is boring—"Joe's Band is proud to announce the addition of more first-rate equipment that will, we're sure, make us an even better band"—the story will never pass the editor's "so what?" filter.

Finish writing the release by giving more details in *descending order of importance.* Squeeze the who, what, where, why, and possibly how, into the first two sentences if possible, and use the supporting, or less important, data in the final two or three paragraphs.

Here are more press release guidelines:

1. *Be brief.* Busy editors won't read through pages to get your story. Try to keep it to one page; two at the most. Don't tell everything you know. If an editor is interested, she'll contact you for more information.

2. *Use short sentences.* Newspaper columns are only around two inches wide, and one typewritten line from your release equals two lines of print in the paper. Keep paragraphs short, too; limit them to two or three sentences each.

3. *Add supporting names toward the end of the release.* Neighborhood and local papers like to print names, so list committee members, band members, and family names when it's appropriate. Larger papers will often cut the story before the names; smaller ones will include them.

4. *Use quotations.* "Strong, appropriate quotations add spice to a story," says Dr. James Traylor, writing instructor at DeKalb College. "Further, they break up the grayness of long paragraphs and they add an expert's authority to your story."

5. *Be accurate.* Sending press releases requires you to be responsible. Be positive that times, addresses, names, and other facts are correct. Have someone else double-check for you. Remember that Johnson sounds like Johnston, Johnstone, Jonson, Jonsen, Janson, and even Jensen. Be sure, of course, that everything is spelled right, but pay special attention to names—because people will complain to the

editor if they're wrongly identified. Don't risk your credibility by in-attention to details.

Press releases usually follow a standard format. First, the release should by typed, not typeset. Always double-space, on one side of the page only. Leave wide margins all around.

You can use a modified form of your letterhead for issuing press re-leases—but you'll need to add the words *Press Release* or *News Release* to show that this isn't just another letter.

In the Appendix you'll find headlines for a press release and a public service announcement. To use this art, carefully cut the page from this book, and have your printer make a stat of the headline you plan to use. (Or, you can photocopy the headline on a Xerox 8200, Kodak Ektaprint 300, or an equivalent machine. The average copy machine will not produce camera-ready copies, so you should check with printers and of-fice supply stores to find one of these high-quality copiers.)

Of course your typesetter can also provide you with the label *Press Re-lease* in your favorite typeface, or you can use press-down letters.

Once you have the artwork, either from Appendix B or your typesetter, use the layout and pasteup techniques from Chapter Six to produce an interesting press release form. Then have your printer make as many cop-ies as you'll need. When you're ready to send a release, follow the instruc-tions below, typing in the headline and copy. You can have them duplica-ted for mailing by the printer, or at a photocopy center. (Whenever you send photocopies, of course, be sure that they're top quality, with crisp, black type, and no extraneous black specs or gray smudges.)

Flush against the right margin, type FOR IMMEDIATE RELEASE, or FOR RELEASE ON JULY 4, 1999 if it's a timely story.

Flush left, type FOR MORE INFORMATION, CONTACT: and give the name and phone number of whoever is available to talk to editors and reporters. Always include a contact name, even if the release is printed on your letterhead.

Use a headline, which can be flush left or centered, and should be all capital letters—KNOXVILLE BAND IS FINALIST IN NATIONAL "STARS OF TOMORROW" CONTEST. (Don't use a period in a headline, though.)

You may choose to run a short "teaser" headline above the main one to attract further attention. "Local rock group is among 'best of the best.' "

If the release is more than one page, type "more" centered at the bot-tom of the first page, and put a short identifying headline, and the contact person's name and number on the second sheet. The second sheet should be a plain, nonletterhead, page.

At the end of the release, type four pound signs (#) or the number *30* centered at the bottom of the page to indicate that there's no more.

PRESS RELEASE

FOR IMMEDIATE RELEASE

For more information, contact:
George Carere: (123)-456-7890

Local rock group is among "best of the best"

KNOXVILLE BAND IS FINALIST IN NATIONAL "STARS OF TOMORROW" CONTEST

Sheer Energy, a four-piece Knoxville rock band, has been named a finalist in NBC's "Stars of Tomorrow" national talent search. The four finalists, best of over two thousand initial entrants, will compete for a record contract and a $100,000 prize on a two-hour live TV special next fall. The exact date will be announced by the network.

Band members Logan Sisk, Don Mack, Steve Tischer, and Rich Peluso, all from Knoxville, are elated. "This may be the break we've been working for," says drummer Sisk. "We've tried other routes to get a record and we're really excited about this chance."

The hard-driving band specializes in a blend of country lyrics with Top-40 energy, but it shuns the high-tech approach that is popular in music today. "No computers, no synthesizers, no drum machines for us. We like the sound of guitars," says Mack, who plays lead guitar.

In the "Stars of Tomorrow" contest, Sheer Energy competed against local, regional, and national-level bands to reach the final four. They are rehearsing new material that, they hope, will power them to a first-place finish.

"We want all our friends in Knoxville to be watching that show and cheering us on," adds Tischer, the group's bassist and lead singer. "If we win, we'll throw a party that Knoxville will remember for years."

Sheer Energy was formed when all four musicians were studying nuclear engineering at the University of Tennessee. They've been together for almost thirteen years, and have no plans to leave the music business.

# # # #

Smaller, suburban papers might print this release exactly as it's written, or they might trim it to fit their available space. Larger daily papers, and TV and radio stations, however, may choose to do their own stories, using their own writers and photographers.

This release should be sent as soon as the contest's finalists are announced, and should go to all the papers in the area, including any university publications, to all relevant radio stations, and to the local TV stations. If Sheer Energy is really interested in maximum publicity, another release would announce the date of the TV special, and yet another release would cover the results. (Of course, if they win the contest, the TV network and the record company would send out their own press releases.)

The news pag here, obviously, is the band's excellent showing in a national contest—its chance at fame and, possibly, fortune. Even if Sheer Energy doesn't win the ultimate contest, it will reap loads of publicity from such efforts as this release, and its name will become synonymous with successful music.

You, too, should get in the habit of using press releases. It isn't difficult, it's the accepted form of reaching media outlets, it looks professional, and it's a very accepted way of tooting your own horn. After all, if you're doing something exciting and worthwhile, shouldn't you share it with the public?

Of course you should. And mark it "For Immediate Release."

CHAPTER 12

Getting Noticed in Print—Newspapers and Magazines

YOU HAVE PRESS RELEASES IN HAND and you're planning a terrific music project that will, you're sure, interest everybody in town. You want newspaper stories—and perhaps a feature in the city magazine. How do you proceed?

You find out what the media want, and what they're now using, and you shape your ideas to fit these guidelines. If you can give them the kinds of stories they need, you'll get lots of coverage. They'll call it "news" or "features"; you'll call it "publicity."

Newspapers exist to provide news, information, and entertainment—but they couldn't survive without selling advertising, and most radio and TV stations also exist through advertising revenue. Always remember that the space devoted to your story represents lots of advertising income—space is expensive. A feature article on your band could easily take up the same space as an $800 ad—or an $8000 one in a major newspaper. An interview with you on a talk show would be "worth" lots of money if it were sold as ad time.

Since your media exposure is worth so much money, it will pay back the effort it takes. Remind yourself, as you're addressing your press releases, that the free publicity you get might be worth thousands of dollars.

On the other hand, no editors will give you free advertising. If they think that's what you're after they'll refer you to an ad salesman. You're trying for free publicity, sure, but it must involve a truly interesting event or personality.

This is such an important point that it should be repeated: *To get publicity from the media, your story ideas must be interesting in themselves.* Don't make editors or writers think you're trying to use them; work to make your story interesting for their readers.

This chapter discusses getting noticed in all kinds of newspapers, newsletters, and magazines. Large daily papers, with circulations of hundreds of thousands, will help your career—and so will PTA newsletters that cover just one neighborhood.

NEWSPAPERS

Maybe you get your daily news from *USA Today* and *The New York Times* but you'll probably get the most publicity from smaller local papers. You might even do best, especially at first, with weeklies, or low-circulation specialty papers. Generally, the more local the paper, the better your chances for lots of publicity, because smaller papers concentrate on local events and personalities.

But, you say, "Newspapers seem so formal and complicated. Is it really possible to get them to notice my band?"

Yes. First, no newspaper can cover everything with its own staff or think of every interesting idea for a story. They do what they can, of course, with their staff people, but all editors welcome ideas—no matter what the source. They may not *use* every concept that's suggested, but if it's a good one they'll at least consider it.

Further, to keep their second-class mailing permits, newspapers *must* devote at least twenty-five percent of their space to editorial matter (such as articles). On heavy advertising days, like Wednesdays or Thursdays and Sundays, they need more articles than usual to maintain their legal ratio. Maybe they'd like to fill up the paper with advertising, but the post office won't let them—and you can benefit.

So it's true. If you have good ideas for stories, newspapers need you.

What's useful to you in the paper? Lots. You'll find potential publicity in every section if you use the right hooks. You can be noticed with extensive coverage, photos, or simply the frequent mention of your name, in news stories, feature articles, reviews of performances or recordings, arts/music stories, business reports, editorials or editorial responses, letters to the editor, regular columns, and calendar-of-events listings.

There are two basic approaches to getting in the paper, and press releases accomplish both. You can write a story yourself (an editorial response about raising the drinking age in your town, for example), or you can interest an editor enough to send a writer and photographer to cover the story. You can even write your own feature articles and submit them for publication—often with surprisingly good results.

Only Frances Wallace knows the Phantom score

By Bo Emerson
Staff Writer

Frances Wallace has accompanied dancers, opera singers, jazz saxophone players — and has also stood center stage as a soloist herself — during a long career as an Atlanta pianist.

Tonight she will accompany the unattractive Lon Chaney as he crawls through catacombs, chews scenery and drops a chandelier on the heads of a crowd of opera buffs.

Miss Wallace will provide the live soundtrack, in others words, for a special presentation of the 1925 silent classic "Phantom of the Opera," to be screened at 8 p.m. in the High Museum's Hill Auditorium.

Her plan for the event is simple. "I'm going to start with something proper and end with something proper," she said. "What comes in the middle I will probably pull out of thin air."

The proper material will come from a score performed as accompaniment for early screenings of the movie. Miss Wallace will use the score only as a prompter, however. She will quote a few of the movie's major themes, many of which were lifted from popular operas of the early 20th century.

The rest she will improvise. As a classically trained jazz pianist, she would rather improvise than read the printed note, and has ad-libbed the accompaniment to other silent films at the High, including short features by Buster Keaton and a grand epic called "Cabiria."

"You've heard people talk about writing a book, about how it's like being a channel," Miss Wallace said of the experience of improvising."It's the same way with me. It's just something that comes through you, and you're fascinated with it. It's a wonderful feeling ... . It's like drawing energy from some other source."

Born in Atlanta in 1921, Miss Wallace has played for vaudeville shows at the Roxy Theater, was a staff musician at WSB radio, WLWA television, and was a member of Albert Coleman's orchestra during the original Atlanta Pops concerts.

Her music was a fixture at the Owl Room in the basement of the Dinkler Plaza, at the Henry Grady Hotel and the old Mayfair Club on Spring Street. Miss Wallace and her trio are now familiar at wedding receptions and parties here.

Linda Dubler, curator of film and video at the museum, said the audience reaction to Miss Wallace's performances at the High has been very gratifying. "There's an emotional directness to the experience of watching a live musician responding to what's happening on the screen," she said.

Here's another story that focuses on a musician even though the peg is about something else—the screening of a silent movie, in this case. A story like this benefits the theater, the movie's sponsor, and the musician, and it's interesting to readers who enjoy both music and old movies.

How to Get in Touch

The organizational chart of a newspaper shows the publisher at the top, editors in the middle, and reporters and photographers at the bottom. Don't approach the publisher or the writers; go straight to an editor with your ideas.

The working, everyday decisions on what to cover are made by the *editors*—men and women who manage one interest-area of the paper. Larger papers have many editors—one for each section—and it's important to approach the right one with your ideas.

It's useful to think of editors as your primary audience; if your ideas don't interest them the story won't get printed. Think of them as *screens,* or *filters*—they're looking for good ideas and discarding the boring, irrelevant, or self-serving ones.

Editors select what to cover and sometimes rewrite articles for publication. At smaller papers they often write stories as well, so remember that editors are always very busy. They'll rarely have time to chat on the phone about your ideas.

Since editors are generally overworked, make your contact with them businesslike and brief—use the standard press release, not a five-page, rambling letter. Also, editors are always under deadline pressure, so try not to call at their busiest times; for morning papers, this is the preceding evening; for afternoon papers, the mornings are most rushed.

Before you call any editor, check the paper's masthead (the little box that lists names and positions) or call the paper and ask for an editor's name. Do your best to stay current and keep up with job changes; editors, like everyone else, want to be addressed properly (with their names spelled correctly).

The easiest, and most direct, route to the proper editor is to simply call her (or her secretary), succinctly describe the story idea you have, and ask if she's the right person to get your press release. If not, she'll tell you who is. *Always send your press releases to a specific editor, never just to the newspaper.*

Which editor should you approach? News stories go to the *city editor.* Send him press releases about awards, fund-raising, school activities, major concerts, new buildings, and so on. Feature stories about your music and lifestyle issues or trends go to the *features,* or *lifestyle, editor* (check your paper for current terminology). Sometimes this department includes the society pages, which can be useful for stories pertaining to country clubs and activities of the well-to-do. And business, education, religion, and sports stories have their own editors on midsized and larger papers. Direct specific ideas to the proper editor.

Reviews are important to every performer, and your paper will either have staff reviewers or use freelancers. Be sure the appropriate reviewer knows of upcoming concerts and appearances, gets plenty of advance information, and has good (complimentary, of course) seats.

Don't assume that the reviewer will be musically educated. You may have to subtly plant ideas and even provide clever phrases that aptly describe your music. If you have previous (good) reviews, include them in your press kit.

If you know when your performance will be reviewed, try to meet the reviewer. (Sometimes this isn't possible, of course, and some reviewers jealously guard their objectivity.) If you can, spend time talking with the reviewer to answer questions, give your own ideas, and to be sure that the reviewer knows what you're trying to do. If your band specializes in original material, be sure the reviewer knows it; and if you do only record copies, tell her that, too.

What if you receive a negative review? Unless it's totally, blatantly unfair, don't respond. You'll rarely win in a battle with the media, so don't complain unless you're the unlucky recipient of a vicious hatchet job—which will probably never happen. If, though, your rock band is reviewed by someone who knows nothing about rock and roll—and hates it, be-

the Bald guy's back

Troubadour in the Lowcountry

By LYNN FELDER
Packet features editor

Musician John Dandurand has been camping at Stoney Crest Campground and teaching at M.C. Riley Elementary School in Bluffton since Monday. During his week as Artist-in-Education there, Dandurand has performed for the students and helped them build 20 clay and rawhide drums which will stay behind when the man moves on.

The campground, near Pritchardville on S.C. 46, is a fine place to meet a modern troubadour. The shade trees and grasses are in the full bloom of late spring. The breezes are fragrant, balmy and spiked with no-see-ums.

While brown rice cooks on his Coleman stove and the vegetables lie ready to be stir-fried, Dandurand moves deftly from Appalachian dulcimer to guitar to mando-cello, singing and talking about his life and times. Dandurand's gypsy caravan is a high-top Dodge van; his traveling companion, an elderly German Shepherd named Carmel.

No stranger to the road, Dandurand has performed in 12 states, the Caribbean Islands and Brazil during his 20-odd years as a musician.

On previous visits to this area, Dandurand was the opening act at the Old Post Office Emporium on Hilton Head Island for Taj Mahal and Stephan Grapelli.

"It was really an honor to open for Grapelli," he said.

Musician

On the TV show "Lowcountry Alive" Tuesday night, Dandurand played "Walking Blues" in Mississippi Delta blues style — plus his special touch and interpretation. His rendition of Lowell George's "Rollin' Easy" was passionate and tender.

Then he played a 15th century Irish fiddle tune on an Appalachian dulcimer — no easy feat.

"It's more fun to do what other people aren't doing," he said.

Exactly what is folk music is open to debate, but if it is music of the people for the people by

the people, then it's what Dandurand is doing.

Folk music generally consists of both traditional songs that are freely interpreted from musician to musician and new songs that reflect or comment on the times or circumstances in which they are composed. Folk songs usually deal with moral issues or social issues or tell stories.

"I grew up with folk music, and it's a challenge to explore these things and do them in a new way," Dandurand said.

He takes blues song, American folk tunes and traditional Irish ballads and performs them in a decidedly new way — new arrangements, even new tunes.

Dandurand started playing bluegrass and folk music during his high school days in San Bernadino, Calif. While a pre-med student at the University of San Francisco, he met Michael Stewart, brother of the Kingston Trio's John Stewart, and joined the young Stewart's college group We Five.

When the group's single "You Were on My Mind" became a hit nationally, Dandurand dropped out of college to pursue his muse full-time.

He went to Brazil in the late 60s with a "not very good psychedelic blues band," called The Sound, which broke up almost immediately. But Dandurand stayed on for two years, making a dandy living ($90 to $100 a night) playing music for American tourists on the streets near resort hotels.

"I wore the raggediest clothes I had at night, and lived like a king by day. I had everything but a chauffeur."

Family man

Times change. Though still a part-time vagabond, Dandurand is also a devoted family man. He recently moved from Savannah to Tifton, Ga., with his wife Gina and their 5-year-old daughter Marrika.

Dandurand says fatherhood has turned out to be an unparalleled delight and credits Marrika

with helping him to relate to the world as a child does. Being open and curious helps him to be a better teacher and a better artist.

"I believe what Aldous Huxley said, that we must 'keep the doors of perception cleansed.' "

Dandurand appears to be a happy person: happy with his family, his life, his work and his unusual appearance.

He lost his hair due to nervous shock during an operation when he was 20. The condition, called alope-

cia, causes the loss of all body hair. The same thing happened to Dandurand's father.

"My father lost all of his hair due to nervous shock when he was 11 years old. He always wears a hat," Dandurand says. "But since my primary role model — my Dad —was bald, it seemed like the normal thing to be."

He said he adjusted to his baldness easily and has learned to like it, because it makes him memorable.

"When I've played somewhere,

people will ask 'When's the bald guy coming back?' "

In addition to performing and building drums, Dandurand teaches dulcimer, guitar, banjo, sound reinforcement and song-writing. His first solo album is being completed in Charleston at Online Audio.

If you're going to Spoleto Festival U.S.A., look for the bald guy singing for his supper. You never know where he might turn up.

There are several pegs in this feature story on a folk singer who roams the South, teaching and performing: his unusual appearance, his work with elementary school children, his gypsylike lifestyle. You could send this story to the features editor, the entertainment desk, or even the education editor; all would be interested.

---

sides—a polite letter of complaint, with copies to the editor, would be appropriate.

Reviewers are usually responsible people who enjoy the music they write about. They'll interview you and give their opinions to their readers. You should help them do a good job by providing lots of excellent background information about yourself, your band, and your music. That's what your press kit is for—so be sure writers and reviewers get a complete packet of all the information you've prepared. Don't hold back; include photocopies of other articles and reviews that will impress the writer, validate your own importance, and perhaps even suggest a few phrases and ideas.

Columns appear regularly, and often deal with the "Who's News" or "Who's Doing What Around Town" kind of material. What you're after here is lots of mention of your—or your group's—name. Many columnists use answering machines to take items for their daily output, so it's a sim-

Chamber Players are magnificent

By Derrick Henry
Staff Writer

Music Review

If further proof be needed of the excellence of the Georgian Chamber Players, that proof was provided Sunday afternoon when the GCP opened its third season, in the Georgia-Pacific Center Auditorium.

That 254-seat hall is in many ways a more suitable site than the Hill Auditorium where the GCP presented its first two seasons. The seats are more comfortable, the setting is more intimate, while the acoustics are equally revealing but cleaner and more flattering.

Sunday's concert attracted a capacity audience; in fact, additional seats had to be added. These music lovers came to hear violinist William Reid Preucil, violist Reid Harris and cellist Christopher Rex — all principals with the Atlanta Symphony Orchestra — join forces with guest pianist Lee Luvisi in a generous and enticing program.

Luvisi, fresh from some magnificent Mozart with the ASO, collaborated with Harris in Brahms' E-flat Major Viola Sonata, Op. 120, No. 2, and with the GCP in two seldom-heard but marvelous piano quartets, Dvorak's Op. 87 and Faure's Op. 45. (The term piano quartet customarily refers not to a piece for four pianos, but rather to the combination of piano, violin, viola and cello.)

Least impressive was the Brahms. Harris is a fine violist, but he does not project a strong solo personality. He seemed ill at ease in the more demanding passagework of this sonata (originally written for clarinet). However, the music's long lyric lines

were realized with becoming sensitivity abetted by an attractively warm but not mushy tone. Luvisi provided extraordinarily supportive collaboration.

The two piano quartets were unqualified successes. To begin with, these are works of considerable substance and originality. The Faure is a hauntingly evocative work, surprisingly passionatic for this normally restrained composer. The Dvorak is romantic, touching, bursting with vitality and full of more good tunes than most composers are granted in a lifetime.

Sunday's performances were vigorous to the point of viciousness, yet this enthusiasm was never allowed to get out of control. And where required, there was delicacy and sentiment aplenty.

As good as the string playing was, it was Luvisi who raised this concert to the realm of the special. Stated simply, Luvisi is an amazing pianist — and a fabulous chamber musician. Everything is shaped with elegance and point. Every gesture sounds perfectly natural. He is never obtrusive, yet his presence is always powerfully felt. There is fervor in abundance. Whatever the music requires, Luvisi produces. The man has taste.

In Saturday's review of last week's ASO concert, I referred to Luvisi as one of the finest Mozartians of our time. Let me revise that statement. He is one of our finest pianists. Period.

Reviews offer good publicity, and most papers print them regularly, though many will review classical music or jazz more seriously than pop and rock. The reviewer's task is to tell the story as he sees it, and you must be able to accept criticism as well as praise.

ple matter to provide a constant stream of jokes, anecdotes, funny or odd events you've seen (all musicians should have lots of terrific stories), and so on—even if it's unrelated directly to your music. You want your name mentioned, that's all.

In a gossip column, you'd be happy with an item such as this: "Big Rick Bell, who mans the piano bar at Danny's Saloon, was surprised last Tuesday when our town's mayor, Jerry Poole, stopped in for a visit. Big Rick reports that Hizzoner's voice is in great shape—and sounds ready for next month's campaign."

The Calendar of Events may take up several pages in the *Saturday Leisure Guide*, or it may be just a few lines in a smaller paper. In any case, all your musical activities that qualify should be listed. Call the Calendar editor for deadline information; send your release, or a short statement of what's happening, to that editor. It wouldn't hurt to follow up with a phone call to be sure the release was received.

The calendar editor may not want to list your appearance at a nightclub, since it's not a nonprofit event. After all, the calendar isn't an advertising vehicle for private businesses. So you may have to use your publicity ingenuity to create a musical happening worthy of mention. (See Chapter Nineteen and use your imagination.)

For example, if you're in a pop band, don't just go to work at the club every week, playing for the same old half-empty room. Instead, think of a special promotion, a celebration you could sponsor, and get it publicized in every calendar of events in town. Hold a celebration of National Cabbage Day, or a Thirties theme party on the day Prohibition was repealed, or an "Aerobics on the Dancefloor" contest. Find an interesting hook and publicize it.

Thus, the calendar of events editor might ignore a notice that simply states, "Joe's Band plays nightly at The Blue Note Lounge" because that looks like free advertising. However, if your notice reads: "Joe's Band welcomes would-be musicians for guest performances every Tuesday night, and holds old-fashioned jam sessions on Wednesdays at the Blue Note Lounge" you'd have a better chance because jam sessions and open microphones appeal to the public.

Does the calendar editor ever print pictures to go with listings? If yours does, be sure to send a photo along.

Cover It

When you send your release to the paper, include a simple cover letter, addressed to the editor you want to reach. Such a cover letter *must be short*—its only task is to introduce the release. Tell, as briefly as possible, what the release says, and why it's important and interesting. If you can think of a short illustration that supports the release, include it.

South Lexington High School

123 Bluegrass Street
Lexington, Kentucky 40502

Dr. B. Joe Picker, *Principal*   Ann Dolan, *Assistant Principal*

11/11/87

Ms. Bonnie Johnson, Feature Editor
Lexington Times-Herald
1000 Corporate Square
Lexington, Kentucky

Dear Ms.Johnson:

Enclosed is a press release about the South Lexington High School
band's fund-raising activities. We're excited about the extensive
community involvement we've gotten, and about the fact that our
new uniforms and instruments won't cost the taxpayers a cent.

The release details our unusual fund-raising methods, some of
which are very creative to say the least. We think that your
readers would be interested in a story on these fine young
musicians who are working so hard for their band.

Thanks for your time.

Yours truly,

Mel Camp
Band Director
South Lexington High School

---

*Don't just send your press releases or stories out to fend for themselves. Use a
short cover letter to explain what you're doing and quickly underscore your
message. Here, the band director reiterates why his band's activities deserve
coverage.*

Don't ask, beg, or cajole the editor to cover your story. Just make your
letter and release so interesting that they demand attention.

Working with Reporters

When an editor likes your ideas enough to send a reporter and perhaps a photographer, you'd better be on time for your appointment. Remind your band that you're scheduled to meet a photographer at ten

o'clock tomorrow morning, and give the drummer a wake-up call if he tends to oversleep. Reporters and photographers are very busy, and won't wait for you—or your sleepy drummer.

During the interview, work to establish good rapport with the writer. If you're at home, offer her a cup of coffee; be relaxed, friendly, and natural. Don't try to impress her, and don't argue with her—just do what you can to help her write an interesting story about your music.

Never tell a reporter what to include. That's her job, and she's proud of her abilities and independence. Answer her questions, and volunteer information, but don't try to dictate the form or content of the article.

Remember that there's nothing wrong with saying "I don't know" when you don't. Evasive or defensive answers can work against you more than an admission of ignorance. "No, I really can't remember when Oscar Peterson made his first record," is a much better answer than, "Nobody cares about that old acoustic jazz anymore." The first is simply an honest answer while the second makes the respondent look narrowminded and uneducated. And, perhaps the reporter is a jazz buff whose favorite pianist is Oscar Peterson.

Similarly, never say anything negative about other performers. Sure, music usually isn't controversial, but reporters always look for something spicy to enliven their stories; if you don't want to be quoted on something the safest course is not to say it; with many reporters, nothing is ever really "off the record."

Don't ask to see, or check over, an article after it's written. Sometimes a writer will ask you to read a piece for accuracy, but usually reporters won't allow anyone except editors to alter their work. Just provide your best facts, anecdotes, ideas, and angles and let them put the story together.

Don't ask the reporter when the story will be printed. That's the editor's decision, and reporters usually can't predict which of their stories will run, or when.

Send a short thank-you note to the reporter and/or editor after your story runs. Don't thank them for running the story because that's their job, after all, but let them know you appreciate the excellent work they did. If you didn't like the way something was presented don't complain unless it was a major error; nitpicking will make the editor think you're a pest, and your access to that paper will disappear.

Keep sending a steady stream of ideas, news releases, column tidbits, and even fully written stories to your paper. To some extent, getting noticed in newspapers is a numbers game—the more you submit, the more mention you get. Don't expect every one of your ideas to be printed, but don't give up. Remember: newspapers must have articles and your ideas are important. Keep them coming.

Bell ringer slips in rock 'n' roll

By David Fox
The Associated Press

CENTRALIA, Ill.— When Charles Collins climbs 140 feet of stairs and sits down at a keyboard, he sometimes slips in some rock 'n' roll with the Bach and Mozart as he tinkles the 65 cast-bronze bells of the Centralia Carillon.

"It's a little bit like listening to the Mormon Tabernacle Choir singing 'You're Having My Baby,'" said Collins, one of only about a half-dozen full-time carilloneurs in the United States. "It's all right, but it's just not the same."

Collins, 23, the carillon's official bell ringer, said he never expected to be doing what he's doing. After graduating from Southern Illinois University with a degree in anthropology, he took the job for two reasons: "I like music, and I needed a job."

Collins makes music by striking the hand batons and foot pedals attached to clappers on the 160-foot steel and stone tower's massive bells. The smallest bell weighs 22 pounds, and the largest is an 11,000-pound behemoth.

The carillon is one of 131 in the United States.

"It's the colossus of keyboard instruments," said William Joy, owner and publisher of the Centralia Sentinel and a major underwriter of the carillon's installation.

The newspaper proposed construction of the carillon in 1957 in this city of about 15,000 people 70 miles east of St. Louis. Residents have been paying for the bells over a period of 25 years, many of them purchased as memorials.

"It's the people's instrument, really," Joy said.

The carillon has been playable since 1983, but its simulated-sand-stone facade and granite base were not completed until this year. Plans call for the eventual construction of a park around it.

Collins plays four one-hour concerts each week from the tower, but hespends most of his time in an office at the Sentinel, where he practices on a smaller version of the keyboard called a clavier.

"Most of what I play is pretty well received," he said. "I think the biggest complaint we get is that we don't play things they know."

But he said playing familiar tunes can lead to embarrassing moments.

"When my predecessor was still playing, he didn't realize there was a funeral going on at the Catholic church across the street," he said. "The very last song on his program was 'So Long, It's Been Good to Know You.'

"Just as he started it, they were bringing the body out."

This is an Associated Press story that was available to hundreds of papers nationwide. The peg—the idea of playing rock 'n' roll on a carillon—is unusual and interesting. Without that angle, the story probably would have had only local interest, but with the added interest of a clever peg, it reached a much wider audience.

DIFFERENT KINDS OF PAPERS

Your publicity needs as many outlets as you can find, so try to get noticed in all the papers in your area. They aren't all the same, however; each has its special niche in the news community, and will be able to help you in a different way, with different readers.

Large daily newspapers are the hardest nut to crack in your search for publicity because they cover the biggest area and must appeal to the broadest range of readers. Further, you'll encounter more competition from other publicity seekers. Don't let this stop you from trying, but realize that your carefully worded press release may be one of a hundred that an editor receives each day.

Smaller, suburban dailies are a better bet. Large metropolitan areas often have several small papers, each serving a specific area—the *Southside News*, or the *Intown Reporter*. Make these a major target.

Weeklies offer excellent publicity possibilities because they often ignore "hard news" and concentrate entirely on feature stories. At smaller papers, try to establish a personal relationship with the editor—deliver your press release in person (but don't stop to chitchat—these editors are busy, too). Arrange to visit on the day *after* the paper comes out, never the day before—call ahead to find out when deadline pressure is at its worst.

The smaller the paper, the more local news is printed, and many small-town newspapers rely heavily on school, community, and arts events. Here's where your press release will often be printed verbatim, and where the stories you write will find the warmest reception. Names are more important, too, to smaller papers, and group photographs have a better chance of being printed here. Emphasize items of community interest and push the neighborhood angles—small papers usually focus on what's close, and of local, immediate interest.

Special interest newspapers are terrific publicity outlets for musicians and performers. Most larger cities have several tabloid-sized papers aimed at specific target audiences. Atlanta, for example, has special newspapers for leisure activities, politically active people, black readers, Spanish speakers, older citizens, intown merchants, attorneys, financial employees, computer users, high school students, and several other well-defined groups.

If you can tie your music to a news or feature story that appeals to these specialized audiences—weekly sing-along evenings for retired citizens, for example—you'll find that these papers provide an excellent path to good publicity.

College papers train journalists and serve college communities. Even if you aren't involved with a local school, keep it informed of musical activities that relate to college students—this is particularly important for contemporary music groups that play to student audiences. Young people are often more interested than the general public in new developments in music, and may be very receptive to what you're doing.

If you now attend, or graduated from, an institution in your area, you have a special reason to have your activities noticed there.

Shoppers are the free advertising tabloids that are distributed in grocery stores, shopping centers, and through mass mailings. While they're primarily advertising vehicles, many of them print feature articles and events calendars to attract readers. Collect these publications, and put them on your publicity list.

All these newspapers need articles, and if you simply slant your story idea to their particular audience your publicity offerings will be well received.

Don't forget to save all the clippings that mention you and your music. Sure, you want to tell the public what you do, but you want to keep proving to yourself that your publicity efforts are paying off. Your personal clip file will keep pace with your growing career, and each piece can be added to your press kit, or quoted in future brochures.

Newsletters

Newsletters are specialized publications for people who are interested in specific subject areas—neighborhood developments, news of interest to banjo players, or information for collectors of old cola bottles, for example. They are usually printed on standard-sized typing paper, and often have only four to eight pages. They may be distributed free, or sold by subscription. Over 100,000 newsletters are published in the United States.

Newsletters provide up-to-date information for club members, company employees, school alumni, hobbyists, and any other group of people you can imagine. You can use such newsletters to get noticed.

Start by getting your musical activities mentioned in local newsletters that serve education, business, religious, neighborhood, or other interests. Think of these newsletters as little newspapers, aimed at a very select audience.

Ask your clients about publicizing your music through their newsletters. Many country clubs produce a newsletter to keep their members updated—the *Hidden Hills Chatter,* or the *Cherokee Club Dateline.* Companies, large hotels, resorts, and even restaurant chains produce newsletters for their employees. When you perform for these clients be sure that you're mentioned, reviewed, publicized, and touted. If you have to write the copy yourself—do it, and slant it toward the newsletter's audience. Tell what your music will do for *them,* and why they'll enjoy your band.

Neighborhood associations publish newsletters, many active churches use them, and real-estate agents often print their own newsletters for past and future clients. When you're playing for a community fund-raiser, school event, church party, or street dance, get it mentioned. What you're after, of course, is constant notice so that your name-recognition grows and stays high.

Don't scoff at a neighborhood newsletter that only goes to 300 homes; there may be twenty prospective brides, two convention planners, and one booking agent who live in the neighborhood, all of whom might need your services for their own events. You never know when publicity will pay off.

To find newsletters in your musical interest area, use such library reference books as *The Encyclopedia of Associations, Ulrich's International Periodicals Directory,* and *The Newsletter Yearbook/Directory.* Thousands of associations are categorized by subject in these annual reference works, and most of them publish newsletters. You'll be surprised at how many relevant newsletters you'll find—and at how easy this library research is. If your

Hot-Jazz & Alligator-Gumbo-Society

A Non-profit Society Devoted to the Perpetuation, Advancement and Performance of Heritage Jazz

Bulletin # 75   September 1986

Information and Bowlines Tied: 1048 S.W. 49th Terrace, Ft. Lauderdale, FL 33317 (305) 581-4310

OKAY, FOLKS, THIS IS THE MONTH WE GO CRUISING!

* * * * * * * * * *

SPECIAL NOTICE TO MUSICIANS!!!

If you have played at any of our regular HAGS bashes in the past two years, you won't need a ticket for our jazz cruise. You sail free, which is our way of saying thanks to you for the talent you have contributed to helping keep Our Music cooking.

If you're not sure whether you've played at a HAGS meeting in the past two years, and are thus entitled to this munificence, call the **Larrikin** at 581-4310 who's laboriously made a list and checked it twice.

* * * * * * * * * *

SPECIAL NOTICE TO EVERYONE!!!

The Jazz Cruise is our September meeting. If you go to the Ramada this month, you will find it filled with Hagonian emptiness because the rest of us will be on the Jungle Queen.

* * * * * * * * * *

TOOT SWEET . . . by Lauderdalius Rotundus

August is a slow month. Ask anyone.

Then howcum **Larrikin** kicked off a tune last month in such a ferocious tempo last month that, before it was all over, a couple of guys in the crowd out front were booking bets as to who was gonna finish first and whether or not **Larrikin's** tang was gonna get all tongueled up in his mouthpiece?

Fortunately, with the super team of **Jack Dixon** on the keys, **Billy Pierce** and **Larry Kenzora** on sax and clarinet, respectively, **"El Rapido" (Pat) Cooke** on bass, **Frank Orilio** on tubs, **Bill James** trombonifying, and **"Dutch" Wiltse** on banjo, the race to the finish line came out a dead heat. The same set was graced by **Lori Lea**, whose attributes are not exclusively vocal.

And slow month or not, we had a goodly crowd of both fans and musicians.

Del Staton, who plays mo' bettah than average guitar, brought **Dick Caruso**, who plays (for more, try Page 2 or 3)

JUNGLE QUEEN IV, seen here unarmed and ferrying refugees from New York and other deprived (depraved?) areas.

Provided herewith are all the facts you'll need to prepare yourself for our **5th ALL PURPOSE TOOT & SLOSH JAZZ CRUISE.**

They are furnished because in last month's missive, we omitted a few minor details, such as when, and where, and how to obtain ducats, having erred in our assumption that all of our readers had were prescient and had gotten top grades in Soothsaying 101.

In rectification, we observe the journalist's Five Ws. The extra odds and ends are a bonus.

Who

You.

What

For our **5APT&SJC,** as with all previous nautical sojourns, HAGS charters for its exclusive use the **Jungle Queen IV.** We spend the afternoon sailing along the Intracoastal and adjoining waterways. We have piano and drums aboard, just as at our regular meetings, and musicians present have been known to play (gasp!) Dixieland and related jazz as we ply the briny. A sizable measure of frivolity and joy seems to be associated with our cruises.

(Cont'd Page 2)

The newsletter is one of the best ways to reach audiences with well-defined interests. Here, the "Hot Jazz and Alligator Gumbo Society," which is composed of traditional jazz players and enthusiasts, uses a newsletter to keep everyone informed of what's going on in the South Florida traditional jazz scene. The lively writing style guarantees that the copy will be read.

band specializes in authentic bluegrass and country music, you should be mentioned in the National Old-Time Fiddler's Association newsletter. If you develop a new technique for teaching a difficult fingering for the classical guitar, why not tell the members of the Guitar Foundation of America through their newsletter?

Many newsletters are published by essentially one person, who does everything from writing to mailing. Often such publisher/editor/writers are desperate for current news items about their subject areas, so help by sending your pertinent news releases. If you can give a newsletter an exclusive *scoop*, the editor will appreciate it and remember you next time you have a project to publicize.

When you find a publication that might be useful in your publicity efforts, save it. You'll be amazed at how many newsletters you'll discover in your own community, so always be on the alert for new ones. Keep samples, even if you don't have an immediate use for them—sooner or later your publicity ideas will include them all.

Publicity Practice

It's time for another list. But this one doesn't require brainstorming; this one depends on research.

As you develop contacts with newspapers, newsletters, and broadcast people, keep a *media-contacts* list. When you reach an editor, work with a writer on a story, or locate a talk-show host who loves your kind of jazz, enter the names, phone numbers, and addresses on your list.

Keep a file card for each contact, and jot down comments that will further your relationship with that person. If an editor not only runs your story but tells you that he's an amateur trombonist—write it down. There may be an occasion when you can combine your need for publicity with that editor's desire to play his trombone.

Your *media-contacts* list should be separate from the target audience list you started in Chapter Two. The media people should get a steady stream of information about your activities, while prospective employers should, in addition, get your sales pitch.

MAGAZINES

Two kinds of magazines will help you publicize your musical activities. The first is the local *general interest* magazine, often published for a city or regional market, that might run a feature article on your band. These *city magazines* focus on people and events of interest to the community. Since monthly magazines have a long preparation time and early deadlines (often three months—or more—before the publication date), they rely on interesting feature stories rather than news.

If your story involves an ongoing event, an annual celebration, or profiles of interesting community people, these magazines provide an excellent outlet; but they won't usually use timely information or news-related, one-time stories. Read a few issues to get a feel for the kinds of features your city or regional magazines like.

You should also take advantage of *professional magazines* written for and by musicians. Whatever your musical specialty, there's a magazine for it—whether you're a drummer, keyboardist, church choir director, electronic music experimenter, or marching band director. You'll benefit, of course, by reading these magazines to stay up to date, but you should also strive to enhance your image by being the *subject* of in-depth articles in professional magazines. The Bibliography lists a sampling of professional music publications.

The Main Feature

Full-length feature articles should be among your primary publicity goals. Work toward having them written *about you and your musical activities.*Or, if you can, write them yourself.

Keep a magazine's audience in mind when you approach an editor or send a press release. Magazines are almost always targeted to a specific group, and your story should offer insight, entertainment, or useful information. Magazine features are often longer and more in-depth than newspaper articles, so they must be informative and interesting to keep readers involved.

Does your town have a business magazine? Why not try to interest the editor in an article called "How Music Can Motivate Your Sales Staff"? You could write it, or work with a staff reporter.

Is there a general-interest city magazine in town? If you've researched the musical heritage of the area for a show your band is producing, suggest an article on it—maybe "Tulsa's Forgotten Music Men," or "Kansas City's Musical Past—How We Found It."

Maybe you're part of the local recording industry—often heard in jingles, but not known by the public. Suggest a feature on local studio musicians—"Tampa's 'Sixty Second' Men (and Women)." If your rock band has been around for fifteen years you probably have enough interesting stories and anecdotes for a book, but send a few of your best tales (the clean ones) to whet an editor's appetite for a piece called "The View from the Stage—Joe's Band Tells All."

When you, your band, or your event gets a feature article in a magazine it means that you're well on your way to a successful performance career. But don't stop—start thinking about your next interesting activity for the next article.

Here are a few more ideas for getting good magazine publicity:

Write a letter to the editor about a controversial issue, to add information to a recent article, or just to praise the magazine for its content and style. If you think *Harmonica Happenings,* for example, did a terrific job covering the annual harmonica enthusiasts convention, write a letter of commendation. Just having your name in print will make your name stand out among harmonica players.

Keep it short. Most magazines use *fillers*—short news items or anecdotes that fill blank space at the end of articles. Jokes, hints, or anecdotes are good fillers, and you'll usually receive credit—and sometimes money—for each one that's used. If you come up with ten clever puns that relate to band directors ("Band Directors Know the Score," and so on) send them to one of the school music magazines.

Or, did your pop band play Christmas parties for every major bank in town? If you can come up with a humorous angle, write a couple of paragraphs about it for a city or business magazine—"Bank Parties Get High Interest from Joe's Band."

More and more magazines run several pages of short *featurettes*—100- to 300-word pieces on an interesting person or event. Match your angle to the magazine's overall slant and regularly submit such one-page items—about you and your music, of course. Thus, do a short piece for a city magazine on "The Ten Most Unusual Places in Town to Hold a Party." Or send a short to one of the drum magazines on "The Drummer's Emergency Tool Kit." Get your name in print, save those clips, and you're on your way to becoming an unrecognized expert in the field.

Most local magazines publish *restaurant/club/entertainment reviews and listings*—often in an on-going calendar format. Send your press kit to the appropriate editor and try for a feature article, review, or at least a listing in the *Current Events Calendar.*

Tourists count, too. A useful subcategory of magazines is the tourist guides you'll see in hotels and at tourist destinations. They always include a "Nightbeat" or "What's Happening After Dark" column (often limited to clubs that buy advertising in the magazine, however). If you play in a club, urge your employer to advertise, and then push for a feature article on your group—or at least listing in the events calendar. This is particularly important if you play a less popular kind of music—jazz, for example—because those out-of-towners looking for jazz will never find you otherwise.

Convention and tourist dollars are important to the economics of many cities—and many musicians. Travelers often spend more time and money on entertainment when they're on vacation—so be sure they know where to find your music.

Such magazines—such as *Where*, or *Key to Birmingham*—are usually found only in hotel lobbies or rooms, or at the Visitors and Convention bureaus. Add them to your media list if they match your needs.

WHAT? ME A WRITER?

Why not write articles on your music and submit them to appropriate magazines? You're already preparing your own press releases, so why not do longer pieces as well?

Professional journals often don't demand perfect writing. The editors know that you're a musician first, and they're more interested in the information you can share with their readers than your writing style. They'll fix your comma errors. So if you've discovered a new way to program your synthesizer, why not share it with other keyboard players?

Most magazines will send a free *author's guidelines* sheet that tells how to submit articles and photographs for publication. In fact, some professional magazines print those guidelines in each issue to encourage readers to share their expertise.

Most, but not all, magazines pay for articles they publish. Even when rates aren't high, it's nice to be paid for your ideas. So, if you have a unique approach to finding new students for your teaching studio, why not write about it? You'll help the readers, and yourself.

As a writer, your status as an expert will grow. If you write an article on "Caring for Your Piano" for *Family Circle*, reprints of that article will add clout to your publicity kit because they'll impress potential clients with your expertise. An article in *San Diego* magazine on "Southern California Jazz—The Laid-Back New Wave" with your by-line will enhance your standing among other musicians as well as editors and the public.

If you're interested in writing for magazines, read one or two of the books listed in the Bibliography. Since you're an expert by now at identifying hooks and relating music to trends and news issues, you'll be a natural. Hooks and trends are exactly what magazines want.

Again, save everything that's printed about you. Send photocopies of relevant articles along with your promotional material, because each article about—or by—you will validate your status, make it obvious that you're important, and will underscore your professional ability.

Help those editors fill their pages, and they'll help you fill your calendar with productive dates.

While The Teacher's Away,
The Children Still Play!

by Sue Heisner

Ten months ago my husband accepted a new job and our family had to leave the security of its familiar surroundings, friends, and Suzuki teacher. My daughter, Elizabeth, had been taking Suzuki violin lessons with Amy Eckert through the public schools in Delaware, Ohio for two years.

I had had no previous exposure to the Suzuki philosophy, but sensed there was something special about a teacher who could be so patient with little children playing uncooperative violins at the end of a full school day. Gradually, I realized that Mrs. Eckert was teaching much more than violin-playing and I was learning as much as Elizabeth.

After observing two years of lessons, reading some Suzuki literature, and attending a summer institute, I was beginning to internalize and reflect some of what I had read and observed. What a wonderful feeling! But how could I leave my model?

Mrs. Eckert showed me the Suzuki Association of the Americas listing of Suzuki violin teachers and, indeed, there were two in our future community. At our last lesson, she also suggested that we might send tape recordings to each other. As in the past, her calm concern for our problems strengthened us.

Thus encouraged, we moved to Urbana, Illinois, hopeful that our Suzuki experience would continue. We soon learned that Suzuki instruction here was not offered free of charge through the public school as it was in Delaware, but for a fee through a private academy. Also, the instructors' schedules were full and we could only be put on a waiting list.

So what did we do?

• Elizabeth kept practicing. We felt more "at home" when she practiced. Practice took on new meaning as we realized we were doing it to please ourselves, and not to prepare for a lesson.

• I spent more time practicing the piano accompaniments for Elizabeth's pieces and she began to accept me as an accompanist.

• We listened more to the Suzuki tapes.

• We listened to recordings from the library.

• We went to concerts.

• We subscribed to Suzuki World.

• I reread Shinichi Suzuki's *Nurtured by Love* and am studying *The Suzuki Violinist* by William Starr.

• About every two months, we recorded a few pieces to send to Mrs. Eckert and she would record the next group lesson or concert and return the tape. Playing for the tape recorder was not easy at first, but the reward of a kind letter and the tape's return made the effort worthwhile. Recently we recorded Elizabeth's whole repertoire with accompaniment.

• We returned to Delaware for a visit and Mrs. Eckert scheduled a group lesson while we were there. How wonderful to talk with all the other Suzuki mothers again!

• We are planning to attend an institute in Ohio again this summer.

The point I would like to make by relating all of this, is that I have found my daughter's break from lessons to be refreshing. It has provided a challenge for me to use what I have learned and a chance for both of us to relax and enjoy our attempts at music-making.

I hope that what I have shared will help parents who face a separation from their children's Suzuki teacher, for whatever reason, to relax and draw on their own strengths and knowledge to maintain their children's musical interests. I hope that this will encourage teachers who need to cancel lessons for short or extended periods to suggest some good literature and recordings, and to view the time apart as an opportunity for their Suzuki parents to grow. It seems to me that parents who can initiate successful practice in the absence of weekly lessons teach a valuable lesson in independence. ♪

Here is a personal-experience article from a special-interest music magazine, Suzuki World. *In this piece, Mrs. Heisner explains her Suzuki teaching experience to the magazine's readers. Such specialized magazines offer you the chance to share your knowledge and experiences, and to raise your profile in your own musical community.*

CHAPTER 13

You're on the Air

ALMOST EVERYBODY LISTENS to the radio and watches television, and that makes these media prime publicity outlets for you. Lots of people don't read newspapers, many don't subscribe to magazines—but most of them watch the Six o'Clock News and listen to the radio while they drive. Shouldn't they hear about your music?

If you can get on the air, you'll have a large audience. The Six o'Clock News will make you famous—for a short time. Stories can be covered live, and broadcast deadlines are measured in minutes, not days or weeks. And TV is dynamic—the addition of sight and sound adds impact to your story. It also conveys the image of success. For some reason, being on TV gives you a kind of celebrity status.

However, there's lots of competition for air time. Many people try to build their entire publicity and advertising programs around radio and TV, so program directors and news editors have lots of requests for coverage.

And broadcasts offer only fleeting exposure. You may be forgotten as soon as you're off the air. People sometimes save newspaper articles, but when broadcasts are over they're usually gone for good.

How can you get noticed on radio and TV? Your activities can be covered on news or feature programs. You can be interviewed on talk shows. You can be mentioned on regularly scheduled calendars of events. You can produce Public Service Announcements (known as *PSAs*). You could even produce your own show. In this chapter we'll discuss exactly how to go about using these publicity outlets.

DIFFERENT STATIONS FOR DIFFERENT FOLKS

There are *commercial, public, community-supported*, and *college* radio and TV stations, so whatever your musical interests, there's a broadcast outlet to match them.

Radio today is a segmented, specialized medium. Rather than try to appeal to the broadest cross-section of the public, most stations target their audiences much as magazines do. There are stations for people who enjoy heavy metal, jazz, classical, country, pop, and ethnic music. There are stations that aim at sophisticated, highly educated listeners while others go for blue-collar audiences. Some stations specialize in news and features all day.

Because of cable's increased availability, television has also changed. No longer is the viewer limited to just three networks—subscribers get up to seventy or eighty channels. Most of these cable outlets won't originate in your area, but some will, and you'll find television a more accessible publicity medium today than it was just a few years ago. Diversity brings opportunity.

Many cable companies provide a "public access" TV channel that's available for anyone's use. Though most public access programming reaches a very small audience, you should investigate the possibilities in your area. At the very least, such free exposure gives you practice with the medium and prepares you to be a prime time player.

It's Happening Now

Sometimes immediate, or live, coverage will be important—the grand opening of your town's restored concert hall as it happens, for example. An FM station might do a remote broadcast of your "Live Monday Night Jazz" from a local club. A TV personality could interview you on the air the day your record is released. And broadcast media can announce the cancellation of your concert because of snow—or the last minute addition of a second performance.

Aside from fast-breaking news, though, most radio and TV stories have special needs. To be interesting, broadcast events must be:

1. *Active.* What's active? A concert, a marching band, a backstage view of a musical theater production, a how-to lesson on playing an instrument, an open rehearsal at the symphony—all would make interesting television.
2. *Current.* Last week's news and events are old stuff to broadcast media. If it's current they'll be interested; otherwise, no. Television producers are very aware of what's hot and what's not.
3. *Aurally or visually exciting.* You'll get the best coverage if your music sounds—and looks—exciting. If you can promise a TV producer that he'll get colorful shots of your high-school band marching in

intricate formations he may be interested; but if all you have to offer is a routine stage concert he probably won't cover it. Television depends on visual excitement.

4. *Simple*. Your story must be easy to tell in a minute or two, because in a news or feature segment that may be all you get. Newspapers can take half a page to tell your band's story but a television station may give you two minutes and fifteen seconds. In such events, try to emphasize the big issue, the most important points, but leave the details for the print media.

GETTING NOTICED ON RADIO AND TV

What kind of publicity opportunities do radio and television offer? Lots. Both news and feature stories will appeal to TV producers and audiences, and the distinction between them isn't always clear. In fact, many TV newspeople try to be like walking feature stories themselves, emphasizing personality more than content, style more than substance. If your event is timely, has lots of human interest, includes a strong visual element, can be summed up succinctly, appeals to a broad range of people, and has an irresistible hook, it may be a natural for TV, regardless of whether it's called news or feature material.

Broadcast News

"News," the old cliché goes, is an abbreviation for "North, East, West, and South." The idea is that the news covers what's happening, everywhere. Of course, it's not possible for reporters to cover everything, so choices must be made. Broadcast news is so limited by time and technical considerations that it has to be more selective—you'll have a better chance for coverage if you emphasize that your event is *timely, controversial, or new.*

Timely events such as concerts, plays, recitals, fund-raising activities, community events, and grand openings all can involve music, be promoted in advance, and be covered live. If your band is producing a local "We Are the World"-type song to raise money for the homeless, try for live coverage of your introductory concert. It's news.

Controversy is a staple of news departments, so watch for it. If the musician's union is on strike and picketing, if the school board is arguing whether to add a course in rock music history, if city police start arresting street musicians, if your rock band is battling the parks commission for permission to hold an outdoor concert on the mall—it's news.

Changes are also news. Did a new band director take over at the only high school in town? Has a landmark jazz club switched to a punk format? If these events would interest many people, they're news.

Features

Often, radio and TV features are an important part of evening newscasts. TV stations with hour-long local news shows rely heavily on *lifestyle* stories, and are excellent possibilities for your publicity. Regardless of whether your event is news- or feature-oriented you should provide ideas—and a visual hook, if you're trying for TV—to grab an audience's attention.

Anything *unusual* offers an excellent peg for broadcast features. Do you collect antique instruments? A radio feature on you playing (or trying to play) the serpent or the cornetto could be the peg for a feature about your hobby. Is your band the first in your area to use only electronic instruments—including drums? Or does your band use only unamplified acoustic instruments? Since radio and television are sound-oriented, why not let the angle be your sound itself?

As with newspaper features, the *oldest, youngest, newest, most advanced* anything can be featured. Is your original high-school rock band— formed in 1955—having a reunion concert now that you're all nearly fifty years old? And are your kids giving their first concert the same night? A "battle of the rock generations" story would be a good TV feature.

Lifestyle stories are popular for broadcast media. Work with whatever trend is hot at the moment to find an angle that will interest the producers. Is the female singer in your rock band pregnant? How about a lifestyle segment called "The Mama and the Rockers"? Is a local part-time big band, "The Second Opinions," composed entirely of doctors and dentists—who are sometimes called to the hospital in the middle of a dance job? It's a natural for a lifestyle feature. Does your pop band change styles one Sunday evening each month to perform old favorites at a retirement home?

When you're thinking about broadcast publicity, remember that on-location segments are expensive to produce—especially for television. Where a newspaper would assign a reporter with a notebook and pencil, a television station must send a reporter, a camera operator, and a sound engineer—and that's just the beginning. Back at the station, editors, mixers, and special effects people may work on the piece with $100,000 worth of electronic equipment. Don't be disappointed if a station doesn't rush out to cover every concert you do, but keep trying to make your events so interesting they can't be ignored.

Talk Shows

Would you like to talk for half an hour about your music on the radio, answering questions from callers—and promoting yourself all the while? That's the opportunity talk shows offer, and that's why they're one of the hottest publicity outlets anywhere. Authors, inventors, politicians, and experts in many fields try to get talk show exposure, which can range from national network shows to small, local outlets.

To get booked on a talk show, do something interesting, controversial, or new that would be a good subject for conversation with the public. If you've written a book or made a hit record you'll have little problem getting invited, but if you aren't yet well-known, you may have to be creative.

Think about what you have to offer—not what you can get. Remember, air time is expensive, and no producer will put you on for an hour of free self-promotion. You've got to have something to give the listeners.

You can offer entertainment, information, or help. You can tell listeners how to save money, attain self-fulfillment, or make themselves popular. You can be a visiting expert who answers trivial or important questions. Whatever you propose, however, must be interesting or important.

For instance, if you're an expert at piano tuning and repair, suggest a talk show segment on "Buying and maintaining a piano." Have you had a couple of songs published? That puts you ahead of most songwriters, and probably makes you a local expert. Try for a "How to Get Your Songs Published" segment. Or maybe you know absolutely everything there is to know about the Beatles. How about a "Stump the Expert" show, possibly timed to coincide with an important Beatles anniversary? Trivia contests are talk-show standards. Use *Chase's Annual Events* and other books of important and unusual anniversaries and celebrations to find a logical date to link with your idea. (More ideas for publicity hooks are provided in Chapter Nineteen.)

Listen carefully to the talk shows you'd like to be on. What kind of guests do they usually book? What's the focus? Is there an angle, a slant that matches your ideas? Would your interests correspond with those of the audience? Listen to the ads—they provide a clue to the makeup of that show's audience. Are the commercials aimed at people who would have no interest in your music—or at those who would share your concerns? You can learn a lot about a talk show by becoming a regular listener.

Every talk show has a producer—the person who books the guests, screens the calls, and probably keeps the show coherent and running smoothly. Often the host mentions the producer's name on the air; if not, call the station and ask. If you have an idea that you think would appeal to her, send your publicity material along with a short cover letter detailing your proposal. Make it interesting and illustrate how it would appeal to the show's audience. Follow up with a phone call—*not* during the show's broadcast time—a week later.

If you have been on other shows, include a cassette of your appearance to prove that you're a good guest. If you haven't, send your press kit and emphasize your tie-in with a larger, important issue. Tell them about the work your band does with ghetto kids, or the money you've raised for urban renewal, or the free concert you played for the women's shelter. Make your proposal relevant. Tell them that you'll entertain the audience with tales of the early days of the big bands, or recent bits of rock trivia. Offer to demonstrate your ability, on the air, to make up calypso songs based on callers' suggestions. It has to be interesting, fun, up-beat, though. You probably won't find any talk show hosts that would like a guest to demonstrate all the members of the woodwind family.

To get ready for a broadcast appearance, practice with a tape recorder (or video camera if you're going to be on TV). Have friends interview you, and ask difficult, even nasty, questions. Don't get flustered, mad, or defensive. If a caller asks, "What makes you such a hot-shot expert anyway?" or, "If you know so much, why aren't you rich?"—what would you say? Practice will give you confidence.

Practice with a recorder will also highlight annoying verbal habits you may have. Do you say "you know" every other sentence? Do you rely on "uh," or have a nervous laugh? You can change these habits, and if you're trying for lots of broadcast publicity, you'll find it helpful to work on how you sound and look.

WRITING FOR BROADCAST

Maybe you're not trying for a personal appearance. Perhaps you just want your event to be covered by radio and television news. Or maybe you want to submit a public service announcement to be aired. How do you write for broadcast use?

Writing for broadcast requires shorter words, shorter sentences, and a very direct approach. Remember, many listeners will be driving, jogging, or doing something else, and won't pay much attention to your announcement. Make it easy for them.

Usually you'll send the same release to newspapers and broadcast outlets—you won't have time to prepare a special release for each one. Sometimes, however, if you only want broadcast coverage, or if you have a publicity committee to help you, you may direct a special release to radio and TV.

If so, make it even shorter than usual. Be sure to include the important facts in the first two sentences, and get the hook in as quickly as possible. If pronunciation is tricky, write it phonetically so there won't be any mistake (" . . . Bill Jordan [JERDAN] said. . . .").

Calendar listings. Each station has its own preferences for calendar submissions—often they'll specify a postcard or three-by-five file card. Ask about, and follow, their wishes. If WXYZ is set up to use index cards for its *Entertainment Calendar,* don't make it difficult by sending your item in a letter.

If yours is a steady engagement, find out what the local stations require for continuing calendar mention. Some may keep repeated items on file while other stations may require you to send a new notice each week. Whatever their requirements are, follow them—use your datebook or wall calendar to remind you. Type up your information but DON'T USE ALL CAPS; IT'S HARDER TO READ. Double space, and leave wide margins. It only takes a minute to type that postcard, but the weekly publicity from these calendars of events will build with each mention of your name. Remember the water dripping on stone—persistence is required to build and maintain name recognition.

Some stations won't run any kind of community calendar. Others schedule such a segment several times a day. Take advantage of this free publicity whenever it's available.

PSAs

You've heard and seen hundreds of *Public Service Announcements* for everything from the symphony to Smokey the Bear. *PSAs* are, essentially, free ten-, thirty-, or sixty-second commercials that stations "give" to worthwhile causes. Often they're aired during slow times—like the middle of the night—but that doesn't matter. If it's free, take the publicity.

What qualifies for a free PSA? Obviously, stations won't give advertising time away. Usually, community-related events or nonprofit activities meet a station's PSA guidelines. Concerts, recitals, auditions, plays, festivals, fund-raisers, and fairs are good possibilities. Are you holding an open rehearsal? An amateur night? A sing-along? Auditions for the community symphony or band? PSAs are ideal for publicizing these events.

Stations usually don't produce public service announcements themselves. You do that, and there are two ways to do it. You can produce a finished audio- or videotape to be aired "as is," or you can provide copy for the station's announcer to read on the air.

Will a station air a PSA for private businesses—such as your teaching studio? Will it announce such events as a high-school band concert via a thirty- or sixty-second PSA? Policies vary, so contact local stations to find out. If they're receptive, take advantage of these excellent publicity possibilities by sending out lots of public service announcements.

If you provide the finished PSA yourself, be sure the production and voice are professional quality or you'll just be wasting time—no station will run an amateurish PSA. If you're working on a PSA for radio, you could begin the announcement with a bit of your music, followed by the message. You must read more slowly than normal, with good voice inflection and pronunciation. For a ten-second announcement, limit yourself to twenty-five words. A thirty-second message should have no more than seventy-five to eighty words, and a minute's announcement should be limited to about 150 words.

For television, provide either finished, broadcast-quality video-cassette of exactly the right length (and you'd probably need to work with a professional video producer), or send several excellent slides to accompany the copy. Most visuals are only on the screen for three to five seconds, so send at least ten slides for a thirty-second spot, and twenty for a full minute. Even if they aren't all used, give the director a choice.

Television copy requires fewer words, since much of the message is visual. For a ten-second TV spot try for only twelve to fifteen words, use about fifty words for a thirty-second announcement, and 120 for a minute spot. It's counterproductive to cram too much into these short messages because people won't hear, and won't remember. Keep it simple. Want proof? Transcribe a few professionally produced commercials. Count the words. Notice the short sentences. Copy their techniques when you write PSA copy.

When you send written copy for the station's staff to read, accepted PSA format is much like a press release, but dates are more important. List the beginning date, and the "kill date," or the last date to use this announcement. Often, professional public relations firms send two PSAs for the same event on one sheet (a ten- and a thirty-second, for example) to increase the chances of it being used.

You can use your letterhead and simply type *PUBLIC SERVICE AN-NOUNCEMENT,* centered, below your name. Or you can produce a special PSA letterhead which will look much more professional. Simply use the *Public Service Announcement* headline provided in the Appendix and create your own PSA format. (As usual, follow the layout and pasteup techniques described in Chapter Six.)

PUBLIC SERVICE ANNOUNCEMENT

FOR IMMEDIATE RELEASE (12/12/93)

KILL DATE (12/16/93)

Contact: Susan Bennett
(123) 456-7890

-30 second-

Like to sing? Got the Christmas spirit? Join the annual *Messiah* sing-along this Sunday night, December 15, at 7:30 at All Saints Church at the corner of Peachtree and Third. All singers—regardless of ability—are cordially invited to join this festive performance. Music will be available at the door. Make your Christmas season special by joining with the Church choirs and orchestra to celebrate Handel's *Messiah.*

-10 second-

Like to sing? You're invited to join the All Saints Church choirs and orchestra in their annual *Messiah* sing-along, Sunday, December 15, at 7:30.

Most stations will limit PSAs to community events of broad interest—sometimes only to government and public-service organizations. If, however, you are planning an event that will be fun, enlightening, or inspiring to lots of people, try for PSA publicity. It's just like free advertising—and it's worth the trouble.

TV APPEARANCES

So you're booked on the *Lifestyle* segment of the noon news to talk about your new computer-assisted music lessons for preschoolers. How do you behave, and what do you wear, to look polished and cool?

Several factors determine how you'll appear on TV. Your demeanor, the way you talk and answer questions, how relaxed you are, and even what you wear all work together to make you seem ill at ease—or to make you look like a video pro.

Clothes are important for television appearances, so think again about the image you want to project. You may have to plan an outfit that will look right on TV—and different broadcasts will have different needs.

If your band is being taped on location there's no problem—just wear what you always wear when you perform. But if you're being interviewed for a news or feature segment, or if you're on *Today in Dallas* as a guest, you'll need to give some thought to what you wear. Jeans and flannel shirts, or metallic pants, may not be right for morning television.

For interview or news segments you should dress more conservatively than usual—especially if there's a question of what to wear. Sure, stars on David Letterman's show look disheveled (with each hair carefully arranged to look carelessly tousled), but you aren't a star, and local television has different expectations from late-night network shows.

Practice with a video camera. Large cities have video-coaching firms that teach business executives how to be telegenic and believable on the air—but such professional coaching is expensive. You can get much the same valuable experience by using a home video camera to tape yourself in an interview, or performance, situation. If you don't have a video camera of your own, borrow one from a friend, or rent it from a video store. All you need is the chance to see yourself on the screen.

The cardinal rule of video is don't look at the camera. Just keep your eyes on the host and ignore the camera. The exception is if you're making an appeal directly to the viewers, but this is rare.

Be sure your clothes fit, are fresh from the laundry with neat creases. If you must eat on the way to the studio be careful—that's the very time you'll spill soup on your tie or blouse. Polish your shoes, too, and wear over-the-calf socks. Also, TV cameras make you look a bit heavier than you are, so if you have a weight problem, wear dark colors and avoid patterns that would make you appear larger. Loose-fitting clothing is also more attractive than tight.

Ask the producer what colors photograph best, or watch the show in advance to see how the host dresses. Bright colors sometimes tend to "bleed," patterns distort, white glares, and black looks dead. If you can, wear earth tones and subtle colors. And avoid dark glasses (or photosensitive ones); they make you look sinister.

Men with heavy beards should shave just before the broadcast if possible. It may be helpful to use a smoothing pancake makeup to cover bags under your eyes (were you playing late last night?) and skin blemishes—but try them out before you get to the studio.

Your Own Show

Well, why not? If you're an expert in a particular kind of music, why not host a radio show specializing in that format? If there is little or no programming for jazz, bluegrass, folk, ethnic, blues, electronic, new-age, Latin, classical, choral, or chamber music in your area, this could be an enjoyable way to publicize your kind of music—and yourself as well.

The most responsive stations will usually be community-supported, public, college, or specialized FM outlets. Smaller stations generally offer more specialized programming than the 100,000 watt giants.

If you're interested in producing such a show, call the station's program director and explain your proposal. Volunteer to bring in a sample tape, or ask for an off-the-air audition.

Try an approach like this. "Hi, Mr. Program Director. I'm Joe Jones, and I have a program idea that I believe WXYZ would be interested in. I'd like to host a weekly jazz hour on your station. Jazz is gaining popularity, and has a devoted following—I've checked with several record stores, and they all report growing sales of jazz albums. Since no jazz at all is broadcast in our area, I'm sure we could attract listeners, and I'm qualified to do the show—I have a degree in music education, and I earn my living as a jazz musician. My performance background has taught me to speak well. I understand mike techniques, and I've worked around electronics all my life. I'd even be able to program the shows from my own record collection if the station's jazz resources are limited. I believe we could develop a new, and loyal, group of listeners for your station with just a little work."

This approach shows the program director that you've done a bit of market research, and that you're aware of how important the audience size is to his station. You've shown that you're qualified, and that this venture wouldn't cost the station a lot of money.

There are plenty of pop and rock music experts already on the air. You'll have the best chances of success with other types—and you'll reap the best publicity if you match your broadcast efforts with the kind of music you perform.

More On-the-Air Ideas

Try to link your performances with someone else's broadcast when possible—and be sure that you're mentioned by name. If your dixieland band is attracting crowds at a car dealer's Sell-a-Thon, and a local station is doing a remote broadcast, be sure your band is featured several times during the afternoon. This way, you *piggyback* your publicity onto the car dealer's advertising.

And don't overlook the possibilities of educational programming. Even a locally produced show such as "How to Play Folk Guitar," or "Reading Music for Beginners" would raise your recognition level, give you valuable experience, and probably pay you a fee. Many educational stations, of course, rely on professional educators, but a creative approach, talent, and enthusiasm might prevail. Who knows? Your idea might work so well that your show gets syndicated—and creates a new career for you.

Also try to publicize your band's music on appropriate programs. If you have a terrific tape of an original top-40-style tune, visit the top-40 stations and try to get it aired. Even though many stations play only what's on the charts at the moment, some will play your work.

Many stations even have a regularly scheduled segment featuring local musicians. If you've produced a record you'll need to really pursue this avenue, with all the publicity tricks you can muster; but even if you only have a demo tape, work at getting it aired during the *Denver Music Scene* show.

If there's an all-news station in your town, let them know that you're an expert on jazz, electronic music, or whatever. News stations keep files of local experts who can comment on news stories—and you may be called to offer your insight into an issue that concerns your kind of music.

Or if there's a local variety show produced in your town, try for guest musical appearances. Such slots often offer excellent publicity. You could even become a regular—the house band for *Salt Lake City Tonight*.

Remember, always get tapes of your broadcast appearances. Call ahead and ask the producer whether the station will make a copy for you (if you supply the blank cassette, of course). If so, find out if they use VHS, Beta, three-quarter, or one-inch tape. It's also a good idea to have a friend record the broadcast at home, too, in case something goes wrong with the station's copy. Several performance tapes will be very useful in putting a good demo together.

Radio and TV broadcasts travel at the speed of light, and your appearances may seem to be forgotten just as quickly. Continue to establish good media contacts and develop ideas for coverage, though, because the net effect of all your appearances will be great publicity. One interview may not make you famous, but several can make you a local celebrity.

People will ask, "Didn't I see you on TV?" You'll smile and answer, "All the time." But don't tell them how you arranged all those appearances in the first place. Let them think that you're just a natural.

CHAPTER 14

It's in the Mail

WHY SHOULD ANYONE GO TO THE TROUBLE to write a letter when it's so easy to pick up the telephone? After all, isn't this the age of instant communication?

True, telephoning is easy and quick—but letters remain an important publicity tool for your performance career. Well-written letters enhance your image—and they'll make your professional life run more smoothly than an unending series of phone calls. Businesspeople rely on letters of all kinds, and you should show your clients and prospects that you understand how things work in the business world. A clean, well-written letter of introduction shows that you care enough about that client's business to spend the time necessary to communicate clearly. Further, your personalized letterhead shows that you're established and serious about your image.

In fact, a well-done business letter, carefully typed on your handsome letterhead, puts you on equal footing with every other business or competitor, regardless of size or reputation. Your client needn't know that you borrowed the typewriter, or that your office is really the kitchen table. If your business correspondence looks good, you look good. In short, a well-done letter says a lot more about you than just the message it carries.

People will read your letters at their convenience, whereas they might not return your phone calls. Businesspeople value their time, and letters give them a way to control it, so letters are often more appreciated than phone calls. Letters don't interrupt important meetings. Phone calls are forgotten, misinterpreted, or ignored—but letters are answered, filed, passed around for others to read, and kept for future reference. Letters last.

Letters also save money if you're dealing with an out-of-town client. Why make a series of long-distance calls when a letter will serve the same purpose—only better? Plus, it always helps to get it in writing. Specific details should be down in black and white to avoid errors. When people read and write letters and sign contracts they pay close attention. You'll avoid mistakes by using written confirmations. For example, a client may forget to tell the band about time or date changes. If you have a written, signed confirmation for Friday night, the client can't blame you for not showing up on Thursday. Letters help you protect yourself.

Mass mailings allow you to deliver a message inexpensively to your target audiences. You should build, and keep, mailing lists of those who need to know about your activities. Is such *direct-mail* publicity effective? Look in your mailbox for the answer. If so many companies rely on it, you can be sure that it works for them—and mailings will work for you, too.

DO YOU KNOW ALL THE LETTERS?

You'll depend on different kinds of letters in publicizing your career, and while they're easy to write, they have different styles and purposes.

1. *Letters of introduction* will tell new prospects about you and your music. Often, introductory letters prepare a client for your sales call so she'll already know who you are—and what you do. *Cover letters* that you send with press releases and other publicity information are like introductory letters—they "introduce" the material you're sending, and reinforce the message.

2. *Other business letters* of all kinds are also important. You'll write to confirm details, to make proposals, to sell your music, to ask for information, or to request overdue payment. Letters have more impact than phone calls, and often get better results.

3. *Confirmations and contracts* aren't really letters—often you'll use standard forms and just fill in the blanks. They are written communication, however, so we'll discuss how you can best use them.

4. *Thank-you notes* are as important as anything else you do in your publicity program. When you've played a job and taken the client's money (whether a little or a lot) *always* send a thank-you note. It's an extra step that every client will appreciate, remember, and probably talk about. And saying "thank you" is not just good business—it's also normal courtesy.

Believe it or not, a simple thank-you note can be one of the most effective aspects of your publicity program. Don't just take the money and run. It's much better to take the money, say "thank you," and run.

Just My Type

Business letters usually follow a well-established pattern. You probably studied this in school, but since you're not aware of the publicity value of everything you do, let's have a review.

Appearance matters in business communication—and this means that your *business letters must be typed*. Handwritten business letters convey just one message: regardless of content, they say, "amateur." There aren't too many hard-and-fast rules concerning publicity, but this is one.

If you don't have a typewriter, why not buy one? Excellent machines cost much less today than they did just a few years ago. Discount stores sell sophisticated electronic typewriters with replaceable type elements at less than two hundred dollars. You don't type? It's not that hard—you can easily teach yourself or take an inexpensive course. An alternative, of course, is to arrange for someone else to do your typing, but this is cumbersome and can be expensive.

Keep your typewriter clean and well adjusted. Use black ribbon only—save the colors for writing to your fiancé. Use only typefaces that look like a typewriter—never use script or other fancy styles in business correspondence because they may be hard to read, and they don't look businesslike.

Use a computer, if you have one, but be sure it has a *letter quality printer*. Unless a dot-matrix printer really produces "near letter quality" results, don't use it to produce business correspondence—it's harder to read because each letter is composed of tiny dots rather than solid lines.

If you do use a computer for correspondence, be sure that the right margin prints uneven, or *ragged right*, just as it would be if you'd typed the letter on a typewriter. Justified (that is, even) right margins look artificial and make letters look impersonal, so even if your computer is generating a mass mailing for you, give each letter a "hand typed" look.

Maybe this sounds too rigid. You're a musician, after all, and not a business tycoon, so why should you conform to someone else's standards? When you're seeking publicity, you'll do better to play by established rules—and with business correspondence that means one thing—type it.

Business Letter Style

Perhaps the simplest, though not the only, format for business letters is the *full block* style in which everything is lined up with the left margin and no paragraphs are indented. If you're interested in other styles consult one of the books listed in the Bibliography.

Mary Jo McCormack
123 Duck Creek Drive – Walden, Massachusetts 01081

September 17, 1989

Mr. Greg Studdard, Manager
Upper Crust Country Club
123 Highbrow Dr.
Newport, Rhode Island

Dear Mr. Studdard:

I know you're busy, but I'd like to take a moment of your time to introduce myself.

I'm a pianist specializing in country-club type music, and have just moved from New York to Rhode Island. While in New York I worked regularly as a single, and with combos, at several well-established clubs.

I sing, know hundreds of tunes, and get along well with country-club members—and I'd like to work for you.

In the next week or so, I'll call your secretary for a three-minute appointment to meet you. I'd like to say "hello" and leave a demo tape and some publicity material.

I look forward to the opportunity of working with you.

Thank you.

Sincerely,

Mary Jo McCormack

Mary Jo McCormack

P. S. My specialty is remembering members' favorite tunes. I'm proud of my memory, and rarely forget a face, name or special request. Club members seem to appreciate this trait. Hope I can demonstrate it for you.

Good business letters look neat and businesslike. They're short and to the point, but friendly and polite. Here Mary Jo is introducing herself and laying the groundwork for a later sales call, and her letter gives a good, professional first impression.

What has Mary Jo accomplished with this letter? Some observations:

- She called the club to get the manager's name, the club's address and zip code. She checked his title, and the spelling of "Studdard."
- She comes right to the point in the first sentence, ". . . I'd like to introduce myself."
- She toots her own horn without overtly bragging, ". . . I know hundreds of tunes. . . ."
- The phrase, ". . . [I] get along well with club members," shows, subtly, that she understands the importance of personal rapport with club members, a key trait in country-club work.
- She follows business protocol when she says she'll call ahead for an appointment. And she shows respect for Mr. Studdard's time by mentioning a three-minute visit.
- She uses "Sincerely" for the *complimentary close* because it is the most popular. She could have used "Yours truly," "Cordially," or "Respectfully."
- She uses a postscript because she knows that is the most read part of any letter. (Notice that the advertising letters you get *always* include a postscript to add emphasis.) Here, the P. S. repeats the idea that Mary Jo is interested in the club members, and implies that she would be a popular addition to the club.
- Mary Jo clips one of her business cards to the letter, but she doesn't include a brochure at this point since she's planning a personal sales call within a week. She'll personally deliver the brochure and demo tape for more impact. (We'll cover sales calls in Chapter Fifteen.)
- The letter is neatly typed in a standard business style.

WHAT DO YOU WANT TO SAY?

Business letters are time savers, and should be brief and to the point. Your time is valuable, and so is that of your clients and prospects. Don't beat around the bush. There's no need to be verbose, vague, wordy, or evasive. The best approach for writing a business letter is to come right out and say what you mean. Even in a letter of complaint, though, always be polite.

Are you writing to introduce yourself? Follow Mary Jo's approach, and say, "I'd like to introduce myself." Are you writing for an appointment? Don't make the reader guess what you're after. Say, "I'd like to set up an appointment to show you how my band can increase the popularity of the Chez Nous club."

Is this a letter of confirmation? Spell out the details as clearly as you can. In such a letter, *always* note the day as well as the date in case the client doesn't have a calendar handy. "Joe's Band will play on Friday, May 13th, 1988, from 6:00 to 9:00 p.m." Maybe the client really wants you for Saturday, and was confused about when the thirteenth will be. Writing "Friday" will catch the error before it catches you.

The Unpleasant Truth

Are you writing about an unpleasant subject—an overdue bill, a broken contract, an unsatisfactory performance? Don't be nasty or ugly (which could even get you into legal trouble), but make your point in a businesslike way.

"I'm writing to request payment for our performance at your company function six weeks ago. While I realize that the check must be issued through your usual procedures, let me point out that you promised payment within two weeks, and that we have been very patient. Please advise when we may expect a check."

Or, "I'm truly sorry, Mrs. Jones, that your daughter felt she had to cancel her wedding on the morning of the ceremony, and I know that you've had a traumatic week, but I must point out that our contract does not allow cancellations on the day of the performance. Unfortunately, we had turned down several other jobs for that Saturday, and we must insist on full payment per terms of the contract. I'm sure you realize that Saturday nights are our prime time."

How does this help your publicity goals? By being businesslike in all your dealings—pleasant and otherwise—your reputation will be enhanced. Your clients will be impressed by your professional approach in this unmusical aspect of your career.

What if an engagement was unsuccessful, and your band really was at fault? Perhaps you'd need to offer an adjustment in your fee, but at least a well-phrased letter of apology shows that you care—and helps mend fences. You can't afford unhappy clients.

So, say "I'm sorry about our drummer knocking over the wedding cake, Mrs. Jones. He tripped on the edge of the dance floor and instinctively reached out for support. It's unfortunate that the cake was within his reach, though in years to come I hope the pictures of him lying amid the fallen cake may be cause for amusement rather than anger."

Face up to problems, and be sincere with your apology—even humorous if it's appropriate. Anger or defensiveness, even when justified, is usually counterproductive.

Form Letters Save Time

In the right situation, forms and preprinted contracts will save time and probably make communication easier, but don't substitute a form for a real live letter. Use forms when a standard, repetitious kind of information is required, design it with your publicity objectives in mind, and make it simple to use.

If you're a union member, you may prefer to use a standard union contract form—in fact, you may be required to file a copy with the union office. If so, you can at least have contracts duplicated onto your own letterhead. You may, however, wish to design a time-saving confirmation form to match your own musical needs.

If you require a legally binding contract, consult a lawyer or use an accepted, tested, union form. If you're comfortable, however, with a less legalistic kind of communication, just devise a simple form that includes all the pertinent data for your kind of music. Your goal is to save time—yours and the client's—and reduce the chances for a communication error.

If a client won't pay, will such a contract help you in small claims court? Again, consult an attorney about the exact form you've devised, but the truth is that in such a situation you may be out of luck, with or without a contract. Sometimes it's just not worth the effort to collect the money, and you'll have to just write it off as a bad debt. If a club goes out of business there may not be any assets for you to claim, or money to pay your bill. A clear, well-written contract, or confirmation letter, however, will help you make your case.

Of course you'll print the form on your letterhead, or add your logo to the top, or bottom, of the page, but also consider having your contract *typeset*, to look extra good. You can pattern the form after a letter, a memo, or a contract. Even though the purpose here is to get detailed information in print you should take care that your professional image is enhanced. You can do this by asking for some kind of specific information that shows your interest in this particular client, and by stating your requirements more like *requests* than demands. Read the sample confirmation agreement on pages 168-169. Notice, particularly, the phrasing of the first three paragraphs. The bandleader is really saying:

1. We charge extra if the piano you provide isn't tuned.
2. We charge extra if we must unexpectedly change locations during a job.
3. We probably charge extra for early set-ups.

But, rather than make such demanding-sounding statements, he phrases them so the client doesn't feel insulted.

If you choose to use a form like this one, tailor it to your own kind of music. Make it as handsome as you can by applying the same design principles you used in preparing your other printed material—be sure that the image conveyed is that of a successful professional.

If you have unusual requirements (large space, power, or lighting needs, for example), attach a rider listing exactly what you need. But if your needs can be included on one sheet, try to phrase them diplomatical-

Joe's Band

123 Homestead Avenue • Fayetteville, Arkansas 72701

Dear Mr. Harvyasi,

Thank you for hiring Joe's Band to play at your upcoming function. We are interested in working with you to be sure that this event meets your needs and expectations.

Please take a moment to check all the information below. The smallest details are important, so if there is any discrepancy, or if you have additional requirements, please let us know.

Over the years we've found that the following concerns will help your affair enjoy the best possible music with the least possible confusion.

1. If you are providing a piano, your music will sound much better if the instrument is in tune and good playing condition. If it's not we'll bring in an electric piano and add a forty-dollar cartage fee.

2. If an unexpected move is required during the course of an engagement it could disrupt your party because our equipment takes time to break down and set up. Should such a move be necessary, additional cartage fees of forty dollars each for the drummer and keyboardist, and ten dollars for every other band member, will apply. We would like to work with you to plan in advance the best location for the band so such moves won't be needed.

3. We always arrive at least an hour before each performance. This gives us ample time to set up our equipment. If an earlier set-up is required, there may be an extra charge for the time involved. We'll gladly work with you to make the logistics of your engagement as smooth as possible.

4. Should you have to cancel this affair, we'll refund the deposit if cancellation is sixty days or more in advance. For cancellations less than sixty days in advance, the deposit is forfeited, unless we are able to book another engagement, in which case we will refund your deposit. If an engagement is cancelled two weeks or less before the event, the entire amount of the contracted price will be due. This does not apply to cancellations due to bad weather when schools and businesses are also closed.

DATE OF ENGAGEMENT: Thursday, November 9, 1989
TIME: 8:00-11:00pm
PLACE: Plantation Ballroom, Hilton Head Inn, Hilton Head Island, SC
TYPE OF FUNCTION: Dinner/Show/Dance music for company dinner
NAME OF BAND: Joe's Band
NUMBER OF MUSICIANS IN BAND: 6, including vocalist
APPROPRIATE ATTIRE: Formal
COMPENSATION AGREED ON: $1850, plus four motel rooms (doubles)
DEPOSIT OF $600.00 REQUIRED
BALANCE OF: $1250.00 IS DUE: at conclusion of engagement
OVERTIME TO BE BILLED AT: prorated per half-hour

SPECIAL REQUIREMENTS: We need access to the Plantation room at least an hour, and preferably two, before the function begins. Stage must be twelve by twenty feet. We provide keyboards and sound equipment.

COMMENTS: Company will advise of exact time schedule for evening, and will provide a script for the awards music, etc.

Signed _____

Joe Jones, Bandleader
123 Anystreet, Anytown, NY
(123)456-7890

Client's signature _____

Company _____
Address _____
City _____
Telephone, office _____
home _____

ly, so the client won't feel that you're making difficult demands. Rock stars are well-known for attaching contract riders specifying everything down to the brand of soft drinks that must be provided. Remember, though, that celebrities can make demands that the rest of us shouldn't try.

"Thank you"

There's an old saying that the most powerful words in the English language are "please," and "thank you." It may be true.

People like to be appreciated for doing a good job, or thanked for spending their money. Since that basic fact of human nature isn't likely to change, get in the habit of sending short thank-you notes.

What if you're a macho guitar player whose band has a mean, masculine image? Should *you* send a thank-you note? Sure. It doesn't have to be on pink, scented, floral-design notecards. Match it to your own style.

Further, the thank-you message doesn't even need to be a full-sized letter. A short note works just as well. In fact, you might produce a smaller letterhead, half the usual size (that is, 8½ by 5½ inches) to use just for such short notes.

And, unlike business letters, thank-you notes don't have to be typewritten, particularly when you're addressing individuals. Just make sure your handwriting is legible.

What do you say in a thank-you note? Not much. Thank the client for using your music and mention some aspect of the engagement to personalize the note. That's all.

Joe's Band
123 Homestead Avenue • Fayetteville, Arkansas 72701

May 12, 1999

Dear Mrs. Bowen,

Thanks for using our band at Jane's wedding reception last Saturday night. We really enjoyed being part of your family's festivities.

We especially liked the serious dancing at the end of the party. Those pictures of the groom doing the "alligator" will probably become family heirlooms.

Thanks again.

Joe Jones

That's all it takes to show the client that you appreciate her business. Such a thank-you note softens the impact of an invoice if you're sending one, and puts your name, again, before the client. Clip a business card to the note, too; if your music was really good and the party was a success, the client will be more likely than ever to save your card.

Sending thank-you notes is just plain courtesy. It's also good business; thank-you notes continue to sell your music after the engagement is over. There may be another job on the horizon, and the client's friends and associates will certainly need your services sometime. Don't let that client forget who you are.

IT'S NOT "JUNK MAIL" WHEN YOU SEND IT

A great way to keep your name before those *affect communities* you listed in Chapter Two is to use *direct mail.* You can send postcards, flyers, form letters, or even your own newsletter or demo tapes, to tell people where you're playing and what you're doing.

Remember, client indifference is a fact of life, and you must constantly work to keep your name, and your music, in their minds. Frequent mailings remind them that you're still around.

If you carefully select your target audiences, mailings can be extremely effective publicity tools—and they're not really very expensive when compared with other kinds of advertising. (Of course, mailing expenses, like other business costs, are tax-deductible, so save all receipts and cancelled checks.)

Mailing Lists

In advertising and publicity, direct mail is big business. Large list companies provide mailing lists targeted to incredibly precise audiences—forty-year-old men who like jazz, drive Jeeps, and live in affluent zip codes, for example. Huge catalogs of available mailing lists are published, and the names of virtually any interest group imaginable are for sale.

You won't *buy* the mailing lists you see, however. You'll *compile* them yourself, and you may have only ten or fifteen names on one list and eighty or a hundred on another, rather than the tens of thousands used by advertising professionals. No matter what the size of your list, you'll get helpful impact from each mailing.

You'll probably find it useful to develop and maintain at least three different lists. First will be a list of regular clients—those who frequently hire you. If your band plays a circuit of ten different motel lounges, you'll begin with ten managers on your list. If you play convention work in a large city, you may have thirty or forty names of booking agents and convention planners. If you play weddings, your list will include wedding planners, photographers, florists, caterers, as well as agents.

The second compilation you'll need is the *friends of the band* list that helps you keep track of people who like your music. If you play in a club, restaurant, or lounge there will be regular customers—perhaps even fans of yours—who should be kept up to date on where you're playing and what you're doing. Keep a mailing list, and you can keep them posted.

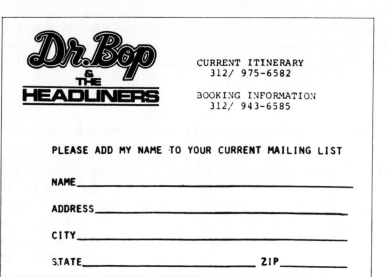

How do you build your "band fan" mailing list? One good way is to distribute cards such as this each time you play. People who like your music fill out the cards, and you add them to your list. It's a simple but effective tool.

A third list, which you're already keeping, is your *media contacts* compilation. You'll send out press releases and announcements of interest to the press, and a mailing list will expedite the process.

Publicity Practice

Start researching a *client list,* including addresses, of all those clients who should know about your music. Include those for whom you've already worked, as well as those who haven't booked you yet. Start with the names you know, and use the Yellow Pages for more listings. There is a thorough discussion of locating such clients in *How You Can Make $30,000 a Year As a Musician Without a Record Contract* (see the Bibliography for publication data).

Next, start a list of all your loyal fans—your *band fan* list. When you talk to people in the club or see the same faces each week, ask for their cards, or get their names and addresses. Perhaps you should keep a legal pad for this purpose at the bandstand, or by the cashier, or at the table where you sell T-shirts and tapes. Add these to your *friends of the band* list and keep them updated about where you're playing. You could distribute preprinted (but not stamped) postcards at the clubs where you play, with the copy "Please add my name to your mailing list so I'll always know where to find Joe's Band."

You should already have a *media contacts list* that you can use for sending out press releases and announcements.

Keep your mailing lists active—add and delete names as people come and go. One way to "clean" your lists is to stamp "return postage guaranteed" on the envelope, so the post office will return the mail when the addressee has moved. When something is returned, delete that person from your list. (This technique adds a little initial cost since return postage adds twenty-two cents per piece that's returned, but it saves money in the long run and improves your mailings.) Using direct mail is easy, but its effectiveness depends on the quality of your lists, so always be on the lookout for potential clients and fans who should be kept informed.

Remember, you don't have to *know* the people on your list, so if you read a newspaper article about a potential new client, go ahead and add her name. Look the address up in the phone book, or call her office to get the proper mailing information.

Nuts and Bolts of Direct Mail

If your mailing isn't too large, use first-class mail for simplicity, impact, and reliability. First-class mail is delivered promptly, and some researchers say that it makes a better impression than alternative rates.

If you expect to do lots of mailings, though, you could benefit from the less expensive *third-class* (also called *bulk mail*) rates. If you're part of a nonprofit organization, you'll be especially interested in this category because such groups have a much lower rate than commercial mailers. Third-class can save money, but to use it you must meet certain requirements. You must:

1. Have a permit, which currently costs fifty dollars a year. In addition, there is a one-time fifty-dollar application fee.
2. Include at least two hundred pieces in each mailing.
3. Sort each mailing by zip code.
4. Include your third-class permit number on each piece.

Third-class bulk mail currently costs 12½ cents per piece, and approved nonprofit organizations can mail for only 8½ cents. You'd have to mail over a thousand pieces a year (if you include the start-up application fee) to save money over first class, and most musicians probably won't need to mail that extensively. And third class mail is not the highest post office priority, and can take days, or weeks, to be delivered.

PRODUCING A MAILING

Who has time to do all that work? You're too busy to spend all day typing addresses each time you have an announcement about your music.

Relax. You shouldn't have to type names and addresses more than once. Modern office technology has made mailing easy. You can use master labels and a photocopy machine or you can use a computer.

The easiest way, if you already have a computer, is to let a mailing-list program do the work for you. Even the most inexpensive computers can run mail programs that alphabetize lists, make address changes easy, and print labels in zip-code sequence. A computer will even let you produce specialized subcategory lists (such as clients who've hired you more than twice, or within the past year, or whatever criteria you want to use).

If you don't have a computer, don't worry. Rather than type each address laboriously onto each envelope, you'll use mailing labels that can be duplicated on photocopy machines. Visit an office supply store, and buy *master,* and *photocopy label* sheets.

Each master sheet has space for thirty-three names and addresses, and you can type as many masters as you need for each list. When it's time for a mailing simply use a copy machine to run off the self-adhesive labels, and stick them onto each mailing piece. It's easy.

What to Mail

Use your mailing lists to keep clients and audiences up to date about all your musical activities. When your band opens at a new club, send postcards to everyone on your *band fan* list. You can probably talk the club manager into paying for this mailing, since he'll benefit from larger crowds.

Why not design your own card for more impact? As long as it meets the post office's minimum size requirements (3½ by 5 inches, no thinner than a postcard) you can be as creative as you wish. Your printer will turn your camera-ready copy into an inexpensive and effective mailing piece—including your photo if you wish. Adding a photo does cost a little more, since the printer will charge ten dollars or so to screen the picture.

Keep your name before agents and regular clients by sending them frequent updates. You could simply send your brochure out a couple of times a year, or you might prepare a different flyer or circular for each mailing. Each regular mailing should bring you more benefit than it costs to produce—though you could overdo it and reach the point of diminishing return. Keep track of results by asking booking clients if they got your flyer.

If yours is a large organization like a school band or a recording studio, you might even produce your own newsletter. Include news of what you've done—concerts, parades, recitals, recordings, new equipment, new repertoire, visiting soloists, fund-raising events, parties, or anything else that might interest your clients. Producing a newsletter, however, is work, so you should have a committee, if possible, to assist in writing, layout, printing and distribution. Perhaps a quarterly or twice-yearly news-

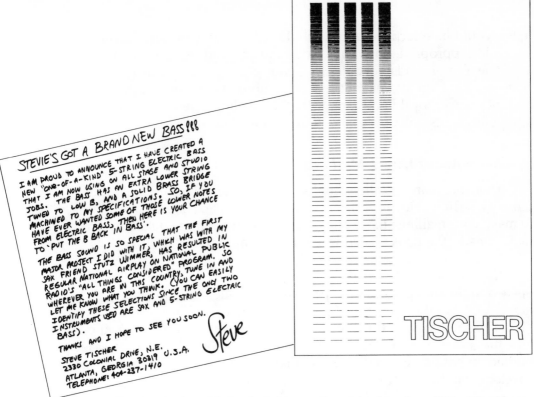

STEVIE'S GOT A BRAND NEW BASS !!!

I AM PROUD TO ANNOUNCE THAT I HAVE CREATED A NEW "ONE-OF-A-KIND" 5-STRING ELECTRIC BASS THAT I AM NOW USING ON ALL STAGE AND STUDIO JOBS. THE BASS HAS AN EXTRA LOWER STRING TUNED TO LOW B, AND A SOLID BRASS BRIDGE MACHINED TO MY SPECIFICATIONS. SO, IF YOU HAVE EVER WANTED SOME OF THOSE LOWER NOTES FROM ELECTRIC BASS, THEN HERE IS YOUR CHANCE TO 'PUT THE B BACK IN BASS'.

THE BASS SOUND IS SO SPECIAL THAT THE FIRST MAJOR PROJECT I DID WITH IT, WHICH WAS WITH MY SAX FRIEND STUTZ WIMMER, HAS RESULTED IN REGULAR NATIONAL AIRPLAY ON NATIONAL PUBLIC RADIO'S "ALL THINGS CONSIDERED" PROGRAM. SO WHEREVER YOU ARE IN THIS COUNTRY, TUNE IN AND LET ME KNOW WHAT YOU THINK. (YOU CAN EASILY IDENTIFY THESE SELECTIONS SINCE THE ONLY TWO INSTRUMENTS USED ARE SAX AND 5-STRING ELECTRIC BASS).

THANKS AND I HOPE TO SEE YOU SOON. Steve

STEVE TISCHER
2330 COLONIAL DRIVE, N.E.
ATLANTA, GEORGIA 30319 U.S.A.
TELEPHONE: 404-237-1410

TISCHER

When bassist Steve Tischer built his own five-string bass, he publicized it with this homemade postcard. He produced the artwork, tracing **Letraset** presstype to retain a handwritten look, and copied the cards on heavy stock using a laser copy machine. The logo of five lines represents the vibrating strings of a bass, and is repeated on all his publicity material.

You are cordially
invited
to the
Atlanta Studios
holiday
Open House

3140 E. Shadowlawn Ave.
Atlanta, GA 30305

Sunday, Dec. 19, 1980   R.S.V.P.
4:00—9:00   231·9888

Have a party and invite friends and clients. You'll enjoy it, and it will publicize what you're doing. If you're part of an institution or business, such as Atlanta Studios, why not hold the party at your office/studio?

letter would be effective—and it would help avoid constant deadlines.

If it's appropriate for your kind of music, send regular schedules of available (or not-available) dates to clients who need such timely information—booking agents, party planners, club owners, concert promoters, and, of course, loyal band fans. Monthly mailings aren't difficult to do, and your clients will appreciate your businesslike approach.

More About Direct Mail

There are many excellent books about direct mail techniques, and extensive research helps advertisers increase response. Here are a few ideas to make your mailings more effective. (If you want more detail on direct mail, consult the books listed in the Bibliography.)

Use a teaser on the envelope. How can you be sure the envelope gets opened in the first place? Many professional mailers use questions, statements, or illustrations to arouse curiosity. "For a Good Time, Call. . . ." Or, "What has ten legs, two horns, and guarantees a good time?" You can type the teaser, have it printed on the envelope, or have your message printed on brightly colored stickers or labels. Or maybe your logo on the envelope will be the only message you need.

Combine a letter with your circular to increase response. Add either a form letter or a personal one to supplement the message in your brochure. (Personal letters, however, require first-class postage.) Remember that most direct mail copywriters believe that the P.S. is the strongest part of a letter.

Plan your mailing date. If you're interested in booking Christmas jobs for your band, do your first mailing in June and follow up in September. Use a strong teaser to get their attention—perhaps "Christmas in June?" or "For best results book now, play later." Plan far ahead—your clients do.

Also think about when you want your mail received. Monday and Friday are the busiest mail days; Tuesday is the slowest. January is the busiest mail-order month when mailboxes are flooded with catalogs and solicitations. Time your mailing, if possible, to arrive on a slow mail day so it will have a better chance of being noticed. First-class mail is the only category that can dependably be planned this way. If local delivery usually takes two days, mail on Saturday for Monday delivery, and so on. Do a couple of tests to find out what day (and time of day) to deposit your mail for predictable local delivery.

Use first-class mail wisely. Emphasize that you're spending the extra postage by stamping "First Class Mail" on the envelope. This will help distinguish your envelope from the mass of third-class advertisements. And use *commemorative stamps*, which cost no more, but are (usually) larger, more colorful, and more likely to draw attention to the first-class treatment you've given this letter.

Do quickie mailings for special events. When the Sheer Energy band (remember the press release in Chapter Eleven?) schedules its final "Stars of Tomorrow" TV show, it should send out postcards to all clients and friends—and press releases, of course, to all media contacts. When your band plays at halftime at the Sugar Bowl, publicize the event with a postcard blitz.

Also do special mailings to celebrate successes. If the Sheer Energy band wins its contest, there should be a "thanks for your support" mailing. If you get a flattering letter of thanks from the governor, or the mother of a bride, or a club owner, incorporate it into a special mailing called "Here's what they're saying about us. . . ."

Write On!

Writing letters takes time. It forces you to sit down and think carefully about what you want to say. Because of that care, however, a letter can be a potent force, and a very useful part of your publicity program. Help your letters work hard for you. Give them a finished, neat appearance, and you'll look like the successful professional you are.

Who else but the post office will deliver your brochure, with a cover letter, to a client across town—or across the country—at such a small cost? Let the postal employees do the walking for you, and keep them busy doing it.

CHAPTER 15

Selling, Meetings, and Presentations

BY NOW YOU'VE DEVELOPED LOTS of ways to publicize your musical activities. The time comes, however, when you must get out of the house and actually face potential clients. Someone's got to tell them—face-to-face—about the band, orchestra, or show you've produced. It might as well be you.

If you're already rich and famous, you'll have a staff of agents and managers who book jobs for you. The rest of us, however, have to do it ourselves. "Wait a minute," you say. "I'm interested in publicizing my music, sure, but I'm not a salesperson. I don't mind playing in front of big audiences, but I'd really be nervous talking about myself to clients. Is this really necessary?"

Yes, it is. Dealing directly with clients, whether on the phone or in a face-to-face committee meeting, is crucial to your career. Your ongoing publicity efforts have already started the process; now you can complete it by booking some jobs.

Publicity, after all, isn't just paper and photographs. It's also how you act, what you say, and how you're perceived. Good results come from good face-to-face meetings just as much as from good press releases. Your letters and printed material have been working hard for you, selling your music at a distance. This chapter deals with how to sell it in person.

"I'm not a salesperson," you may be thinking. Of course you're a musician who's worked years perfecting your art. Your goal is to play the kind of music you want—and get paid for it. (If you don't care about getting paid, don't worry about this chapter—or this book. Your music is a hobby, not a profession.)

All the publicity ideas described so far, from business card design to feature articles, are geared toward raising your recognition level and giving you the status of a successful musician. All that work, however, has one ultimate goal—getting you hired to perform. All your publicity efforts ultimately lead to this point of contact with potential clients.

Here, in a nutshell, are the steps to follow in selling your music. (Excellent books on sales are listed in the Bibliography, and if you're interested in this important part of the music business you'll benefit from the advanced sales techniques discussed by these experts.)

First, locate potential clients and contact them. Use the techniques discussed in *How You Can Make $30,000 A Year As a Musician Without a Record Contract* to develop a client list from past engagements, referrals, and brainstorming about the kind of prospects who'd *need* your kind of music. Use the Yellow Pages and your experience to create as long a list as possible of those who might hire you. Remember, the more prospects, the more jobs.

Once you've located these potential clients, let them know who you are. Write letters of introduction. Tell them, as Mary Jo did in Chapter Fourteen, that you'll be calling on them soon to talk about your music. Send enough promotional material to warm them up, but save some— perhaps your demo tape and letters of recommendation—to deliver, or demonstrate, in person.

Prepare for the sales call by thinking about your music from the client's point of view. Go back to the list of advantages you developed for your brochure, and *personalize* them in your mind as you think about your music and this particular client. After all, why should he hire you, and not Band *X*? Be sure you're convincing. Practice the sales pitch until you know it backward and forward and are confident of what you'll say.

Have your spouse or a friend role-play the client's part in practice sales sessions. They should ask you hard questions, because the client will. "Well, Joe, your band sounds pretty good, but we're running on a tight budget this year. Why should we pay you $700 when we can get another band for $450?"

If you prepare in advance and are confident of the quality of your music, hard questions won't be difficult—they'll just give you the chance to tell another aspect of your story.

Now, let's look at how to act when making the sales call itself.

THE SALES CALL

Before the call, make an appointment. If you've written to introduce yourself, you already have an advantage—the prospect knows who you are. If there's not time for a letter, call ahead for an appointment.

Call the client's office and ask to speak to her. Often you'll have to deal with a secretary who carefully shields her boss from unwanted calls. That's why a letter will help—it will get your name known, show you're a professional, and demonstrate that you know business protocol and won't waste valuable time.

Speak clearly, a little more slowly than usual, and confidently when you call. "Hello. This is Joe Jones. I'd like to speak to Ms. Smith, please."

The secretary will probably ask what company you're with, and you should have an answer ready. If you have a business name, use it—or just confidently say why you're calling. "I'm with 'Joe's Band' and I'm calling about music for your Christmas party. I understand that Ms. Smith is the person in charge this year."

The secretary's job is to guard her boss's time by not letting you through. Your job is to be polite but persistent. You're actually doing Ms. Smith a favor by telling her about your terrific band, so don't give up.

Never be rude. No matter what the provocation, don't get angry. Sooner or later you are bound to encounter arrogant, dumb, or abrasive secretaries, prospects, or clients. Maybe even a few musicians will be less than perfect. Resist the urge to tell them the truth about their abilities— just keep a smile in your voice and be businesslike. Everything you say can directly affect your reputation.

You: "Hello. This is Joe Jones. May I speak to Ms. Smith?"

Secretary: "What company are you with, Mr. Jones?"

You: "I'm with 'Joe's Band,' and I'm calling about music for your Christmas party. I understand that Ms. Smith is the person in charge this year."

Secretary: "Well, she won't start planning the party until November, and she's much too busy to talk to musicians. My son's band, 'The Electric Amplifiers,' will probably play for our party, anyway."

Here's where you'll have to remember that *everyone you deal with is important*. Word-of-mouth is the strongest kind of publicity, and making anyone mad is counterproductive. Instead of telling this secretary what you think, be polite—even friendly or humorous if you can—and persist in your request for a short meeting.

You: "Well, I'm sure your son's band is terrific, and I'll listen out for them. Our band specializes in corporate functions, and we played seventeen company parties last December. We'd like to work for you, since we've heard good things about Apex Industries, but December is beginning to fill up. All I need is five minutes to drop some material by, and meet Ms. Smith. How would next Friday morning be?"

You may have to keep trying for days, or longer. You may have to write letters. But if you're persistent, you'll eventually get to see Ms. Smith.

The Office Visit

Appearance is important to businesspeople, and many of them scrutinize clothes and personal grooming. An old sales cliché says, "You never get a second chance to make a good first impression."

When planning a sales call or presentation, then, try to dress the way your clients dress. If they wear three-piece suits, you should too, if possible. Don't wear jeans or glitzy, show-biz-looking clothes. And, don't make sales calls with your shirt unbuttoned to show your collection of gold chains, either.

You may think IBM's dress code is silly—but when you're selling music to IBM, how much chance will you have if you wear jeans to a presentation? Be realistic and play by their rules.

A popular book among businesspeople is John Molloy's *Dress For Success*, in which he demonstrates—through research—that the way you dress directly affects your success in the business world. You may not want to study the subtle power implications of charcoal versus dark blue suits but you should pay attention to how you look, and how you're perceived.

So, for sales calls and meetings wear conservative business clothes and be neat and well-groomed. This includes fingernails, breath, hair, and polished shoes. (Suits don't go well with running shoes—forget the Woody Allen look when you're making business meetings.)

Always be on time. Leave home early enough to deal with traffic, possibly get lost, and find a parking place. The slickest publicity piece in the world won't help you if the client doesn't think you're trustworthy. Lots of musicians are pretty casual about time; the business world isn't.

Similarly, don't be too early—you'll seem overeager and too anxious. If you get to the building twenty minutes before your appointment, find the cafeteria and have a cup of coffee. Use the twenty minutes to review your proposal and practice your sales pitch. Then stop by the restroom to be sure your hair and clothes are neat.

Carry your publicity material in a briefcase if you have one, or in a file folder or large envelope. It doesn't hurt to carry a newspaper with you in case you have to wait; you'll project a better image if you're catching up on the news than if you're staring into space.

Confidence is crucial in making calls. When you enter the outer office, smile at the secretary and say "Hi. I'm Joe Jones, and I have an appointment to see Ms. Smith at nine fifteen." Don't make her guess who you are or what you want. Don't mumble, and don't let fancy office furnishings intimidate you.

When Ms. Smith comes in, stand up, smile, introduce yourself clearly, and shake hands. *You must appear confident, and at ease.* The best way to attain confidence is to believe in your product and be comfortable with your presentation. Practice is the answer.

If you're nervous about meeting clients, remember this: your prospects *need* music. You've identified that fact. And they're going to book someone, some band, to do the job. It might as well be you. In fact, it *should* be you because your music is the best. (If you're not convinced that it is, go back and rehearse until you're a believer.)

When you're in the prospect's office don't sit down until you're invited to. Take a minute to talk about the weather, or whatever small talk seems natural, then get right to your presentation. Make it simple and clear, but don't rush. Ask lots of questions to be sure you're going in the right direction.

Try to maintain a professional, friendly attitude. Don't be a pest, and be sensitive to the client's time; if she glances at her watch it's time to finish your presentation. And never talk negatively about other musicians. If you say "Our band is lots better than Band *X* because our vocalist sings in tune," chances are that the vocalist in Band *X* is the prospect's daughter. It's much safer to stick to business.

Similarly, off-color stories and jokes have no place in these discussions. While you may be trying to relate as "one of the guys," you may offend someone without knowing it. You'll make a better impression if you're pleasant and businesslike.

Know exactly what your prices are for different situations, and how much you'll give up to get the job. You'll often do better in the long run if you refuse to work below your own bottom line; sometimes a client just can't afford you. Decide in advance how far, if at all, you'll bargain. One useful idea is to insist that any price concession be matched by a reduction in hours, in size of the band, or be made up another way—meals and rooms to be provided, for instance.

If a prospect comes up with a question that you can't answer, just say, "I'll have to work up an answer for you on that one, and I'll call you with it first thing in the morning." In a sales call, don't promise anything that you can't deliver or that will cause trouble later. Don't let yourself be swept away by the possibility of booking a job.

Are You Listening?

While meeting with a prospect, listen to what she's saying. In fact, learn to listen between the lines for extra information. For example, if she's planning a four-day sales meeting at the Ritz, and is flying in her entire national sales staff, you can assume that she's not counting pennies. She's more interested in quality than in cutting costs.

On the other hand, if she mentions that this year's meeting is much smaller than last year's and is being held in the company auditorium rather than at the Ritz, you should be sensitive to her concerns about expenses. She may not *tell* you directly, but if you listen carefully you'll know that expenditures are being closely monitored. Such clues will help you tailor your proposal to her requirements, and such awareness helps guarantee success.

Your publicity material points out that you're sensitive to clients' needs. Meeting with the client gives you a chance to prove it. If you listen to what's on her mind you'll be able to offer genuine help, and make yourself indispensable.

When you've told your story, *ask for the booking* (called the *close* by professional salespeople). Don't make the prospect wonder why you're wasting her time. Present your ideas, tell her how much you'll charge, put a contract form on her desk, and say "Shouldn't we go ahead and fill out this confirmation now so you'll be sure of having the music you need?"

When you leave her office, make notes on what you proposed, how she reacted, when to call again, and any personal characteristics you should remember. Write a thank-you letter whether or not you got a booking. Plan follow-up letters or visits, and mark the calendar to remind you.

PRESENTATIONS

Sometimes you'll need to make official presentations to a prospect—perhaps even to a committee. Such a presentation is a formal sales meeting, and it gives you the opportunity to publicize your music to several people at one time.

In a one-on-one sales call you'll usually just talk naturally with the client, but in a presentation you may need to prepare a script. Don't write a speech, word for word, to get through a presentation, but an outline of your major points will help keep you on track.

Maybe your band wants to be booked into the show room at the Great Americana theme park, and you've been invited to make a presentation to the management team. What should you do?

First, research the job you want to book. Find out as much as you can about it—who played it last year, how many hours were involved each day, how much rehearsal time is required, who writes the show and arrangements for the band, and so on. Find out, if you can, what the musicians were paid last year.

More important, find out who the audience will be. Will your show be aimed toward middle-aged tourists, or teenagers? Will it be a dinner show, or a late evening's entertainment?

How do you get this information? Ask around. Ask the client what's expected—he'll at least give you the general guidelines. You or your friends probably know someone who was in last year's show band, so talk with him (unless you're competing for the job). Ask at the local union office. You could even get information from waiters and waitresses who worked in that show room.

Such background information gives you a head start—it keeps you from beginning at point zero. You at least know what's been done—and if it was successful, you can duplicate it. If it was unsuccessful last year, you can offer constructive suggestions for changes.

The Press Kit

For an important presentation, you'll provide complete press kits for each person at the meeting. Tailor the kit to this prospective engagement. Include your brochure, group pictures, pertinent press releases, and photocopies of press clippings and reviews. Also include copies of thank-you letters from satisfied clients. Include the strongest material *that relates to the presentation you're making.* You might even want to include an audio demo tape in each kit.

So, if you're trying for the show-room job at the Great Americana park, emphasize your show experience. Tell what famous acts, if any, you've backed, or opened for. You might even write a special *fact sheet* or a new resume that includes *every* show-related experience you—and your group—have had.

On the other hand, if you're trying for an engagement at the new-wave rock club, don't include your wedding and bar mitzvah promo material. And, most people looking for wedding bands won't need to know about your months at the punk rock club. Target the press kit to the needs of each client.

If you're a show band, you'll have a good strong video demo. Take it to the meeting, and be sure that playback equipment will be available—in the right format.

Tell Them Now

Your presentation will be like a little speech. Tell them, simply, what your music can do for them. Remember that business people are results-oriented, always interested in the bottom line. Offer specific, concrete ideas of how your music will help meet their objectives. Plan ahead and work hard (brainstorming helps) to come up with real-life situations and actual examples—concrete suggestions make your presentation much more effective.

Be specific. "The manager at the Golden Nugget told us that he sold more drinks when we played than the weeks before or after, and he attributed that to our fast-paced, upbeat show." You're demonstrating here that you know what's important to the management team and that you'll be interested in working with them.

Show them, with the demo tape if possible, what you're talking about. Prepare them for viewing your demo by briefly pointing out your special strengths—"Notice the pacing, if you will. Once we start the show, the momentum builds to a powerful finish that leaves the audience calling for more." Offer to leave the video behind for further viewing. (If you only have an audio tape, playing it during the presentation could cause a boring lull, so you may prefer to leave tapes for the clients to listen to at their leisure.)

Tell them *again* how you'll help them. It won't hurt to repeat a bit— salespeople and preachers constantly repeat to be sure the point is being made. Prepare for this by using the Publicity Practice list from Chapter Five, where you brainstormed the ways you could meet a client's needs. Review the list, and apply those ideas to this presentation. Does the client want sophistication, a show, a rowdy good time, an exciting sales meeting, or music for a theme party? The more you can relate your music to his needs, the better your chances of being hired.

Emphasize your experience. Refer to other, similar, jobs you've done. Drop a few names, if you have them to drop. "Our band spent last summer in Atlantic City, working in the lounges at the Golden Nugget and Bally's. We opened for a different 'name' act each week, and we never felt that we were outclassed by all that top-flight entertainment."

Make your presentation short and simple. Look at your audience, smile, speak clearly. Don't think that you should use big words because you're in a formal setting—be as natural as you can. And stay away from musical jargon and "inside" cleverness.

End your presentation by passing out press kits to each member of the committee. Tell them, as you hand out the material, what's inside, and emphasize that each kit contains its own demo tape. Many professional salespeople think it's a bad idea to hand out your material *before* the presentation because committee members will tend to look at your material rather than listen to your remarks.

Thank them for coming, tell them that you look forward to working with them, and leave. Never say that you need this job—even if you do. Remember, they care about *themselves*, not about you.

Should you discuss money at the first presentation? You should be prepared to, in detail, but you should take your cue from the prospects. At the initial meeting they may simply want to meet you and get your ideas. Money talk can come later. Find out when they'll make their decisions, and check back with your contact then. If you're working on a really big account, you may schedule another meeting. If it's a smaller job you're after you can probably follow up by telephone and send the contract by mail. In any case, don't forget the thank-you note.

To Close

Sales meetings and presentations give you a chance to put your publicity material and skills to practical use, to try them out on the ultimate consumer of your music.

If you've done a good job preparing these tools, you'll find that they reinforce your image as a competent professional. From the time she first sees your letterhead the prospect knows that you take your career seriously, and will do a good job for her.

In fact, your publicity material will have a *synergistic effect* in which the results are greater than the sum of the parts—everything works together to create good publicity, which generates more publicity, which generates even more.

As a musician, you're used to being on stage. Nervousness is likely a thing of the past—you can perform before thousands without flinching. If you look at your sales meetings and presentations the same way—as performances—you may be surprised at how much you enjoy them.

After all, you can be on stage in more than one way—and a virtuoso sales performance can bring you as much satisfaction as a perfectly executed solo. The big difference is that instead of applause from the audience, your sales performance is rewarded with a contract.

CHAPTER 16

People and Publicity

IS PUBLICITY WORTH ALL THE EFFORT? Does it really work?

A famous story among public relations professionals tells how the right kind of publicity helped make Bing Crosby a superstar. Many powerful people in the entertainment industry felt that his popularity would be limited to women, that he'd never be a major star. They thought he was too much a crooner to appeal to men.

Crosby's publicity people looked for a hook that would broaden his appeal—and they found it in the masculine sport of horse racing. Soon, stories appeared in newspapers and magazines about Bing Crosby's interest in racing, his constant visits to the track, and his friendship with jockeys. His show was peppered with racetrack jokes, and newspapers carried pictures of Bing at the track.

Did Bing Crosby really like racing? Probably. But his publicist saw this identification as a way to demonstrate that he was a real *macho* character who liked masculine things. His popularity soared.

This is how publicity works. You plot specific ways of getting your message out—whether it's that you're a macho horse lover, or that your band is the best in town. You use major media—newspapers, radio, magazines when they're appropriate, but you don't stop there.

Publicity comes from everything you do. Bing Crosby was a singer, but racing provided the publicity hook he needed. You're a musician, but who knows what you'll find useful in tooting your own horn? You can tailor your image just as Bing Crosby's publicity advisers did.

A good understanding of publicity, then, shows you that almost *any-thing you do* can get you noticed. You aren't limited to the standard publicity approaches we've already discussed. Sure, news and feature stories are wonderful, but don't stop there. The world of good publicity is as wide as you can make it.

We've discussed *hooks* linking your musical event to a larger cause that broadens its appeal. By now you should be finding hooks everywhere, and thinking about the publicity potential of all kinds of activities.

This chapter discusses several very simple, direct ways of creating, or advancing, good publicity. These are down-to-earth ideas. You can start using them *tonight*. You probably won't decide to associate yourself with horse racing to demonstrate your macho toughness, but you can devise publicity activities to suit your music.

The music business, like most others, is a *people business.* You deal with other musicians, agents, brokers, planners, club owners, and audiences. You play for nice folks and boors; you work for gentlemen and jerks. You meet so many people that you'll never remember them all. And you interact with them on many levels. With care, you can turn these daily personal interactions into positive publicity.

EVERYBODY'S TALKING ABOUT ME

Get people talking. *Word-of-mouth* is the strongest and most direct publicity medium of all. In fact, all the publicity you create is really aimed at getting people to talk about you. So work at it.

Talk yourself up. Don't be shy. *Be proud of your profession.* Keep a high profile—wear your band T-shirt around town. When someone asks what you do, don't mumble, "I'm a musician." Say, "I'm the drummer in Joe's Band—the best band around. Maybe you've heard us—but if you haven't, you will." If you don't believe in yourself, why should anyone else?

Ask people to talk about you. When you've done a particularly good job for a business client, for example, ask her to recommend you. Tell your clients, "Please talk about us. Tell your friends how much fun you had at this party. We love it when you make our ears burn."

People will talk about you anyway, so work to make it positive. Be sure your band members all understand that they're salespeople as well as musicians. One sloppy drummer eating at the guest's buffet table, or a horn player who scoffs at a client's request, can do lots of harm to your reputation. Sandra Dean, in her book *How to Advertise*, recommends "supercourtesy" as a good way to inspire positive word-of-mouth publicity.

Work with your band to be sure everyone shares the same goals and ideas. When you're on break at the club, mingle with the audience. Ask for their feedback and requests; let them know you appreciate them. Don't forget to get names and addresses for your *band fan* mailing list.

There's an old publicity cliché, "I don't care what they say about me as long as they spell my name right." You do care about what they say—and about the spelling of your name—but your goal is really to *keep them talking*.

Keep Them Talking

Here are a few specific ideas to spread the word:

Offer finder's fees to people whose referrals result in more bookings for your group. Car salesmen and wedding photographers do this all the time. Mention in your thank-you note that you'll pay twenty-five dollars for each referral that works out. (Some musicians won't feel comfortable with this, and it won't work with corporate clients who might see it as a bribe, but it's a useful technique for many situations.) Many "casual" engagements depend on a network of people; to book weddings, for example, you could work closely with photographers, caterers, wedding planners, and florists—and devise a reciprocal finder's fee arrangement with each of them.

Use your mailing list to send Christmas, Hanukkah, or New Year's cards. Do it because you really care about your clients—your "best wishes for the coming year" are genuine. And it doesn't hurt to remind them of your existence. (Remember that image without substance won't last, so let your clients know that you honestly appreciate their business and work hard to do a good job for them. Don't let them feel that you're just using them.)

Make yourself a recognized authority. If you're an expert, exploit your knowledge. Work up a speech and present it to civic clubs, the PTA, conventions—any audience you can find. Talk about music, children, education, history, trends and fads, give demonstrations, show slides or videos—whatever. And publicize your speech, of course.

Try an "Understanding Rock and Roll" speech for the Lions club, or a "Why School Band Programs Are Important" talk before the Kiwanis club. You'll publicize your cause, and gain recognition. And civic clubs and church groups always need speakers.

What else could you do to demonstrate that you're an authority?

Teach a noncredit class through the "personal enrichment" program of a local community college. These courses are very popular—many cities even have private adult "learning centers"—and your experience and personality will be more important in getting hired than academic credentials. Teaching a class in "The History of Jazz," "Beginning Improvisation," "Playing Blues Harmonica," or "Rock and Roll Roots" will give you important credibility, enhance your image and even pay you.

It's not as important that these courses be traditional as that they be interesting. If you have a good idea, prepare a presentation for the director of a continuing education department. They're looking for appealing courses that will involve the community and attract students, and you can help.

If you're an expert, you should send your name to the news media in your area for their "experts file," as discussed in Chapter Thirteen. When they need a comment, explanation, or interview about your area of expertise, they'll call—and you'll get wide exposure. Perhaps a famous jazz trumpet player dies, and you're the local jazz trumpet expert—a local radio station might interview you about his influence. Or perhaps the school board has just cut funding for music programs and a TV station asks for your reactions. They won't interview you if they don't know that you're an expert.

Be good. Be the best at what you do. Most of your audience, let's face it, will be musically illiterate, but sometimes you'll play for people who recognize quality—and they'll be impressed enough to talk about you. If you're a piano player, don't get lazy on those boring single jobs. Pretend that Billy Taylor is in the room every night. Who knows—someday he may be. It's easy to forget that quality counts.

Help Others and They'll Help You

There are lots of ways your music can help worthy causes and create good publicity at the same time, so you should be willing to give your music away—sometimes. Develop a policy for donating your music, and stick to it. It's true that you'll get "exposure" by playing free for this cause or that fund-raising drive, but you can't eat exposure. If you perform for a living, your talent is valuable.

You could easily spend all your time helping all the good causes that exist in every city. Since each important disease has its own fund-raising professionals, and since many of them sponsor well-publicized society events, you must know how often you can afford to donate your time and music. Decide how many free events you'll play a year. Maybe you'll do one, or two. If you're popular, you'll probably be asked to do ten or twelve—or more.

It's not inappropriate to think about which donations of your talent will bring you the most good publicity. Ask if you'll be mentioned in the official program or if you can get a photograph—or a page—devoted to your music. Find out if you'll be publicized by the organization through the media—"The Tampa Zoo's Fifth Annual Wildlife Ball Features Joe's Band."

You can, and should, bargain for publicity in exchange for donating your music. Work with the committee—usually volunteers who may not know much about publicity—in preparing their press releases, brochures, and programs. Provide them with your own bio sheets, photos, and background material, and insist that your music be mentioned in their publicity program.

Always remember what your music is worth, and act accordingly. If your band normally gets $1000 for a night, be sure that the charity you're working with knows it. Get written acknowledgement of the amount of your donation for use in filing your income tax return.

Musical ability is a gift and you should be willing to share it. There are so many worthwhile causes, however, that you'll have to make careful choices. You'll find that limiting your donations will, in the end, raise your prestige and gain you more respect.

CULTIVATE THE PERSONAL TOUCH

Develop personal relationships with press people and clients. If you are friendly and naturally like people, this will be easy for you. Everyone appreciates being remembered by name. If you have trouble recalling names and faces, read a book on memory development (see the Bibliography). Business cards help you remember people if you jot a few facts on the back. You can also keep a small notebook handy to write down bits of personal information. If you read in the paper that your client John Smith has just returned from a canoeing trip in the Yukon, make a note to ask him about it next time you see him.

You *are* keeping a clip file of interesting publicity ideas, aren't you? There's another simple way you should use clippings—this time to keep your name before your clients. When you see an article about a client, or a client's interest, clip it and send it to him with a very short note. If shows that you're interested in him and his activities. Thus, if you see an interesting photo essay on canoeing in Northern Canada in *Popular Photography* magazine, clip it and send it to Mr. Smith. Attach a short note that says simply, "I thought you'd be interested in this." You might even write the message on the back of your business card.

Do the same when you see an article by, or about, clients or contact people. It only takes a moment, and is an excellent way to build relationships while reminding them of your existence. Best of all, it focuses attention on the client's interest—not on you.

Reach Out and Grab Someone

Involve others in your music. You can pull in regular folks from your audience, or you can work with local celebrities. For example, say you're looking over the media contacts list you've compiled and you notice that the feature editor of your newspaper is an amateur trombone player. Why not invite him to play with your band for a particular event? Perhaps he'll accept, perhaps not, but he'll appreciate—and remember—your invitation.

This idea can be expanded to fit whatever kind of music you do, and can involve all kinds of public figures. It's the old piggyback-publicity idea, and it works. But celebrities are busy—sometimes booked solidly for months ahead. If you'd like to involve a TV sportscaster, say, in judging a dance contest, you'll have to plan ahead. (And, when you have a commitment, write a confirmation letter *immediately*, and follow up with a reminder or two. These folks are busy, and you need them more than they need you—so don't let your function be overlooked.)

Is the mayor of your town an amateur conductor? Invite him to conduct a march at your high-school band's concert, and publicize the event widely. (It doesn't matter whether he's a good conductor or not—in fact, it could be more interesting and amusing if he's inept—and has a good sense of humor.) Harold Macmillan, the former Prime Minister of England, was an accomplished amateur conductor and generated lots of publicity for the orchestras he visited; perhaps there's a celebrity "closet conductor" in your town, too.

Involve a popular TV personality in one of your events. Most television people enjoy the spotlight—many of them, in fact, have sizable egos. So invite the anchorwoman of the Six o'Clock News to narrate "Peter and the Wolf," or to judge an amateur-night singing contest, or to be in the video you're making. She'll love the publicity, and her station may well decide to cover the music-related activities of one of their own personalities.

Sports figures are very popular in many cities, and if you know one who has a musical interest, work on a special event to involve him. Maybe the quarterback of the local college team writes songs about football. Perhaps you could hold a "world premier" party to introduce his compositions to the public.

Public personalities can be given recognition, invited to make speeches, and join panel discussions. They might even be "roasted" by your group. Their fame and reputation will enhance yours, and they will often be happy to work with you on worthwhile projects.

If you are involved in a community-wide charity project, work with one—or more—celebrities when planning the entertainment. Perhaps you're playing for a fund-raiser for the homeless in your city. Why not invite a local celebrity to be the evening's emcee, judge a dance contest, pick the best costume, or just be the on-stage host to welcome the crowd?

Move Over CBS, I'm Forming My Own Network

As you work with more and more people you'll develop friendships that are also business relationships—and you'll realize that most business is done at a personal level. Susan meets you, you get along, and she hires your band. If she doesn't meet you, or doesn't like you, she'll probably hire someone else.

Networking is an old activity with a new name. In past years, people met to do business at "the club." Today they're just as likely to go to a "networking meeting" that exists solely to expand their circles of potential clients.

You're building a network of clients and referral sources anyway, and if you're organized about it you'll get more from—and give more to—your relationships. Always working at meeting new people who need your music will help solve the most basic problem faced by most musicians: finding new clients.

Do what insurance salespeople do. After each sales call, whether they've sold insurance or not, they ask, "Do you know anyone else who would benefit from hearing about my product?" Thus, each sales call leads directly to several more, and the salesperson's base of contacts grows quickly.

You should do the same. After each job, ask your client if there are any business associates or friends who should know about your music. If the client makes suggestions, write them down and ask if you can use his or her name in introducing yourself.

Thus, you can say, "Hello, Mrs. Johnson, I'm Joe, of Joe's band, and we just played for Mary Bernard's wedding reception last week. Mary told me that your daughter, Helen, is planning a wedding, and suggested that I give you a call to tell you about our band."

When you use a mutual acquaintance's name your position is strengthened, and the recommendation gives you a boost. Don't neglect, then, to ask for referrals. While you're at it, ask for letters of commendation or thanks from clients who seem especially appreciative of your work. In a short time, you'll have a file bulging with good recommendations that will be very useful in developing more publicity materials.

"Mr. Jones, we've had a great time playing for your company party, and I think your employees enjoyed themselves, too. I wonder if I could ask you a favor? Would you mind writing me a letter of recommendation based on our work for you tonight? We try to keep a file of letters from our clients." Mr. Jones, of course, will be glad to dictate that letter. It won't take him very much time and he'll be flattered that you value his opinion.

Also, after successful jobs ask your clients if you might use their names as references. Let them know that you won't overdo it and have them pestered with lots of phone calls. Often you'll find that a prospect needs to talk with a past client or two to feel comfortable about hiring your band.

Keep building a network of satisfied clients. Use your mailing list to stay in touch, and use their influence to build your career.

- *Unions and other professional groups* keep you in touch with your peers and let you know what's going on in the musical community.
- *Civic clubs and associations, neighborhood groups, and religious organizations* are great places to meet people. Join in the activities of the group for their own sake—but also be alert for the opportunity to meet potential clients.
- *School groups*, from PTAs to college alumni, offer chances to make new friends, get involved in useful work—and expand your network of acquaintances.
- *Networking clubs* exist in most cities today. These groups charge a small membership fee, and meet for breakfast, lunch or cocktails on a regular basis, for the sole purpose of networking—swapping business cards and ideas. If your kind of music can be used by businesses—and with creative marketing, it probably can—you might find a networking club to be very useful.

I'LL TRADE YOU . . .

We discussed bartering your music for professional help in Chapter Nine, but this can also be an interesting way to expand your musical influence. You'll be surprised how often people will be willing to trade goods or services for music—and you'll profit by expanding your list of clients, working in more situations, and increasing your network of contacts. Plus, you'll get whatever you've bartered for.

You'll have most success dealing with small businesses and professionals. Large companies won't usually be flexible enough to engage in a barter transaction.

When would you trade your music? And for what? Trade it anytime, for anything. You'll have to be the creative brains behind these transactions, but if you approach it right you can really profit. If you're part of a group, of course, the trade will have to benefit everyone equally.

Do you need some dental work? Ask your dentist if he's planning a garden party, houseparty, anniversary celebration, or whatever—and exchange your solo guitar performance for fillings and X-rays.

Do you need a brochure printed or a photograph made? Find a printer or photographer whose daughter is getting married, who is about to throw a "grand opening party" for his new shop, or who needs a jingle written for a radio commercial.

Are you ready for a week in the mountains? Find a small resort that will trade you a cabin with meals for a week in return for your music. In cases such as these, a barter may not work out to be equal, and you may require a small payment as well as the rooms.

Do you buy drumsticks every time you pass the music store? Why not arrange with the store owner for a Saturday afternoon clinic to demonstrate a new line of drums—in return for a year's supply of sticks.

A good use for barter is to fill up slow nights, weeks, or months. Do you rarely work on Mondays? Try to arrange your bartered jobs for times when you wouldn't expect to have a paying job. You've gained, without losing anything.

There's no limit to what you can barter. In fact, there are national organizations, or clearinghouses, that arrange multi-party barters. When you set up such a swap, trade *value for value*. Don't cut your quality just because you aren't getting paid in dollars, and insist that your trading partner do the same. A good barter is a "win/win" situation.

Exploit the publicity angles of bartered jobs just as you would any other engagement. Use each job to locate others, and to add to your file of good publicity material.

These are just some of the ways you'll be able to expand the effects of your publicity by dealing positively with people. Talk it up, help others, show them you're interested, invite them to participate in your events, trade your music, and create a network of contacts.

The benefits of meeting lots of people are very clear. The more people you know, the more people know you. And the more they know you, the more they hire you.

CHAPTER 17

Good Publicity Is Everywhere

HOW MANY MORE PUBLICITY IDEAS are there? As many as you can devise—and they certainly aren't all discussed here or in any book. You'll invent better, more useful, ideas as you work on your publicity program.

Here are more ideas, though, that you can use to spread the word about your music. Most of these, in keeping with the idea of avoiding advertising (which costs money) are free, or very low cost, projects. Several of them have been mentioned in earlier chapters—they're included here to remind you, or to expand their value as publicity generators. It will be useful to occasionally reread this chapter so you won't forget these ideas, or get in a publicity rut. Even after you're a PR expert, there will be lots of avenues you haven't explored, so work at being alert, creative, and flexible.

You've already turned your band members into salespeople, and worked on spreading the word about your music through the best of all media—word of mouth. You've worked at involving yourself in the community to elevate your image, and at involving community leaders in your music. What else can you do?

A lot. Turn everything into publicity aids. You can start wherever you are.

KEEP YOUR PUBLICITY MATERIAL HANDY

Remember the Boy Scout motto, "Be prepared." When you're asked about your music, be prepared to answer in the most effective way you can—with your publicity material. Don't wait a few days and mail it—do it now.

Always keep a few complete press kits in your briefcase, instrument case, or car. Handing out business cards is good, but when people express an interest in your band, strike while the iron is hot by giving them the requested information—now.

Whether you use fancy presentation folders or simple envelopes, always have a few sets ready to hand out. Include your brochure, photo, a few press releases, and photocopies of news stories, and maybe even a demo tape.

If you're playing a private party and the catering manager of the hotel asks about your band—give her the entire press kit. If you're playing a country-club dance and someone inquires about your availability for a wedding reception, give them your high-quality materials.

Being prepared this way will take advantage of a client's interest on the spot. It will impress him that you're efficient and businesslike. And the excellence of your publicity material will reinforce your image as a competent professional.

Phone Machines

Does your phone machine actively expand your publicity—or is it just a bland business helper? Make it a publicity tool—have the message tell part of your story. It needn't be a full-scale thirty-second commercial, but it can subtly spread the word. Here are two real-life examples.

The leader of a group called Best Bet uses this message: "Hi. You've reached 123-4567, your best bet for musical entertainment. If you'll leave your message at the tone, we'll get right back in touch. Thanks for calling."

That's short, and very low-key. The band's name is mentioned naturally, and the message is short. Nevertheless, the caller gets the message that this band is his best bet.

Best Bet's answer is much better than, "Hello. We're using this answering machine to take messages. When you hear the beep, you'll have thirty seconds to leave your message." After all, everyone knows how to leave a message by now; there's no need to sound like you're reading from the phone machine instruction book.

A guitarist/singer I know always uses song parodies for his phone machine messages. His machine allows outgoing messages of various lengths, so he can add the beep when the tune ends. The trick here is to make the words appropriate, and clearly understandable. Such messages are made more effective, too, if the music reaches a logical quitting point just before the beep sounds. Here's an example—a blues:

> Well, I know the phone's ringing,
> But I just ain't around.
> I'm probably playing my guitar
> For some happy folks downtown.
> If you'll leave your name and number
> I'll call you when I can,
> 'Cause I'm your friendly, soulful,
> Rock-and-roll guitar man. (BEEP)

Now that looks silly in print, but it sounds great on the phone, because the music and words work together so well. The message demonstrates his singing, playing—and sense of humor.

Writing clever words and getting the timing to work right, takes practice—but you can do it. And don't use the cheap plastic mike that came with the answering machine if you can find a better one.

If you try this musical approach, keep your message-tune short, and change it frequently. People who call you regularly may not enjoy hearing your sixty-second "Telephone Machine Blues" several times a week.

Use Body Language

Why not wear your message and turn yourself into a walking ad for your music? Your own T-shirt or other imprinted clothing will travel with you and carry your message to everyone you meet. T-shirts are easy to produce, can be creatively designed, are a great advertising/publicity medium, and don't cost much. You can also produce golf shirts, sweatshirts, jackets, caps, and visors. After all, you've got to wear something.

Shirts, and other imprintable wearables, are available in all sizes and colors. You design the illustration or copy, and have the shirt *silk-screened* to transfer your art to it. The silk-screening process handles very fine detail and uses inks that are bonded permanently to the fabric. The silk-screen process, from your standpoint, is much like working with a quick-copy printer. You simply provide finished camera-ready artwork, which is transferred to cloth rather than paper.

There is a standard set-up charge for turning your artwork into a film positive, and then into the silk screen. The fee varies, but currently should be in the area of twenty-five dollars. The set-up price is doubled if you want printing on the back, and is charged again for each additional ink color.

Some printers can print only limited image sizes; others can print across the entire shirt. Remember that people probably won't want to stare at your shirt to get the message, so make the copy simple and the letters large. Maybe your logo by itself will be all you need, or you can come up with a good design using your band's name or even a photo.

To find a silk-screen shirt printer, consult the Yellow Pages under "T-shirts," "screen printers," or "advertising specialties." You'll probably be most successful with a small—perhaps one-person—operation. Large T-shirt printers often have high minimum orders, but a smaller operator will be happy to work with you.

Most T-shirt printers have minimum orders of at least two or three dozen shirts. If you are part of a five-piece band, for example, you may not need that many. Explain your situation to the producer—you may be able to have just a few shirts printed, at a higher per-shirt cost. If you have to order the full minimum you could give (or sell) the extras to your *band fans*.

The per-shirt price does drop significantly as you order more shirts. You may pay five dollars per shirt if you order two dozen, but only three dollars each for larger quantities. Shop around, and look at samples of the shirts you're considering. You should be able to get a first-quality cotton/polyester blend that will last well—and look good. In fact, your shirt could be the exact same brand as the expensively imprinted shirts sold in fashionable boutiques.

When ordering large numbers of shirts to be distributed to the public, one rule of thumb is to order twice as many medium and large shirts as small and extra-large ones. Or, if you can take size orders in advance, you'll be sure to get a shirt to fit everyone.

If you're likely to reorder, be sure to tell the T-shirt producer. While the screen probably won't be saved, the film positive will be filed away to await your next order.

Some colors print better on T-shirts than others. Look at samples of the shirt/ink color combinations you like to be sure that the shirt color doesn't bleed through. Thus, a light gray shirt with black printing should present no problem, while a bright red shirt might turn white ink into a sickly pink. Get assurances from your printer that the combination you like will work.

While you're dealing with the T-shirt printer, look at the entire line of imprinted items. Would umbrellas with your logo be useful? If you're a country band, how about truck-driver style caps? You can even work with corporate clients to provide shirts specifically made for one single event— "United Computer Systems July Fourth Bash" with, perhaps, your band's picture or logo on the shirt. In such a case, the company would pay for the shirts and give them to its employees and guests—and to the band, of course. Make this suggestion to your corporate contacts when a large, informal party is being planned.

If you can wear your message, and get others to do the same thing, you'll get noticed everywhere you go. Let your shirt do the talking.

Throw a Party

Why not have a party once or twice a year for your friends and business contacts? It needn't be elaborate, and it will give you a chance to enjoy yourself and do some serious networking if you like.

Many musicians, particularly those who work six nights a week in clubs, don't have much social life. You can't go out with friends if you're always working, and it's easy to become isolated. Parties help get you back in circulation.

You could have a music-oriented party, at which your band plays, or you could have a full-scale jam session and invite all your musical friends to sit in. If you're inviting clients and prospects, however, think carefully about whether a jam session would appeal to them—it might seem chaotic, or boring, and actually be counterproductive. Perhaps you'd benefit from a party to present your new demo tape, or introduce your new vocalist or manager.

If you're working in a club, try to talk the manager into letting you use the club's facilities, perhaps on a Sunday afternoon, for your festivities. Perhaps he'll even provide beer and hors d'oeuvres. You could, of course, have the party at your house, or even rent a facility.

Maybe you should plan a one-band showcase and invite only potential clients, business associates, and media contacts. If so, be sure to attend carefully to all the details that will make your party a completely positive experience. (And be sure to save all the receipts, since business expenses are tax-deductible.)

Sponsor a band picnic, softball game, swimming party, snowball fight, jam session, road race, volleyball game, or street dance. If your group can work with another organization, why not join forces to do something really elaborate—a Halloween party, or theme party that encourages creativity?

When you have a party, no matter what kind it is, try to arrange everything so that your guests have a good time. Don't hit them over the head with your "hire me" message—if they enjoy themselves, that's enough.

Join Forces

Find an organization to work with—or even sponsor—your group. This approach gives your music more impact, because you are linked with the sponsor's reputation, and you can share its publicity.

Established musical groups—such as civic symphonies—often have corporate sponsors for an entire season, or a series of concerts. "Noontime Concerts in the Park are sponsored by Citizens' First National Trust Company"—and advertised widely by the bank.

Corporate sponsors are usually interested in supporting kinds of music that have artistic merit and aren't widely popular or self-supporting. Thus jazz, opera, classical music, chamber music, and so on probably have better chances than pop bands for encouraging corporate support.

Community arts councils often offer grants to worthwhile musical endeavors. You could get a grant to present programs to schools on jazz, chamber, folk, or whatever your specialty is. Or you might secure funding from a historical foundation to locate, transcribe, and record the indigenous music of your area. Many times grants are made for decidedly noncommercial projects, so search for worthwhile, even academic, ideas that relate to your kind of music. Read a book on *grantsmanship* to learn how to locate such funding.

Radio and TV stations like to keep a high profile, and you can join with them to co-sponsor a celebration. Perhaps a local radio station is producing a massive "Spring Fling" festival—you could provide the music at a reduced price, or even free, in exchange for lots of publicity. In this case, be sure to work out *how much* publicity you'll get, in what form, and when it will be aired.

Corporate sponsors like to work with musicians because they get excellent publicity from these events. Musicians benefit financially, and reap good publicity, too. When a corporate sponsor is paying you to perform weekly concerts in a downtown park, the company's advertising and public relations staff will work hard to publicize the event—and you.

To locate possible corporate sponsors, think about the largest industries and companies in your area. Are any related in any way to your kind of music? (A beach-wear manufacturer could logically sponsor a series of beach-music parties.) Have any of them done this kind of thing before? A large bank that's sponsored noontime concerts in a downtown park, for example, would be a good prospect for a similar series in suburban areas. Are any of them notably civic- or arts-minded? Contact their public affairs offices with your ideas, and if they're interested they'll ask for a full presentation. Again, show how the project will benefit *them*.

We're in the Directory . . . and the Program, Too

In many cities, special directories are published that list what's available—and good—in the area. Some of these are distributed free, others are sold at newsstands and bookstores. Some describe a wide range of community services while others concentrate entirely on entertainment and leisure activities.

When you see a book such as *The Best of Atlanta* for sale, notice who published it, what the emphasis is, and how it covers the music world. Is your competition listed? Is your own kind of music described? Ignored?

Some of these directories are really high-cost advertising vehicles that charge hefty fees for each listing. Others, such as the guides printed for newcomers to your town, probably give free coverage to interesting people, places, and events. Your city magazine likely publishes such a guidebook, or devotes one issue a year to describing "the best" of your town. Find out what's available, when it's published, and what it costs.

These publications are aimed at well-defined groups. If their reader profile matches your *target affect communities* (remember Chapter Two?), work hard to get listed or reviewed in such special directories.

Symphony and theater programs may offer another good source of publicity. Even if you're not a classical musician, this captive audience of music and arts-oriented people should know about your music. Normally, you would buy a small ad in the program, but if you're creative you could barter an evening of your music for an ad in each program of the season.

Music teachers, classical musicians, and chamber groups will find symphony and theater programs to be excellent publicity vehicles. But don't limit your thinking to the obvious. If you're a jazz guitarist, suggest that the owner of the cabaret where you're working buy an ad in the theater program for a "late-night jazz breakfast," a new name for the hours you already work. The cabaret is already serving the late-night breakfast, but your idea is to *repackage* it to appeal to a specific audience. The ad could offer a discount with a theater ticket stub—and you could do an evening of show tunes for the after-theater crowd. The club owner will thank you—and you'll have been discovered by a new audience.

Your goal is always to raise your recognition level. Special directories and programs, if they find the right audiences and don't cost too much, will help.

TEST TO LEARN WHAT WORKS

Big advertisers use scientific techniques to find out if their advertising and publicity are working. This is called "testing" and all smart advertisers do it. You can do the same thing; you'll work more effectively when you know what publicity and advertising efforts work for you.

Watch what others do. If your competitors are getting good publicity, find out how they're doing it, and copy them. Keep your clip file active—clip and save all the articles you see about other musicians and arts groups. Ask yourself, "How did she go about getting that story in the paper? What kind of press release did she send?" "How did Jack's Band get a segment on the *Entertainment Review* on channel two?"

If it's appropriate (that is, if the article isn't about a *direct competitor*), call and ask. "Say, Susan, I really enjoyed reading that feature story on your innovative piano teaching techniques. I'm trying to expand my class of voice students, and I wonder if you'd mind telling me how that story came to be in the paper?" Most of the time people will be glad to tell you—because most people like to talk about themselves.

Ask clients and prospects where they heard of your band. Keep track of their answers. "Referred by Sandy at the Ritz hotel." Or, "Saw flyer at music store." You'll quickly get a feel for which of your publicity efforts bring the most response, and you'll know to continue, or reinforce, them.

Go Where the Clients Go

Put your publicity material where it will be seen by the right clients. Often store managers will let you leave brochures or flyers at their shops, or they may have a bulletin board where you can display a poster.

If you play for weddings, leave brochures and cards at formal-wear shops, with wedding photographers and florists, and with wedding planners and caterers. Notice that most formal-wear shops display the work of local wedding photographers, and you should distribute your material the same way.

Be innovative. Does the formal-wear shop, or the photographer, use videotaped presentations? If so, arrange to leave one of your tapes for their clients to view.

You may work out a referral fee and agree to pay a commission for jobs you book with the help of these shops. Sometimes this will be appropriate, and sometimes not. Make it clear that you're not trying to buy the business unethically, but are offering the same kind of commission you'd otherwise pay an agent.

Are you playing in a hotel lounge or restaurant? Arrange to have your video played periodically on the hotel's in-house video channel. Or are you working in a club or restaurant that has a window facing a busy street or mall? Show your video on a monitor in that window to attract the interest of shoppers who pass by.

Use Unique Printed Material

We've discussed brochures and letterheads, and how to design them. Use the same techniques to devise specialty pieces to promote your music.

Rolodex cards. Most business and professional people use a Rolodex to keep up with names, phone numbers, and addresses. Why not have Rolodex cards preprinted with your band's name and a short message? Your clients and prospects can insert the card right into their filing system, and presto! you're in their network.

The Rolodex has become more than a filing system—it's a prime networking aid. Sometimes having your number in a busy executive's Rolodex is a status symbol—so make it easy for them by giving them the preprinted cards.

If you use a computer, you can buy continuous Rolodex file cards from computer-supply stores (see the Appendix) and produce your own—or you can have your printer do them for you. This specialty card stock is available in many colors!

Table tents, request cards. If you play in a restaurant or club, why not design your own promotion piece for each table? You could incorporate your logo or a picture of your band. Such pieces can be self-standing triangles, printed on two sides and flat on the bottom, or they can be simple cards to fit the plastic holders that many restaurants use. Of course you'd need the manager's permission to add promo items to the tables, but why not work with him—and convince him he should pay for the printing? After all, increasing your popularity also increases his business.

If you enjoy taking requests and interacting with the audience, print your own request cards, again with your logo and name prominently displayed. You'll be surprised how many people take such cards home; the publicity is always worth the cost.

Some bands distribute preprinted postcards to build up their mailing lists. The copy reads: "Yes, I'd like to be the first to know where Joe's Band will be playing next. Add me to your mailing list." Space is then provided for name and address.

Posters are useful in lots of ways, and there are at least three kinds that you might need. Photographic posters are basically just big prints, and their quality can be excellent; they are best used inside—in a hotel lobby, say. If you need posters to put on telephone poles and fences, you'd get them *silk-screened* to last longer. If you need posters to *sell* to band fans, you'll get them *printed*, so they'll be affordable.

Photographic posters of you or your group can be made from any good photograph, and can be used to promote your band at the site of your job. Check with local photo labs and printers to get the best prices, and look for specials that photo stores may run. If you just need one or two posters you can order them from companies that advertise monthly in photo magazines.

For a good poster start with a *very good* photograph. Be sure it's as sharp as possible, and is on glossy paper. Don't have a poster made from a very contrasty picture, because it will get even more contrasty, that is, the midtones will tend to disappear and the poster will look too harsh.

To effectively present your large photo, have it mounted on foamcore or similar material at a picture-frame shop, and sprayed with a protective coating. Display the poster on an easel or in the window of the club or restaurant where you're working.

Many silk-screen printers do both T-shirts and posters, though some specialize in one or the other, so check the Yellow Pages for a screen printer who does posters. Many offer typesetting capabilities as well, so they can quickly produce a long-lasting, brightly colored poster for your upcoming blues concert.

If you need a wall-size poster to sell, or give, to band fans, check with several printers to get competitive prices. Many quick-copy printers can't print anything larger than eleven by seventeen, so for bigger posters you'll need to find a printer with a web, or sheet-fed, press.

Use the same layout and pasteup techniques we've discussed to prepare camera-ready posters. Use large letters for the headline or caption, and smaller type for the details—and use as few words as possible.

Posters pack punch, so use them.

THE SKY'S THE LIMIT . . .

Are there more ideas for publicity? Of course. They're invented every day. There's a list of lots of ideas to stimulate your own imagination in Chapter Nineteen.

Here's an example of creative publicity. Recently the Greyhound bus company in Atlanta ran a very special promotion. For one hour on a certain day anyone could buy a bus ticket to any destination in the United States for fifty-nine cents. During that hour, Greyhound sold *five thousand* tickets.

Did they lose money? Yes, of course. Fifty-nine cents won't buy a crosstown bus ride, much less a cross-country one.

But look what they gained by this bold publicity ploy:

- Big newspaper articles, with pictures, both before and after the promotion.
- Extensive television coverage, both locally and nationally.
- Extensive radio coverage—including live broadcasts from the bus station and interviews with passengers and company officials on several stations.
- Magazine stories—many still to come—in both consumer and trade publications.

What did Greyhound get by giving away its product? Thousands and thousands of dollars worth of free publicity. The amount lost on cheap tickets is tiny when compared to the extensive, positive national publicity they got.

And—they got people talking about bus travel. During the same week, the airlines were offering fifty-nine dollar fares, but Greyhound stole the spotlight by massively undercutting them.

Is a fifty-nine cent fare silly? You bet. Did the publicity program work? Absolutely. What would have happened if the bus company hadn't come up with this publicity idea? Nothing would have happened. There would have been no stories, no talk, no live interviews. All the transportation news that week would have gone to the airlines, as usual. But Greyhound took the publicity initiative—and won.

Of course you're not running a bus line. But you can use the same creative approach. Think big. Be bold. Take risks. Be willing to lose money—in the short run. Don't even be afraid to look silly. Greyhound didn't, and they stole the headlines for days.

CHAPTER 18

Basic Advertising

MOST OF THE IDEAS WE'VE DISCUSSED so far focus on free publicity. Getting noticed in newspaper articles and encouraging people to talk about your music, for example, are ways to spread the word without spending money.

Why is publicity so helpful for performers? It's simple. You can toot your own horn without breaking the bank. Your message—"look what we're doing"—gets through without your ever buying an ad. And most of your publicity is more believable *because* it's not bought.

Sometimes, though, you'll be able to benefit from advertising—also known as "paid publicity." You won't buy full-page ads, nor will you invest in expensive TV time, but you may augment your publicity program with a bit of well-selected advertising.

Large companies use professional advertising agencies to produce their ads, but your budget won't be enough to interest most agencies. That's no problem, though, since you've already learned how to create your own publicity. The same techniques apply to ads.

YOUR AUDIENCE

In pursuing your publicity campaign, you focus on an exact target audience, a precise group that needs to know about your music. You don't reach for everyone in town but to aim at those who can make a difference in your career. Thus, your publicity goes to people who can hire you, buy your records, or come to your performances. You'll approach advertising the same way.

There are so many expensive advertising media that you could easily spend all your publicity budget on ads and never reach the right people. You could waste lots and lots of money on high-priced advertising that looks good—but doesn't work. It's done every day.

Before you even think about buying advertising, ask again, "Who needs to know about my music? How can I reach them at the lowest cost?"

Do you want to reach corporate meeting planners? Nightclub owners? Booking agents? If so, you wouldn't use newspaper ads or radio commercials, because those mass media aren't targeted at your prospects. Sure, booking agents read the newspaper and listen to the radio, but so do hundreds of thousands of people who don't need to get your message. Why pay to reach all those extras?

What Should an Ad Do?

Different kinds of advertising have different aims. *Image-building ads* promote a brand name in general terms, with no specific event in mind. Full page car ads in slick magazines are a good example—they promote a brand, but not a dealer or a sale price. Since your publicity is already doing this for you—raising your profile—at little cost, you probably won't need image-building ads.

Specific event advertising tells about something concrete—a concert, new record, or a grand opening. Small newspaper ads to promote club appearances and concerts are examples of this kind of advertising, and the money you spend producing flyers, handouts, and posters could be considered "advertising expenditures," even though these items are part of your low-cost publicity campaign. The line between publicity and advertising is not always a sharp one.

Continuing ads such as Yellow Pages listings or directory entries, help people locate you. Maybe a prospect knows your name—but not your telephone number. A Yellow Pages ad could send him directly to you.

What kind of advertising do *you* need? Maybe none. Or maybe quite a bit. We'll discuss a few possibilities that might help. Choose carefully, though, and think about how you're spending your money.

It's important to remember that advertising salespeople work on commission—if they sell ads, they make money. Don't expect them to give objective information about whether or not you need an ad. They'll always say yes, and they'll have reams of facts and figures to show how their ads will help you.

A good ad is really more of an *investment* than an expenditure. It should pay for itself, and then some. So, a good ad doesn't really cost anything in the long run. The difficulty lies in deciding which ads will be good, and which ones won't work. How do you know what to do? Simple research will help you decide.

ANOTHER COURSE IN THE MEDIA UNIVERSITY

You're already keeping a clip file of good publicity ideas for study. When your city magazine runs an interesting profile of a local actor, you should automatically ask, "How did he get that article written? How can I do the same?"

Now take the same approach with advertising. Use the same free "media university" to learn what will likely work for you. Here's why: *in the world of small-time advertising there are no secrets.*

What does that mean? Simply that advertisers who have limited budgets *must* spend wisely; they can only afford advertising that works. (Large advertisers, by contrast, often have enough money to do the kind of *image advertising* that's not designed to yield specific results.)

Doing the following Publicity Practice will help you decide if ads are effective for other people in the entertainment business. If something works for them, it should work for you.

Publicity Practice

Start a clip file for *competitors' ads.* Look in special sections of the newspaper (entertainment guides, wedding planners), and read specialty newspapers and advertising circulars. Look for ads from other musicians, performers, and arts or drama groups. Pay special attention to those whose target audience matches yours.

Clip the ads and *record the date of each one.* If you see the same, or a similar ad, repeated every week or month, you can be pretty sure it's working—but you can't draw any conclusions from just one ad. What you're looking for in your competitors' ads is *continuity.*

Perhaps you see a slick, well-designed ad in a local business magazine for a jazz trio—trying to sell its music for business meetings. You know that the ad cost several hundred dollars to produce and also several hundred dollars to run. Was it worth it to the trio?

How can you find out if this ad generated enough jobs to pay for itself? Look at the next several issues of the magazine. If the trio repeats the ad for several months, it's almost certainly working. (However, if the leader of this trio is independently wealthy, such research is invalid. Be alert for such extraneous facts.)

RESEARCH BEFORE YOU LEAP

Looking for repeated ads is a useful, simple way to judge an ad's effectiveness, but there are other routes you can use to decide if an advertisement would be worthwhile.

Ask the person who's running an ad if it's working. Perhaps a competitor will tell you, perhaps not. Perhaps he'll tell you an ad is working even if it's not, or vice versa, just to throw you off the track. You'll have to use common sense and intuition to decide if you're getting good information.

As you know, many musicians are jealous of their success and nervous about losing their clients and jobs. If you ask for information, make it very clear that you are not a threat, that your target is a different market entirely. Explain that your efforts won't infringe on their turf.

Thus, try to find another musician who advertises, but whose music isn't enough like yours to be directly competitive. "Hello, Chuck. This is Mary Smith. I have a pop/rock band, and I know that you're in a country band. I've seen your ads in *Cincinnati* magazine, and I wondered how they're working out for you." If Mary makes it clear that she's not trying to steal the country-music market from Chuck, he may be happy to tell her about his advertising results. Or, he may not.

You can also talk to the advertising department of the media you're interested in. Remember that above all they want to sell you an ad, so don't believe everything they tell you, but ask anyway. Request a demographic breakdown of their readers—age, sex, education, income, and so on—to see if it matches your target audience.

And you can even ask ad salespeople about the success of your competitors' advertising. Perhaps they'll tell you, if they know, how the ads for Chuck's country band are working. It doesn't hurt to ask.

If you do decide to buy an ad, don't sign a long-term contract until you've proved, from experience, that the ad will work for you. Even though the rates are much lower for ads that repeat regularly, don't obligate yourself until you've tested a few ads and carefully monitored the results.

If you're thinking about running ads in newspapers, magazines, or on the radio, a visit to your library will tell you how much you'll have to spend for the space or time. The reference departments of all large libraries carry *Standard Rate and Data,* a multivolume set of periodicals that list the advertising rates for virtually every media outlet in the country. Of course, you may be able to negotiate a special deal—bargain hunting works with advertising, too—but the rate books will provide a starting estimate of ad costs. And, of course, you can call the advertising department of each media outlet you're considering and ask for rate information.

Rates vary with circulation, type of paper, size of ad, how often the ad runs (one insertion costs the most, of course), whether the ad runs week-days or Sunday, and other factors. As a comparative example, an Atlanta alternative weekly with a circulation of 40,000 charges $175 for an eighth of a page (four by three inches, which is technically twelve column inches); a suburban daily with a circulation of 27,500 charges $146 for the same size ad, and the largest metro daily, with combined morning and evening circulation of 439,000 charges $911. (However, the larger paper offers *regional* editions along county lines that are much less costly; one county edition, circulation 33,000, charges $130 for a twelve-column-inch ad.) To get a true comparative cost, divide the cost by the circulation to get the cost per thousand (or *cpm*). Remember, large circulation may not be the most relevant consideration for your specialized message, and the lowest *cpm* may not be the best deal; analyze the readership carefully to be sure it matches your needs.

Test, Test, Test

All smart advertisers are *testing experts*. They tabulate results to learn which ads work, and what can be done to improve them—and which ones aren't effective at all.

You must do the same thing. In fact, you're already testing each time you ask a prospect, "Where did you hear about my band?" *You must know which publicity or advertising methods are working, and which ones aren't.* If you don't keep test results, your publicity and advertising could be wasting your time, effort, and money.

Let's say that you've bought a classified ad in the Sunday newspaper's "Wedding Planner." The ad costs thirty-five dollars a week, and you've signed up for four weeks. (Too short a run won't give accurate results, so you've committed $140 to this test, deciding that a month will give a fair trial.)

From now on, for the next couple of months, you must be sure to ask each prospect, "Where did you learn about our music?"—and to record the response. Pay particular attention, during your test, to those who cite the Sunday paper as their source. Record the results for each ad on a separate sheet, and be sure to keep careful records.

Perhaps the ad generates ten calls a week, but no one books your band. The ad seems to be arousing interest, but maybe your music doesn't match the callers' expectations. Or maybe your follow-up material is faulty. You might reword the ad, or change your selling pitch, because you should certainly book a job or two from ten prospects.

Perhaps you don't get any inquiries at all that can be traced to the newspaper ad. For some reason, the ad isn't working. Drop it, and concentrate your efforts somewhere else.

Maybe you get ten calls because of the ad—and book five jobs. In this case, the ad pays for itself many times over, and you should continue to run it until it quits working. You might, from time to time, change the wording slightly to experiment with different emphasis, but don't change it every week. Continuity is important, and the same weekly ad helps build your name recognition.

Judging how much to spend on advertising—if anything at all—requires close attention to the results of each ad. And you can't stop testing, so get in the habit of tracking the effectiveness of each ad—and publicity ploy—you try.

A famous saying in advertising is, "I'm sure I waste half the money I spend on ads—but the trouble is that I don't know which half." Testing helps you know what works.

The two principal kinds of ads you could use are specific ones that promote a particular event, and long-term ads that work for months or years. We'll discuss both. *Specific* events can be advertised through small ads in newspapers or with flyers, posters, handouts, and banners. *Long-lasting media* include the Yellow Pages, other directories, and advertising specialty items that you give away.

NEWSPAPER ADS: THINK SMALL

Newspapers sell advertising by the inch, or by fractions of pages. They also have *classified* sections that charge for each word. You'll rarely, if ever, buy a large ad; the cost is usually hundreds of dollars, at least. But you may, in some instances, use small ones. Here are some ideas.

Study the small ads you're clipping for the Publicity Practice on page 213. Many papers and magazines have lots of one- and two-inch ads, some of which are very effective. Study the ones you've clipped that reappear. They're working, even if they're small. (Such ads are called *space* or *display* advertising, as opposed to classified ads.)

Small ads usually don't try to tell the whole story. They just try to attract attention and a phone call from prospective clients. Small ads rely on one- or two-word headlines to grab attention, so you can't afford to waste a word. A one-inch ad captioned "FIREWOOD" delivers a direct message and, if you need firewood, you'll notice it. You can learn useful techniques from any effective ad, so when you're studying the ones that reappear don't limit yourself to entertainment. Many small businesspeople and professionals face the same budget limitations you do, and spend advertising money carefully. Watch what they do.

Would a one-inch ad captioned MUSIC be effective? Probably not, because music is such a general term. Something more specific, however, like DIXIELAND, or SALSA, or JAM SESSION would attract the attention of people who enjoy those particular kinds of music.

You can design and produce the ad yourself, or have the newspaper do it for you. If you do it yourself, get their "mechanical requirements" sheet, and be sure you understand the specifications; measurements may be in picas rather than inches, and there will be other technical terms that could be confusing.

It's easier, especially at first, to let the paper design and typeset your ad, though you should provide a sketch of your idea as a guide. Make the sketch as close to the finished size and proportion as you can, and look at a proof before the ad is printed. Most papers charge very little if anything to prepare such small ads.

It's Classified

If your paper has special classified sections devoted to nightlife, wedding planning, business needs, and so on, you may find them to be useful. Since classifieds are divided into precise headings, people who read them are already interested in each category. Nobody reads the classifieds for fun.

Like small display ads, classifieds don't try to tell the whole story—all they need to do is attract interest and curiosity. You tell your story when you answer the phone—a classified ad is only intended to make your phone ring with good prospects.

How are classifieds used? Here's an example. Several piano teachers in Atlanta advertise each week in the free leisure-time newspaper. Their classifieds are inexpensive, and they're *always there*. Thus, a reader who isn't interested in taking piano lessons in June can change his mind in October—and still find the same teachers' ads. When the price per ad is low, continuity is important.

When asked why he runs the classified ad each week, one teacher replied, "Well, I probably do waste some of my advertising money, because some weeks I don't get a single call. But I don't know in advance which week will be good and which won't get any response, so overall it's better to run the ad constantly. And, really, one new student pays for a year's ads."

Remember OPM

In the business world, *OPM* refers to *Other People's Money*. When you're planning newspaper advertising, use *OPM* when you can.

If your band is working in a nightclub that advertises each week in the Saturday newspaper, encourage the club owner to mention your name. Tell him about your loyal following, your *band fans* who want to know where you're playing. Let him promote his club—and your band—at the same time.

If you're a piano teacher, try to do the same thing with a music store, or even a piano manufacturer. Perhaps you're presenting a demonstration at a mall, or giving a concert on a particular make of piano. Contact the

If you pay for ads yourself, limit them to small classified or space ads that generate inquiries. "Piano lessons for adults" is a good example—it's direct and to the point, and adults interested in piano lessons will call for more information. This ad is from a symphony program, so the audience is already interested in music.

sponsoring store or manufacturer and ask their ad manager to advertise your performance, tying it in with his product. You'll both benefit, and it won't cost you anything.

Newspaper ads can be useful if you're very careful with where and how you spend your money. Don't forget, though, what happens to yesterday's paper, so be sure that the ad you buy is really the ad you need.

WILL THEIR FINGERS DO THE WALKING?

Mrs. Johnson, whose daughter is getting married, has never hired a band before. In fact, she's never spoken face-to-face with a live musician. Now, however, she needs to find a band for the wedding reception but she doesn't know how to go about it. She's never met a booking agent, and she certainly doesn't know you.

She thinks, "Aha. The Yellow Pages." She looks under "Musicians." Does she find your name? Should she?

For many businesses, Yellow Pages listings are very important. In fact, many businesses and professionals do no other advertising except for their phone directory entries.

However, the cost of Yellow Pages advertising is high and it's going up each year. Unfortunately, you can't just sign up for a Yellow Pages listing. You must first have a business phone, and as you might expect, business phone installation and monthly charges are much higher than residential costs. It's possible to use a business listing *as your home phone*, of course, but the cost is still high. Business charges are two to three times higher than residential rates.

Yellow Pages advertising costs vary according to the population served—small town directories charge less, big cities more. As an example, the Atlanta Yellow Pages, with 1.2 million books in use, charges $55 to $250 per month for expanded in-column listings from one-half to three inches. (If money's no object you can buy a half-page ad for $1800 a month.)

(With deregulation of the telephone industry, you may find other telephone directories published in your area. Some may have different requirements from the "real" Yellow Pages, and their rates may be lower. Check carefully, however, to be sure that alternative directories will be as widely used.)

Despite the expense, should you be listed? After all, if an ad pays for itself, it's worth it. Again, you'll be guided by research. Check the Yellow Pages under "Musicians," "Entertainers," and other listings that may be relevant to your kind of music—"Wedding Planning," for example, if that's your specialty. See if other musicians are listed.

If you find such entries, simply call them and ask if the Yellow Pages ads work, or see if the ads are repeated year after year. (To complicate things, however, remember that Yellow Pages rates are increasing sharply, and an ad that might have worked three years ago may not pay for itself today.)

A survey of musicians advertising in the Atlanta Yellow Pages indicates that those *whose phones are still connected* are happy with the service. One disc jockey is listed in five different categories, and a small booking agency uses four different listings. Both these advertisers prefer several small listings to one larger ad. (Several of the phone numbers for musicians listed, however, have been disconnected. For whatever reason, Yellow Pages ads didn't work for them.)

If you have an established name that's widely known in your area—Joe's Band, The Blues Kings, or The St. Louis Pops Orchestra, it may pay you to be listed so prospects who already know your name can locate you. You'll get one free listing in the Yellow Pages with use of a business phone. Everything else—boldface type, larger ads, inclusion of your logo, multiple listings—costs extra.

The standard advertising theory the Yellow Pages uses is that every listed business stands an equal chance—shoppers don't know you and can't tell over the phone who is established and who isn't. By this theory, those with the bigger, dominant ads will get more calls.

Some phone directory companies publish neighborhood directories aimed at well-defined communities. If your work is mostly limited to such an area you may find it useful to be listed only in such a regional directory. If you're a teacher, and most of your students come from nearby neighborhoods, why waste your money on a listing that covers the entire city?

The Yellow Pages, or other spin-offs from this venerable directory, may be very useful to you. Or a listing could cost you a hundred dollars a month that you can't afford. Do as much research as you can, and then sign up for the shortest possible time.

Ultimately, you'll have to take a chance with Yellow Pages ads—you really can't know whether an ad will work without trying. To make it more difficult, you'll have to contract for a year's time, since telephone directories are annual publications—and pay for that business phone each month as well.

If you do get a business phone and a Yellow Pages listing, try diligently to keep the number active. It is *bad* publicity for callers to find that "this number has been disconnected." They'll assume the worst about you, so if you get listed, stay listed.

FLYERS AND HANDOUTS

Flyers have always been a great advertising medium for performers. They're like little posters, but are so inexpensive that you can cover an area with them. They can be considered to be low-cost publicity, of course, but

The flyer is an inexpensive way to publicize an event. You can make a single sheet of paper do the work of a small poster and a mailing piece at the same time. If you limit the copy and artwork to black, you can even use photocopy reproduction (or you can easily include photos by having them screened). Here, even though the illustration is extensive, it is still limited to black and white, so it can be printed or photocopied without additional expense.

we'll discuss them in this chapter since they're also like little ads, promoting specific events.

Flyers and handouts are really just small posters, usually 8½ by 11 inches, and you can make them yourself. Use press-down letters, have the copy typeset, or even use a black marker to hand-write the finished copy. A quick-copy printer, or even a photocopy machine, will inexpensively produce as many flyers as you want—on bright paper, if appropriate, to attract attention.

Where would you use flyers and handouts? Everywhere. Put them on car windshields, in store windows, on school, library, or laundromat bulletin boards. Hire teenagers to distribute them door to door. You can even fold them over, staple them together, and mail them.

You can use handouts to make special offers, or to do last-minute publicity for a concert. The Red Garter Dixieland Club in Florence, Italy, gives flyers to American tourists who would enjoy a touch of old-fashioned jazz. The flyer includes a map and a special offer. A jazz club at Hilton Head Island distributes handouts at tourist centers promoting the featured music of the week. Wherever there are crowds, flyers and handouts are effective.

What should a handout or flyer (or poster) tell? As little as possible. Study the professionally produced billboards in your area. Even though they cost thousands of dollars to create, they use only four or five words. Advertisers often go for *impact*, not *information*.

You should take the same approach. Limit yourself to the "who, what, where, when, and how much" that your audience needs to know. A short headline, set in the biggest possible type, will grab attention, and the copy (set in smaller type, of course), should give exact, succinct information.

LIKE BIG BAND MUSIC? Join the Capitol City Big Band for dancing and fun. Gainesville Civic Center, Saturday, April 11, 8:00-12:00. Tickets only $5 at the door

STREET DANCE. The Fabulous Songbirds play Big Chill Music. Saturday Afternoon, June 4, Elm Street between 4th and 5th Aves. Benefits the Elm Community Restoration Project

PIANO LESSONS. Experienced teacher with advanced degrees will come to your home. Amy, 123-4567 for information

In each case the headline grabs attention, and the smaller type gives the fewest possible details to complete the story. The big, simple headlines will attract people who are interested in each subject—big bands, street parties, or piano lessons. Don't use flyers (or posters) to tell the *entire* story—just get their attention, and give the main message.

Flyers need to be noticed, and colored paper stock—even fluorescent *brights* can be attention-getting and effective. You might experiment with unusual, or smaller, sizes, but be aware of the printing, cutting, and trimming charges.

Remember the KISS rule and use it in preparing your flyers and handouts. "Keep It Simple, Sir" and leave out as much as you can. Just attract attention, tell "who, what, when, where and how much," and your flyer will have done its job.

Banners

Banners that stretch across the street or a storefront attract lots of attention. You can make them yourself using paint, cloth, and rope, or you can have signpainters prepare them for you. Kinko's, a nationwide chain of photocopy centers, offers computer-generated banners that are quite inexpensive, and most screen printers will prepare professional-looking, long-lasting banners.

A banner must be *timely* to be effective. And if it is hung where the event will take place, so much the better. If you're planning a street dance, neighborhood festival, or grand opening, use a banner to mark the spot.

You'll have to get permission to stretch a banner across a street—and it may be denied for many profit-making enterprises. Check with the police department or your city's Streets and Environs bureau. (For banners on buildings, even zoning commissions could be involved.) Get permission then, and use them when you can, because a colorful banner stretched between two trees can be an excellent way of publicizing that concert in the park.

ADVERTISING SPECIALTIES

Do you have a bank calendar on your wall? Is there a book of matches from a restaurant in your pocket? Are you writing with a pen inscribed with an insurance agent's name? These are *advertising specialties,* and they're a great medium for you to consider.

There are, incredibly, over 15,000 different items in the advertising specialty market. Most of them can be imprinted with your name or message, and many are inexpensive enough to be given away.

This is a different kind of advertising, with a different purpose. You don't use such giveaways to *sell,* but to *remind* people that you're still around or thank them for using your services. These little items don't tell your story; they just carry your name.

To get an idea of what's available, request catalogs from a few of the companies listed in the Yellow Pages under "Advertising—Specialties." You'll be surprised at how many firms compete in this area, and you'll be amazed at the number of products you can buy.

You can have your name or logo imprinted on bumper stickers, shirts, guitar picks, binders, calendars, Christmas cards, pens, pencils, key tags, buttons, decals, matchbooks, lighters, balloons, tote bags, umbrellas, mugs, paperweights, scratch pads, plastic bags, rulers, and thousands of other items.

Is this kind of advertising effective? Yes, if you choose wisely and don't spend too much money. Before you buy, however, ask:

1. *Is it useful?* A wooden nickel imprinted with your name might be cute, but what will it do? It will be lost or thrown away within a week. A scratch pad, however, with your logo, name, and message printed on it, will be used constantly. An Atlanta comedian gives giant four-inch cubes of scratch pads to all his clients, and each time they write a note they think of him. The recipient of each note also gets the built-in publicity message.

2. *Is it inexpensive?* Don't waste a lot of money on these items if you can't afford it. If you're choosing between felt-tip pens that cost twenty cents each and coffee mugs that cost a dollar, decide how far your budget will go. You could give away 250 pens for the same cost as fifty mugs. Which would your clients use more often?

3. *Is it unusual?* As useful as calendars are, most people don't need more than one or two—and banks, service stations, and insurance salespeople will provide those. Search for a free gift that's unique as well as useful.

4. *Is the price competitive?* Get several quotes from different suppliers, and don't buy more than you need. Specialties are like printing, the more you buy, the less expensive each unit is. But—can you really use 2000 pens with your name on them—even if they only cost 11½ cents apiece?

Today's Bumper Sticker Is. . . .

Bumper stickers are a very popular specialty item—almost like T-shirts for cars, and they're an effective advertising medium. You use them on your own car (and instrument case), of course, and give them to fans, supporters, and anyone else who's interested.

Silk-screening is the best way to produce high-quality bumper stickers, but you'll have the same set-up charges as for T-shirts. Screened bumper stickers last the longest, and can handle very fine detail. (Again, find these printers in the Yellow Pages under "Screen Printing" or use a mail-order service such as those listed in the Appendix.)

Offset printing produces bumper stickers that don't last as well, but they're cheaper to buy. Most printed stickers will fade after about ninety days in the sun—and your long-term message may disappear with it.

Do-it-yourself bumper stickers can be made with a simple kit that's widely advertised through classified ads in such magazines as *Popular Mechanics*. This method uses a metal backing plate, a blank piece of vinyl, and magnetic letters that stick in place. Once you've spelled out your message with the magnetized letters, you use a special spray paint to color the sticker, let it dry, and remove the letters. Such stickers are very inexpensive to produce, but are time-consuming, and don't look very exciting because the colors are usually harsh and they all use the same type style.

Bumper stickers are so popular for serious—and funny—messages, that you can get lots of mileage from them. If you can think of a clever message, or a pun, that's short and simple—and publicizes your music, why not use it? You're going to be driving around anyway, so your car might as well become an advertising vehicle. With bumper stickers, your advertising dollars will go a long way.

To Repeat

You're tooting your own horn as many ways as possible, and you may find that inexpensive advertising will be an important component in your overall plan. Always remember, though, that advertising should *pay for itself*; if it doesn't, it's not helping you. No matter how slick or "pretty" an ad is, it's worthless if it doesn't sell.

Actually, of course, a poor ad is worse than worthless because it brings no benefits, and costs money to produce and run.

If an ad works, use it. If it doesn't, concentrate your efforts on other ways of getting noticed. When you use advertising wisely, it can help, but it should never be more than a part of your entire publicity program.

CHAPTER 19

Events to Publicize

BY NOW YOU HAVE THE TOOLS and knowledge you need to publicize your music—in the media, by word-of-mouth, with T-shirts, and lots of other ways.

Throughout this book we've used *brainstorming* as a way to discover ideas and get out of mental ruts. It's a great technique to find, or create, events to publicize; brainstorming often provides the creative kick you need. It gives you an idea, and you suddenly realize, "Aha! That's it!"

You know you'll benefit from publicity—that's the point of this book. But you also know you need a hook, a peg, a point of interest where your music intersects with a bigger idea or a popular issue. It's up to you to find connections that work.

Here are more ideas. Some will quickly bring good publicity, others may not work at all. Don't be discouraged, however, if each project you undertake doesn't result in all the publicity you want, every time. Just keep trying.

Remember, every organization, business, committee, school, individual entrepreneur, and government group is after publicity, too. They're spending just as much time and effort as you are—to tell the world about *their* causes and projects. You can't expect to win every time.

Keep looking for new angles, fresh ideas, unique approaches, outrageous stunts. Watch what publicity professionals do to attract attention. Perhaps you won't hire sky-writing planes, or parachute to center field during the World Series, or even burn guitars on stage. But you can profit from planned events. Planned, that is, with publicity in mind.

This chapter presents ideas for music-related publicity. Use them as a springboard to jolt your own brainstorming, and apply them when they fit your own needs. Some of these ideas have been discussed earlier; they are included again to provide a quick review of the myriad ways you can get noticed. The exciting thing is that there's no limit to your creativity, so this list is really just a beginning, a nudge to get you started.

Are you a classical musician? A rock band? A country group? A Broadway singer? Do you write songs? Teach improvisation—or classical guitar? Many of these ideas apply to all different kinds of music; others will be limited to one genre or another.

Can you invent something to celebrate with music? Of course. Whether you're working in a club or directing a marching band you can come up with good ideas. Maybe it hasn't been done before. Then you'll have a "World Premier" to publicize. Or maybe it's been done each year— but without your music. Then you can join the tradition.

You know what catches an editor's eye: it's a hook, an angle that interests him—and his audiences. You're creative, so go ahead and devise your own events to publicize if you can. That's exactly what public relations professionals get paid to do.

So use this chapter as a nudge to your brainstorming, or a quick review of the ideas and techniques discussed in this book, or an overview of what publicity is all about. It's up to you.

IS IT NEWS?

You're already working on events to publicize with a press release and with other techniques that you now know. Some of these events need the full treatment; others require subtlety. Be sure to include anything that's:

An anniversary. Is your band celebrating its fifteenth year of playing rock and roll together? How many times have you played "Louie, Louie"? How many clubs have you worked? It's a story. Other anniversaries to note include

- The date of a famous composition
- The birth, or death, of a well-known composer, artist, or performer
- The fifth birthday of the bistro where you play guitar
- The fifth year you've played for a company picnic
- The seventy-fifth birthday of a church, theater, concert hall, pipe organ, or whatever; birthdays are anniversaries to celebrate.

A social event. Has your band been booked to play a Mardi Gras Ball in Mobile, Alabama? Publicize it in your town, and in Mobile. Social events include

- Annual country-club functions
- Debutante balls and parties
- Large weddings and receptions
- Annual parties, and fêtes, sponsored by prominent people and organizations
- Openings of galleries, elegant restaurants, country clubs
- Black-tie events related to concerts, showings, fashion shows, fund-raisers for charities

Be sensitive to what's appropriate when publicizing your part in someone else's event—don't make too big a deal of the fact that you're playing for a deb party, say, but do let the society columnist of your paper know that you're an important, continuing, part of the social whirl. You don't want to offend a client by publicizing *her* party for your purposes, but you should subtly spread the word.

An election. Has your college band elected officers? Did the board of the Music Arts Society vote on this year's schedule of concerts? If you're elected, you reap the benefits of the publicity; if not, publicize the results to raise the organization's profile. Common elections to publicize are

- Officers of music fraternities, sororities, and clubs
- Working committees that plan programs, raise money, sponsor events
- Union elections

A civic project. Are you donating your music to raise money for a park? The homeless? A community center? Other civic projects include

- Participation in a neighborhood clean-up day
- Playing for a party for March of Dimes volunteers
- Working as an unpaid music therapist for a community mental health center
- Teaching free, or at reduced price, poor (or handicapped) people
- Joining city leaders to celebrate an important local anniversary

A special achievement. Were you named first-chair flutist in All-State Band? Has your album gone Platinum? Did you win the Metropolitan Opera's regional audition? Also note such achievements as

- Winning any kind of contest
- Receiving any kind of scholarship
- Performing in a prestigious forum—your first Carnegie Hall recital
- Getting a job through competitive evaluation—you passed the first round of the Metropolitan Opera's national auditions
- Having a song or book published
- Signing a record contract

An upcoming event. Is your annual Christmas concert scheduled for December 10th? Is your piano class giving a graduation recital? Is your band playing for the grand opening of a new club in town? Also, of course, publicize such events as

- Your first night at a new club
- Your band is the opening act for a major rock concert
- The first performance on the new piano bought with community donations
- The first performance in a new, or renovated, auditorium, club, concert hall
- The premier performance by your new, or re-formed, band

A celebrity or out-of-town group is involved. Is the Music Lover's Club sponsoring a clinic by Bruce Bonvissuto? A concert by Van Cliburn? A festival featuring the New York Brass Ensemble? A fund-raiser with the Count Basie Band? Other celebrity-related events are

- Guest appearances by famous musicians with any band, at any venue
- Speeches, presentations, awards, given to—or by—the celebrity
- Homecoming events featuring famous alumni, graduates, or former members of your band
- Record, or book, autographing parties sponsored by your organization, usually in conjunction with a record company or publisher

An introduction. Is your record finally coming out? Are you introducing new band uniforms—that were paid for by the students themselves? Did you build your own five-string bass from a solid block of oak—and you're introducing it with a special concert? Introductory events can include

- Presentation of a new band member, soloist, conductor, or arranger
- The grand opening of your teaching studio, renovated con-

cert hall, redecorated music store, or expanded bandroom
● The first performance—or first *local* one, anyway—of a new, or famous, or newly discovered work

A personnel change. Is a new conductor making his debut? Is the concertmaster retiring? Have you hired a recent Juilliard graduate to teach at your studio? Also publicize these:

● A new player of exceptional ability joining your group
● A new management agreement or agency contract
● A new band director, assistant director, music teacher—any addition to your group or staff

CAN IT BE FEATURED?

As you know, there's often little distinction between *news* and *feature* material—and feature stories are frequently longer, with more pictures. *Lifestyle* pieces are popular with the press, so your ideas' can generate good publicity if they're:

Unique. Is yours the first all-girl country band in town? Are you reverting to unamplified, acoustic jazz? Have you built a pipe organ from parts bought at the hardware store? Do you play the glass harmonica?

Trendy. Aerobics, walking, jogging, retro-jogging, macrobiotics, digital electronics, video and neon art—these are trends that catch the media's attention. Does your band do aerobic exercises together? Have you commissioned a piece of neon art to display on the bandstand? Have you composed and produced a tape of jogging music—to be used "on the road" with personal Walkman-type players?

First or earliest. Is your band the first in town to do away with "real" drummers? Are you playing a violin that was made in 1837? Does your "Early Music Consortium" use hand-made instruments to re-create the hits of the fifteenth century?

Inspirational. Did you overcome arthritis to learn the piano? Did you take up the flute because your doctor wanted you to exercise your lungs? Did you start writing songs to ease your post-divorce depression? Did you succeed?

Largest. Forget the musical quality—is your Music Teacher's Association sponsoring a Play-a-Thon at which 200 students will simultaneously play "Fur Elise"? Does your marching band have 400 members?

Ethnic. American cities are dynamic melting pots, so emphasize your unique ethnic knowledge. How about a Mariachi night in the park? What is a Greek restaurant without Greek music? Do you play Japanese, Chinese, Indonesian, Russian, Italian, or any other special kind of music? Tie it in with restaurants, churches, festivals. Combine it with costumes, foods, drama, other arts.

Do You Have a Date?

We've talked about this one before, but it offers such creative possibilities that it deserves more discussion. Virtually every day of the year can be celebrated. Sometimes the anniversary is serious—Beethoven's birthday. Sometimes it's frivolous—Sadie Hawkins Day or Hat Day. It doesn't matter; if you can link up with a birthday or anniversary, you share the publicity.

Every week, and each month, are also devoted to causes that can be celebrated with parties. There is "International Pickle Week," "Lefty Awareness Week," and "American Music Month." Look for a sponsor who would also benefit from the publicity, and who may be able to financially support the project. Plan ahead, using all the publicity techniques you've practiced in this book, and reap the rewards. If, for example, you'd like to celebrate International Pickle Week, look for a pickle processing plant nearby, or a deli, or a grocery chain to sponsor a party. If it's "Lefty Awareness Week," plan a party for left-handers—and look for a sponsor such as a bar, club, restaurant, or radio station to support this light-hearted event. "American Music Month" could be cosponsored by a music store, manufacturer, music teachers' association, radio station, record store, or music school.

Chase's Annual Events lists at least one celebration for each day. Your library will have other sources, too. (See the Bibliography for titles.)

Do It

Plan an event, put on a party, make a statement with your actions. Perhaps you can do the entire project, or maybe you need to find a cosponsor. You can publicize an event that's:

Extraordinary. Try for a *Guinness Book of Records* entry with the world's loudest trumpet solo, biggest dance contest, longest version of "Shout," or largest Christmas carol sing-along.

Enriching. Teach your kind of music at a community college, private learning center, retirement home, ghetto school, or civic club.

Free. Why not hold a chamber music concert in the park—or from the deck of a sailboat moored in the harbor? Could you give weekly noon-time jazz, bluegrass, or classical concerts in a downtown office building? Could your choir, band, or group perform at a shopping mall for Christmas, July Fourth, or Thanksgiving?

Worthwhile. Did you give free saxophone lessons to ghetto kids? Make a local record to raise money for displaced workers? Hold monthly musicales at a nursing home?

Plenty of dancing, Cajun food will greet Queen Ida and crew

by Sharon Thomason

In the bayou country of Louisiana, the legend goes that Cajun music bubbles up out of the swamps and great caldrons of gumbo.

Zydeco music is basically Cajun music with plenty of other influences thrown in — reggae, calypso, rock, rhythm and blues and western swing. The word "zydeco" evolved from the French "haircot" and denotes a snappy, dance beat. Queen Ida and the Bon Temps Zydeco Band make dance music with a button accordion, a Cajun fiddle, washboard, triangles, trap drums, electric guitar and electric bass. In short, the music is guaranteed to get just about everyone dancing.

Queen Ida, a Louisiana native and the acknowledged queen of zydeco music, is a well-established performer in Europe, though a cult figure in America. In 1983 she won a Grammy (best ethnic-folk category) for the album *Queen Ida and the Bon Temps Zydeco Band on Tour.* The group now has seven albums. Queen Ida has played her button accordion on Saturday Night Live, A Prairie Home Companion and All Things Considered, in addition to numerous U.S. and European tours. But even

with all of this exposure, and the country roots of zydeco, the group is better known to fans of WRFG rather than WPLO.

For the group's Atlanta show, the floor of the Center Stage will be reserved for dancing, with polkas, two-steps and Cajun waltzes the order of the night. Center Stage's Encore Restaurant will serve Cajun food featuring items from Queen Ida's new cookbook to keep with the tone of the evening.

Ida Guillory was born in Lake Charles, Louisiana, raised in East Texas and later migrated to California. In the late 1970s, after her own three kids were grown, she decided to start a band centered around the accordion she had learned to play in her Louisiana youth. A San Francisco newspaper writer soon caught her act at a church festival, wrote her up in the San Francisco Chronicle and things began to happen.

In her concerts Queen Ida tells her audiences that in the Bayou country, every night is Saturday night, and every day is Sunday. In other words, when she's ready to play, you'd better be ready to dance.

This article is from a weekly "alternative" newspaper in Atlanta that covers the entertainment and leisure scene. Often, smaller papers provide the best publicity opportunities, are most receptive to your ideas, and will reach your target audience better than the larger daily papers.

Festive. Hold your own "Old-Time Bluegrass Festival." Or "Old-Time Blues Festival." Or "Old-Time Barbershop Quartet Festival." Any kind of music that can attract several groups can have a festival—especially if it can be called "Old-Time. . . ." Perhaps it could be competitive, with celebrity judges to award prizes. A battle of the bands, a jazz-trio play-off, a country fiddling contest—all will attract musicians, crowds, and publicity. Maybe it shouldn't be competitive, but an evening of a particular kind of music, just for fun.

You could hold such a festival at a large park (perhaps co-sponsored by the park's management), at a community college or cultural center, or even in a hotel ballroom (if you can find a sponsor to underwrite the expenses).

MORE MISCELLANEOUS IDEAS

These, and hundreds of similar ideas, can be turned into good publicity—and can also be enjoyable activities for you and your group. Include a hook to assure media attention, of course, but be sure that the event itself is interesting, fulfilling, and fun.

And, when you've planned an event—with that interesting hook—don't forget to publicize it to all the usual sources. Let them know what you're doing, so they can tell the world.

Sponsor a dance contest. The Twist, Jerk, Shag, Waltz, Texas Two-Step, Jitterbug, Charleston, or anything else can draw attention, and crowds. Square dances and clogging exhibitions are popular, too. As discussed in Chapter Sixteen, you can enhance the publicity value of such an event by using local celebrities to judge—TV people, sports figures, politicians, or prominent businesspeople. Or, of course, you could ask dance (or even ballet) instructors to judge, which could be an interesting juxtaposition of formal training and spontaneous energy.

Hold open rehearsals. Your band, chorus, or orchestra can invite music lovers to a free rehearsal, serve coffee, and even present an explanatory program. You could also schedule regular jam sessions. Many nonprofessionals and former musicians like to play and sing, and would love the chance to perform with you. This idea works as well for single pianists as for community orchestras; welcome the amateurs to an "open microphone" and watch your popularity soar.

Or try a classical sing-along. This is often done with the *Messiah* at Christmas, but you could do the same thing with Gilbert and Sullivan, and other popular works. People love to sing, so give them a chance. If you're part of a community orchestra, church choir, or school music department, this would be a relatively simple project for you, since you already have access to performance halls—and it would directly involve lots of people in your music.

Pick a charitable cause that hasn't yet become popular, and donate your music for a fund-raiser, dance, banquet, or picnic. The zoo, botanical gardens, a hospital, children's home, retirement home, inner-city community, restoration project, a disease-research organization, or many other good projects will benefit from your gift. (You'll benefit, too, by sharing your talent.)

Theme parties are always great, whether you sponsor them yourselves or work with another organization. The possibilities are unlimited—Beach parties, Wild West, Costume, "M*A*S*H," Fifties, Thirties, Old South, Murder Mystery, Pioneer—whatever you can devise will work. The more effort you put into such events—with costumes, special food, decorations, as well as music—the more publicity you'll generate.

Hold alumni reunions or weekends. Invite all former members of your group to reassemble for jam sessions or concerts. The Auburn Knights—a venerable dance band at Auburn University—has such a reunion each spring, with attendance in the hundreds.

This idea will work well for any long-established group—school bands, church choruses, community orchestras, dance bands, and even barbershop quartets.

Search, with appropriate publicity of course, for the *oldest or most famous* graduate of your group. Is an astronaut a former member of your dance band? Did an eighty-two-year-old clarinet player come to this year's reunion—and take a sizzling solo?

You could also hold a *going away* or *welcome home party* for your band before, or after, a tour. Are you going on a three-month USO tour? Throw a "M*A*S*H"-style military theme party to let everyone know you're leaving—or returning.

Hold a musical garage sale. Have everyone in your group bring old music, records, instruments, accessories, magazines, books, and so on. You'll be surprised at the depth of community interest in music—and in garage sales.

Sponsor a music auction if you can get enough donated material. You'll benefit particularly from items used by celebrities—guitar picks from Mick Jagger, Bruce Springsteen's T-shirt, James Galway's coffee cup. Anything musical can be auctioned—but items with local or national celebrity associations will bring the most money. (Acquiring such items, however, takes lots of advance planning. Booking agents and reference librarians can help you find addresses for celebrities' press agents. Write them, explain what you're doing, emphasize that it's for a *very worthwhile cause* and that the celebrity will receive good, nearly free, publicity. Ask for a donation of something that can be auctioned off—anything from a coffee cup, T-shirt, or autographed albums on up will be salable.)

Hold a musical art exhibit. Collect serious—and whimsical—art that's music-related and show it in a mall, bank lobby, or shop window. Make a sculpture from all your broken drumsticks. Show off your collection of antique Appalachian instruments. Have the school art students draw their impressions of a concert. Display your photos of famous jazz, or rock, or country musicians.

Issue an annual report for your group. This works especially well for larger organizations—recording studios, school music groups, and so on. Make it a newsletter format, with photos included of your major activities during the year.

Write an article for the local paper, magazine, or Sunday insert. Make it a list-type piece—they're easy to write; (for instance, "Ten Ways to

Help a Piano Survive Your Children"; "The Fifteen Funniest Events in My Musical Life"). Or write how-to articles for music trade magazines. "How to Hold a Celebrity Music Auction," or "How to Record a Demo Tape." All magazines like "how-to" pieces. Other ideas: "How to Form Your First Rock Band," "How to Improvise—for Classical Pianists," "How to Move Equipment Without Hurting Your Back," "How to Understand Today's Music."

If you are a part-time musician, work for publicity in your "real" career's professional journals. If you're a banker, try for a profile in banking magazines about your Fifties rock band. If your entire band is made up of stockbrokers, the interest you could get from the business pages will pay big publicity dividends—a valuable commodity for any musician.

Atlanta has a rock band whose members are all attorneys, and a big band composed mostly of doctors. A young banker in New York recently was featured in a *USA Today* story because he also has a popular society combo—but the story focused on his banking background more than his music because it was an interesting hook. If your profession offers that chance to develop publicity, use it.

Look for interesting personal hooks from every member of your band. Was your drummer's father also a drummer? Does your mother sing in the local opera company—and hate the rock music you play? (Or does she love it?) Can you trace your musical heritage back through four generations?

Produce a historical festival complete with period music, food, costumes, drama, and sports. This kind of project needs co-sponsors, but can be very successful, as the Renaissance Festivals around the country illustrate.

Perhaps the club or restaurant where you work could co-sponsor such an event on a small scale—a "1935 night," for example, with music, costumes, and prices from that year. Add a look-alike contest—for movie stars and singers from that era. Perhaps senior citizens, who remember those years, could judge such a contest—and generate more publicity.

Is it your city's centennial? The seventy-fifth anniversary of a local club? Find out what music was popular that year, and offer to take part in any official celebration.

Prepare a program to celebrate a local composer or artist. Did Stephen Foster write about your area? Did "the Blues" start here? Write a show, prepare a program, produce a concert to honor the local hero. Work with the Chamber of Commerce or the Convention and Visitors Bureau— they're interested in local promotions, too.

For a particularly worthwhile event, you may be able to get an *official proclamation* from the mayor or governor. Sponsor a day to honor a retiring band director, or an award-winning group, or a scholarship award. Remember that the Beatles were knighted.

Get involved in political events that affect your music. When the Atlanta Police Department tried to force all musicians to be fingerprinted and carry special identification cards, the entire musical community joined together in opposition—and created lots of publicity. Support your music when it intersects with public policy.

Hold a demonstration —with picket signs, or sandwich boards. Publicize your concert, or the weekly jam session, or raise the community's awareness of your music by holding a "positive protest." Check with the police department to see if a parade permit or other permission is required, or you may really make news by being arrested—and you probably don't want publicity that badly.

Be a sidewalk musician for a day. (Get city permission first if it's needed.) Play on a busy street corner, at a subway station, on the front steps of city hall to publicize an event. You'll get noticed—just don't get arrested.

Do a one-time promotion for a widely supported music project—a symphony concert, say, or summer concerts in the park—by playing on *buses, trains, subways, or ferries.* Wake up the morning commuters by strolling through the bus playing your banjo—or have the soloist from your choir sing a couple of duets to people waiting for a commuter train. Outlandish? Of course. Effective? You bet. (Official permission is necessary, though.)

Recently, a Washington D.C. troupe did several days of improvisational theater in subway trains for morning rush hours. While reaction was mixed (some riders preferred silence), the group got lots of publicity, and made its presence known to thousands of people. It also generated lots of coverage in local—and national—media.

You get the idea, don't you? Be creative, unique, first, last, newest, oldest, youngest—whatever. Just do something interesting, follow the steps to make your activity known, and you'll get noticed.

Will you be embarrassed to toot your own horn?

Why should you be? You're proud of your music, aren't you? You enjoy performing, don't you? And people are entertained, uplifted, or excited by your music, aren't they? If you'd rather sit home alone and play sad songs for yourself, go ahead. But if you want people to notice you, hire you—pay you, you've got to let them know that you exist.

Because, in the long run, if you don't tell them—who will?

Press Release

FOR IMMEDIATE RELEASE

Starting today, thousands of musicians across the United States are taking a new approach to their careers. They're finding new opportunities and markets for their music—by tooting their own horns. They're working to get themselves noticed by more clients and larger audiences.

"We've practiced scales and songs for years," says Joe, of the famous Joe's Band. "Now we're going to practice public relations, too. We already play great music, and now we're going to tell the world about it."

Musicians like Joe are using the information from Getting Noticed to link their music to interesting issues and ideas. They're learning that sitting alone in their rooms won't build a career, so they're taking their messages to the public.

These energetic musicians are producing press releases and writing feature stories to spread the word. They're making bumper stickers and T-shirts to promote their music. They're designing handsome letterheads and unique business cards that demonstrate their professionalism, and they're creating posters and flyers, hosting parties, making sales calls, and using dozens of other techniques to let people know about their music.

No longer are musicians sitting around waiting for the phone to ring. They're generating interest in their music—and bookings—by telling the world what they do.

Performers of all sorts, from country fiddlers to symphony violinists, now realize that nothing happens until they play for an audience—and that finding that audience is, ultimately, up to them.

"I know I'm creative," says Joe (of Joe's Band). "I just never thought before about the importance of being creative in other areas than music. Now you're going to hear about us everywhere you look—newspapers, magazines, TV—even telephone poles. Joe's Band is getting noticed. And we're doing it ourselves."

APPENDIX

These companies are only suggested to illustrate the kinds of businesses that can help you get noticed—there are many similar firms around the country that can meet your needs as well as these. Most of these companies publish catalogs or price sheets that will show you what's available, and will provide quality and price comparisons.

ABC Pictures, 1867 E. Florida St., Springfield, MO 65803. Reproduces photos inexpensively and adds your name at the bottom.

Business Envelope Manufacturers, Inc., 900 Grand Blvd., Deer Park, Long Island, NY 11729. Sells all kinds of business stationery, including imprinted letterheads and envelopes, often at good prices.

Calumet Carton Co., P. O. Box 405, South Holland, IL 60473. Manufactures shipping cartons, including a stiff "self-mailer" that's useful for sending photos without additional reinforcement.

Chartpak, One River Road, Leeds, MA 01053. Manufacturers a complete line of press-down letters and other graphic aids.

Day-Timers, Inc., Allentown, PA 18001. Produces an extensive line of calendars, datebooks, and time-management tools.

Dexter Press, Route 303, West Nyack, NY 10994. This company prints a wide variety of materials in color—from postcards to brochures.

Dover Publications, 31 East 2nd St., Mineola, NY 11501. Publishes several "copyright-free" books of musical illustrations. Also lists books on logo and trademark design, reprints of musical scores, and a large catalog of useful and interesting publications.

Eva-Tone Soundsheets, Inc., 4801 Ulmerton Rd., Clearwater, FL 33520. Produces flexible soundsheets and does cassette duplication. Their "Soundsheet Idea Kit" is filled with creative ways to publicize your music via their products.

Letraset USA, 40 Eisenhower Drive, Paramus, NJ 07652. Produces an astounding variety of press-down letters and other graphic materials.

The Maine Photographic Workshops, Rockport, ME 04856. If your interest in photography is intense, you'll find a workshop in photography or video production to match your abilities and need.

Mass Photo Co., 1439 Mayson St., Atlanta, GA 30324 and 1315 Waugh St., Houston, TX 77019. Produces publicity photos from your original, and adds your name at the bottom.

National Repro Service, PO Box 56, Pickerel, WI 54465. Provide all kinds of reproduction services—photographic and printed. Also offers printed guitar picks, posters, brochure design and other services of interest to performers.

NEBS Computer Forms, 500 Main St., Groton, MA 01741. Sells all kinds of computer supplies, including continuous letterheads, file cards, and Rolodex cards.

Promotion Products, 1114 E. Colonial Dr., Orlando, FL 32803 and 6065 Roswell Rd., Suite 301G, Atlanta, GA 30328. Sells every kind of advertising specialty item you can imagine, from pencils to Chinese fortune cookies.

Zipatone, Inc., 150 Fenci Lane, Hillside, IL 60162. Manufactures a complete line of dry-transfer, press-down lettering and other graphic material.

Press Release

PSA Public Service Announcement

BIBLIOGRAPHY

BOOKS

The resources available in libraries and bookstores are overwhelming. Here are a few ideas—your bookseller or librarian will be able to suggest more. When you're planning your publicity program you'll take ideas from every possible source—so browsing in a library or large bookstore can really pay off with new concepts and fresh outlooks.

The Advertising Answer Book, by Hal Betancourt, Prentice-Hall, 1982.

Advertising Woodcuts, by Stanley Appelbaum, Dover Publications, 1977.

Antique Musical Instruments and Their Players, by Filippo Bonanni, Dover Publications, 1964.

Basic Magazine Writing, by Barbara Kevles, Writer's Digest Books, 1986.

Basic Typography, by John R. Biggs, Watson-Guptill Publications, 1968.

Business Letter Writing Made Simple, by Irving Rosenthal and Harry Rudman, Doubleday, 1968.

Calligraphy Now, by Margaret Shepherd, G. P. Putnam's Sons, 1983.

Complete Book of Model Business Letters, by Martha Cresci, Parker Publishing Co., 1976.

Confessions of an Advertising Man, by David Ogilvy, Atheneum, 1985.

Getting Back to the Basics of Selling, by Matthew J. Culligan, Ace Business Library, 1981.

The Guinness Book of Music, by Robert and Celia Dearling, Guinness Books, 1986.

How to Advertise, by Sandra Dean, International Self-Counsel Press, 1985.

How to Advertise and Promote Your Small Business, by Connie Siegel, John Wiley and Sons, 1978.

How to Barter and Trade, by Jack Trapp, Cornerstone Library, 1981.

How to Master the Art of Selling, by Tom Hopkins, Warner Books, 1982.

How to Sell Anything to Anybody, by Joe Girard, Stanley H. Brown, 1979.

How to Set Up and Operate an Office at Home, by Robert Scott, Charles Scribner's Sons, 1985.

How You Can Make $30,000 a Year As a Musician Without a Record Contract, by James Gibson, Writer's Digest Books, 1986.

The Language of Layout, by Bud Donahue, Prentice-Hall, 1986.

Logo Design: Design Your Own Logo, by Mark S. Haskett, International Self-Counsel Press (Canada), 1984.

The Memory Book, by Harry Lorayne and Jerry Lucas, Ballantine, 1974.

More Than You Ever Wanted to Know About Mail-Order Advertising, by Herschell Gordon Lewis, Prentice-Hall, 1983.

Music: A Pictorial Archive of Woodcuts and Engravings, by Jim Harter, Dover Books, 1980.

The Perfect Resume, by Tom Jackson, Anchor Books, 1986.

The Photographer's Handbook, by John Hedgecoe, Alfred A. Knopf, 1977.

Plain English Handbook, by Martyn Walsh, McCormick-Mathers Publishing Co., 1972.

Publishing Newsletters, by Howard Penn Hudson, Charles Scribner's Sons, 1982.

Resume Writing, by William Lewis, Monarch Press, 1980.

Stalking the Feature Story, by William Ruehlman, Random House, 1977.

Stop Forgetting, by Dr. Bruno Furst, Doubleday, 1972.

Studio Recording for Musicians, by Fred Miller, Amsco Publications, 1981.

Studio Tips for Artists and Graphic Designers, by Bill Gray, Van Nostrand Reinhold, 1978.

Teach Yourself Typing, by Nathan Levine, Arco, 1982.

Tips on Type, by Bill Gray, Van Nostrand Reinhold, 1983.

The Unabashed Self-Promoter's Guide, by Dr. Jeffrey Lant, JLA Publications, 1983.

Video Production Handbook, by Gerald Millerson, Focal Press, 1987.

Write on Target, by Connie Emerson, Writer's Digest Books, 1981.

PERIODICALS

Magazines are like "books that keep coming out," and give you the chance to keep up with your field. Most of them are very inexpensive—compared to record albums, CD's, or hamburgers, and provide the kind of information that will put—and keep—you ahead. Many specialized magazines won't be in your newsstand or library; write to the magazine for subscription information. Some will even send you a sample copy. This listing is only a tiny sample of the thousands of magazines published in this country. A reference librarian will help you find magazines directed to your special interests—whether in music, publicity, photography, art, writing, or anything else.

Advertising Age, 740 N. Rush, Chicago, IL 60611. The Bible of the advertising world—but won't have a lot of how-to information.

Calligraphy Idea Exchange, Suite 159, 2500 S. McGee, Norman, OK 73072. Articles on calligraphy.

Frets Magazine, GPI Publications, 20085 Stevens Creek Blvd., Cupertino, CA 95014. News and features about banjo, mandolin, guitar, bass, and other fretted instruments and their players.

Guitar Player Magazine, GPI Publications—address above. News and features of interest to guitar players.

Keyboard Magazine, GPI Publications—address above. News and features of interest to keyboard players.

Mix: The Recording Industry Magazine, 2608 9th St., Berkeley, CA 94710. Covers recording news and techniques.

Modern Drummer, 870 Pompton Ave., Cedar Grove, NJ 07009. News and features of interest to drummers.

Music Magazine, Suite 202, 56 The Esplanade, Toronto, Ontario M5E 1A7 Canada. Covers classical music.

Petersen's Photographic Magazine, 8490 Sunset Blvd., Los Angeles, CA 90069. If you're interested in photography, a magazine such as this one can teach you a lot.

Public Relations Journal, 845 3rd Ave., New York, NY 10022. Covers the field of public relations, with some how-to and case studies.

Rolling Stone, 745 5th Ave., New York, NY 10151. The standard magazine for those interested in contemporary music. When you're covered in *Rolling Stone,* you're noticed.

Writer's Digest, 1507 Dana Ave., Cincinnati, OH 45207. Articles of interest to every writer.

INDEX

Other Books of Interest

General Writing Books

Beginning Writer's Answer Book, edited by Kirk Polking (paper) $12.95

Getting the Words Right: How to Revise, Edit and Rewrite, by Theodore A. Rees Cheney $14.95

How to Get Started in Writing, by Peggy Teeters (paper) $8.95

How to Increase Your Word Power, by the editors of Reader's Digest $19.95

How to Write a Book Proposal, by Michael Larsen $9.95

Just Open a Vein, edited by William Brohaugh $15.95

Pinckert's Practical Grammar, by Robert C. Pinckert $14.95

The 29 Most Common Writing Mistakes & How to Avoid Them, by Judy Delton $9.95

Writer's Block & How to Use It, by Victoria Nelson $14.95

The Writer's Digest Guide to Manuscript Formats, by Buchman & Groves $16.95

Writer's Encyclopedia, edited by Kirk Polking (paper) $16.95

Writer's Guide to Research, by Lois Horowitz $9.95

Writer's Market, edited by Glenda Neff $21.95

Nonfiction Writing

Basic Magazine Writing, by Barbara Kevles $16.95

How to Sell Every Magazine Article You Write, by Lisa Collier Cool $14.95

How to Write & Sell the 8 Easiest Article Types, by Helene Schellenberg Barnhart $14.95

Writing Creative Nonfiction, by Theodore A. Rees Cheney $15.95

Writing Nonfiction that Sells, by Samm Sinclair Baker $14.95

Fiction Writing

Creating Short Fiction, by Damon Knight (paper) $8.95

Fiction is Folks: How to Create Unforgettable Characters, by Robert Newton Peck (paper) $8.95

Fiction Writer's Market, edited by Laurie Henry $18.95

Handbook of Short Story Writing, by Dickson and Smythe (paper) $8.95

How to Write & Sell Your First Novel, by Oscar Collier with Frances Spatz Leighton $14.95

Storycrafting, by Paul Darcy Boles (paper) $9.95

Writing the Modern Mystery, by Barbara Norville $15.95

Writing the Novel: From Plot to Print, by Lawrence Block (paper) $8.95

Special Interest Writing Books

The Children's Picture Book: How to Write It, How to Sell It, by Ellen E.M. Roberts (paper) $14.95

Comedy Writing Secrets, by Melvin Helitzer $16.95

The Complete Book of Scriptwriting, by J. Michael Straczynski (paper) $9.95

The Craft of Comedy Writing, by Sol Saks $14.95

How to Sell & Re-Sell Your Writing, by Duane Newcomb $10.95

How to Write Tales of Horror, Fantasy & Science Fiction, edited by J.N. Williamson $15.95

How to Write & Sell a Column, by Raskin & Males $10.95

How to Write & Sell Your Personal Experiences, by Lois Duncan (paper) $9.95

How to Write the Story of Your Life, by Frank P. Thomas $14.95

Nonfiction for Children: How to Write It, How to Sell It, by Ellen E.M. Roberts $16.95

The Poet's Handbook, by Judson Jerome (paper) $8.95

Poet's Market, by Judson Jerome $17.95

Travel Writer's Handbook, by Louise Zobel (paper) $10.95

TV Scriptwriter's Handbook, by Alfred Brenner (paper) $9.95

Writing Short Stories for Young People, by George Edward Stanley $15.95

The Writing Business

A Beginner's Guide to Getting Published, edited by Kirk Polking $10.95

Complete Guide to Self-Publishing, by Tom & Marilyn Ross $19.95

How to Bulletproof Your Manuscript, by Bruce Henderson $9.95

How to Write Irresistible Query Letters, by Lisa Collier Cool $10.95

How You Can Make $25,000 a Year Writing (No Matter Where You Live), by Nancy Edmonds Hanson $15.95

Literary Agents: How to Get & Work with the Right One for You, by Michael Larsen $9.95
Professional Etiquette for Writers, by William Brohaugh $9.95

To order directly from the publisher, include $2.00 postage and handling for 1 book and 50¢ for each additional book. Allow 30 days for delivery.

Writer's Digest Books, Dept. B, 1507 Dana Avenue, Cincinnati, Ohio 45207
Credit card orders call TOLL-FREE
1-800-543-4644 (Outside Ohio)
1-800-551-0884 (Ohio only)
Prices subject to change without notice.

For information on how to receive Writer's Digest Books at special Book Club member prices, please write to:

 Promotion Manager, Writer's Digest Book Club, 1507 Dana Avenue, Cincinnati, Ohio 45207